The Just Shall Live by Faith

Galatians 3:11

(Articles and Stories of Faith and Courage and Answered Prayers)

Linda Clore

"But without faith it is impossible to please him: for he that cometh to God must believe that he is, and that he is a rewarder of them that diligently seek him." Hebrews 11:6

World rights reserved. This book or any portion thereof may not be copied or reproduced in any form or manner whatever, except as provided by law, without the written permission of the publisher, except by a reviewer who may quote brief passages in a review.

The author assumes full responsibility for the accuracy of all facts and quotations as cited in this book. The opinions expressed in this book are the author's personal views and interpretations, and do not necessarily reflect those of the publisher.

This book is provided with the understanding that the publisher is not engaged in giving spiritual, legal, medical, or other professional advice. If authoritative advice is needed, the reader should seek the counsel of a competent professional.

_____

Copyright © 2019 Linda Clore

Copyright © 2019 ASPECT Books

ISBN-13: 978-1-4796-1013-6 (Paperback)

ISBN-13: 978-1-4796-1014-3 (ePub)

Library of Congress Control Number: 2019907658

Scripture quotations marked The Message are taken from The Message. Copyright©1993, 1994, 1995, 1996, 2000, 2001, 2002. Used by permission of NavPress Publishing Group.

Scripture quotations marked NASB are taken from the New American Standard Bible®, copyright © 1960, 1962, 1963, 1968, 1971, 1972, 1973, 1975, 1977, 1995 by The Lockman Foundation. Used by permission.

Scripture quotations marked NIV are taken from The Holy Bible, New International Version®, NIV®. Copyright©1973, 1978, 1984, 2011 by Biblica, Inc.™ Used by permission. All rights reserved worldwide.

Texts credited to NKJV are taken from the New King James Version®. Copyright © 1982 by Thomas Nelson, Inc. Used by permission. All rights reserved.

Scripture quotations marked NLT are taken from the Holy Bible, New Living Translation, copyright © 1996, 2004, 2007 by Tyndale House Foundation. Used by permission of Tyndale House Publishers, Inc., Carol Stream, Illinois 60188. All rights reserved.

Scripture quotations marked REB are taken from The Revised English Bible, copyright © Cambridge University Press and Oxford University Press 1989. All rights reserved.

Introduction and Words from the LORD

The Lord gave me the titles for my two books: *The Just Shall Live by Faith*, Galatians 3:11, and *Dreambook*. While writing on my book, *The Just Shall Live by Faith*, Galatians 3:11, I was having my morning worship and asking the Lord in prayer to please give me the title for the stories of faith and courage and answered prayers that I was writing. I wanted the readers of my book to have faith and trust in God as they faced the trying days ahead of us all when the Sunday Law will be passed, and we will all have to decide whose side we'll choose to be on: Christ's side or Satan's side, the 7th day Sabbath and all God's Ten Commandments or choose to be on the side of the Sunday Law, the 1st day of the week and obey man's laws. I knew it would take great faith and trust in God to stand true to God and His 7th day Sabbath and all His commandments and not go along with the majority of the world to keep Sunday, but remain true, when the majority of our fellow believers give in when the Sunday Law is passed. Like Sister White says in *5T* 136, "To stand in defense of truth and righteousness when the majority forsake us, to fight the battles of the Lord when champions are few—this will be our test." On p. 137 she makes this quote: "Now is the time when we should closely connect with God, that we may be hid when the fierceness of His wrath is poured upon the sons of men. We have wandered away from the old landmarks. Let us return. If the Lord be God, serve Him; if Baal, serve him. Which side will you be on?"

With my Bible in my hands and down on my knees, I prayed, "Lord, please open my Bible to the title you want for the book you're helping me to write!" I then opened my Bible and my eyes fell on Galatians 3:11, and I had this underlined in my Bible, "… The just shall live by faith." I prayed and thanked the Lord for hearing my prayer! I thought, "That's just what it's all about!" Praise the Lord!

Then, the Lord gave me a dream to name my other book, *Dreambook*. This was at the time I was writing on my other book, *Don't Be Trapped in the Cities!! Get Out <u>Now</u>!* I prayed and asked the Lord if I should include my dreams He gave me with the book, *Don't Be Trapped in the Cities!! Get Out <u>Now</u>!* I also asked the Lord what He wanted me to name my book of dreams and if He wanted it to be in a separate book? That very night, in a dream, God showed me the word, *Dreambook*. Praise the Lord! God showed me to put my dreams in a separate book and call it, *Dreambook*.

Then, another night in a dream He said to me, "These dreams are for real. Tell others what I have told you." Then, in another dream I was saying this to the people: "These things have been given me of the Lord." Joel 2:28–29, "And it shall come to pass afterward, that I will pour out my spirit upon all flesh; and your sons and your daughters shall prophesy, your old men shall dream dreams, your young men shall see visions: And also upon the servants and upon the handmaids in those days will I pour out my spirit."

In a dream one night, Jesus showed me how He wanted me to sign my name on my book, "Linda Clore." Jesus is really the "Author" of my books written. I'm not trying to be a prophet. I'm just sharing what God gave me and told me in a dream to write and share with others that goes along with the Bible and the Spirit of Prophecy. Isaiah 8:19–20; Revelation 12:17; Revelation 19:10.

In Sister White's book, *1T* 569, she writes, "But dreams from the Lord are classed in the word of God with visions and are as truly the fruits of the spirit of prophecy as visions. Such dreams, taking into the account the persons who have them and the circumstances under which they are given, contain their own proofs of their genuineness. May the blessing of God attend this little work."

> *Jesus is really the "Author" of my books written. I'm not trying to be a prophet. I'm just sharing what God gave me*

Matthew 7:20: "Wherefore by their fruits ye shall know them."

God gave me a dream that said, "You haven't much time left to work!" Another dream said, "NOW is the time to work!" Also, these words were spoken in a dream to me, "Work while you can, the day cometh when no man can work!" John 9:4–5.

In another dream, I heard God call my name, "Linda."

There was a time while writing on my book that I felt like quitting and putting it all away. Then that night in a dream, God spoke to me and said, "Finish your book!" So, I kept writing and working on my book with the Lord's help! Thank you Jesus! Psalm 9:1–2. It's my prayer that these dreams God gave to me to share with others will be a help and strength and courage to those who read them. God bless you my friends!

Sister White says in Vol. 5, *Testimonies for the Church*, p. 573, "Time is very short, and all that is to be done must be done quickly. The angels are holding the four winds, and Satan is taking advantage of everyone who is not fully established in the truth. Every soul is to be tested. Every defect in the character, unless it is overcome by the help of God's Spirit, will become a sure means of destruction. I feel as never before the necessity for our people to be energized by the spirit of the truth, for Satan's devices will ensnare every soul who has not made God his strength. The Lord has much work to be done; and if we do what He has appointed for us to do, He will work with our efforts."

Also, on pp. 576–577, Sister White says, "The spirit and work of Christ must become the spirit and work of His disciples… Christ must be abiding in us, and we in Him, in order to do the work of God. Each must have an individual experience and put forth personal efforts to reach souls… They must make it a business to study His word and hear God's voice addressing them from His living oracles in reproof, in instruction, or in encouragement, and His Spirit will strengthen them, that they may, as God's workers, advance in religious experience. Thus they will be led on step by step to greater heights, and their joy will be full."

In Vol. 6, *Testimonies for the Church*, Sister White writes on p. 393, "The Bible is God's voice speaking to us, just as surely as though we could hear it with our ears. If we realized this, with what awe would we open God's word, and with what earnestness would we search its precepts! The reading and contemplation of the Scriptures would be regarded as an audience with the Infinite One."

God gave me a dream. In my dream, I was talking to God's people telling them how Sister White says we're to get ready and prepared for what's coming! I was quoting her writings. I was telling them how God had given me dreams too, to get ready and prepared for what's soon to come! The people were listening.

Read *Early Writings* by E.G. White, pp. 119–120, about getting ready. The whole book should be read and studied along with books like: *The Great Controversy*, *Maranatha*, *Last Day Events*, etc. by E.G. White.

Dedication

I dedicate this book God has helped me and inspired me to write to my two most loved and appreciated ones, my husband, David, and our son, Jonathan. I could have never written this book without their help and prayers and encouragement! Thanks Dad and Jonathan! I love you both and appreciate your support and encouragement! God bless you both!

I also want to dedicate this book to Jesus. He's the One who has inspired me to write and impressed me through the Holy Spirit and through much prayer, how to write it. I want to give Jesus all the praise and honor and glory and thanks for what He has done to make this book possible. Praise the Lord for the stories and experiences and dreams He's given us to share with others. Just recently God gave me this poem in my dream:

"Take us by the hand—

Guide us to Your land!"

On the same night, I dreamt this poem, David dreamt these words. He said it was a part of a song being sung and this is all he remembers of the song; it was the last of the song: "Christ anew—Alive in me!"

Acknowledgements

I want to acknowledge and thank the staff at my publishing company for all they've done to help me make my book a reality! Thank you and God bless each one of you for letting God use you! You're very much appreciated and loved.

Also, I want to acknowledge and thank the readers of my book for taking the time and interest in reading this material. May it draw you closer to Jesus and His word and have faith and trust in His promises to care for you through the trying days ahead of us all and let the Lord have complete control of your life and plans and surrender all to Him. God bless you!

Contents

The Just Shall Live by Faith, Quotations, Poems, and Songs 11
God is Always Right There! 25
The Shaking! 29
A Red Bird Answers Our Prayer 31
For with God Nothing Shall Be Impossible! 33
Our Two New Friends 39
Update on Our Two New Friends 41
The Search 43
Lost 47
The Fall 49
God to the Rescue 51
A Walk of Faith and Works 53
God Hears the Prayers of Faith 59
"I Sing the Almighty Power of God" 62
When We All Have to Decide! 63
Coming to a Town Near You! 66
Destruction Is Coming to These Cities! 71
A Call to Leave the Cities: Parts 1 90
A Call to Leave the Cities: Parts 2 93
Preparing for the Issue! 100
A Storm is Coming! 102
Our Encounter with the Devil! 107
Preparing for the Sunday Laws!! 110
"Breathe on Me, Breathe of God" 117
Linda's Dream on The Alpha and The Omega 118

Robe of Christ's Righteousness 120

Watchmen, What of the Night?! 123

Ye Are My Witnesses 126

It Is More Blessed to Give Than to Receive 137

Hunger and Thirst After Righteousness 141

You Can Gain the Victory Over Sin! 144

"I Surrendered All" 150

"Is Your All on the Altar" 153

"Jesus, I My Cross Have Taken" 154

The Schools of the Prophets: 1, 2, 3 155

"The Ark" Poem 162

Experiences 165

Be Ready and Be Prepared! 169

What Do People See in You? 173

The Seizure 179

Jesus, Come into My Heart, TODAY! 181

The One Lost Sheep 187

Linda Clore's Dream About "The One Lost Sheep." 190

Now—Don't Put It Off! 192

My New Song! 194

LORD! Make me New! 198

Do It Today! 203

Getting Ready for Jesus to Come! 207

More Time 210

Have Faith in God! 213

PICTURES 215

"The Just Shall Live by Faith"
(Galatians 3:11)
Quotations, Poems and Songs
Written by Linda Clore

October 11, 2017

Read all of Hebrews 11, the "faith chapter," especially verses 1, 6, 7. "Now faith is the substance of things hoped for, the evidence of things not seen… But without faith it is impossible to please him: for he that cometh to God must believe that he is, and that he is a rewarder of them that diligently seek him. By faith Noah, being warned of God of things not seen as yet, moved with fear, prepared an ark to the saving of his house; by the which he condemned the world, and became heir of the righteousness which is by faith."

Mark 11:22–24: "And Jesus answering saith unto them, Have faith in God. For verily I say unto you, That whosoever shall say unto this mountain, Be thou removed, and be thou cast into the sea; and shall not doubt in his heart, but shall believe that those things which he saith shall come to pass; he shall have whatsoever he saith. Therefore I say unto you, What things soever ye desire, when ye pray, believe that ye receive them, and ye shall have them."

Matthew 9:22: "But Jesus turned him about, and when he saw her, he said, Daughter, be of good comfort; thy faith hath made thee whole. And the woman was made whole from that hour."

Luke 7:50: "And he said to the woman, Thy faith hath saved thee; go in peace."

Luke 17:5: "And the apostles said unto the Lord, Increase our faith."

Matthew 17:15–21 (verses 20, 21 quoted): "And Jesus said unto them, Because of your unbelief: for verily I say unto you, If ye have faith as a grain of mustard seed, ye shall say unto this mountain, Remove hence to yonder place; and it shall remove; and nothing shall be impossible unto you. Howbeit this kind goeth not out but by prayer and fasting."

Matthew 21:22: "And all things, whatsoever ye shall ask in prayer, believing, ye shall receive."

Luke 18:1–8 (verses 7, 8 quoted): "And shall not God avenge his own elect, which cry day and night unto him, though he bear long with them? I tell you that he will avenge them speedily. Nevertheless when the Son of man cometh, shall he find faith on the earth?"

Acts 3:1–26 (verses 6, 7, 16, 19 quoted): "Then Peter said, Silver and gold have I none; but such as I have give I thee: In the name of Jesus Christ of Nazareth rise up and walk. And he took him by the right hand, and lifted him up: and immediately his feet and ankle bones received strength… And his name through faith in his name hath made this man strong, whom ye see and know: yea, the faith which is by him hath given him this perfect soundness in the presence of you all… Repent ye therefore, and be converted, that your sins may be blotted out, when the times of refreshing shall come from the presence of the Lord."

Galatians 5:22, 23: "But the fruit of the Spirit is love, joy, peace, longsuffering, gentleness, goodness, faith, meekness, temperance: against such there is no law."

Read in *Patriarchs and Prophets*, by E.G. White, chapter 11, "The Call of Abraham"; chapter 12, "Abraham in Canaan"; chapter 13, "The Test of Faith"; chapter 14, "Destruction of Sodom." On p. 126 we read, "By faith Abraham, when he was called to go out into a place which he should after receive for an inheritance, obeyed; and he went out, not knowing whither he went." Hebrews 11:8. Abraham's unquestioning obedience is one of the most striking evidences of faith to be found in all the Bible… Relying upon the divine promise, without the least outward assurance of its fulfillment, he abandoned home and kindred and native land, and went forth, he knew not whither, to follow where God should lead… God has spoken, and His servant must obey; the happiest place on earth for him was the place where God would have him to be. Many are still tested as was Abraham." On p. 139 we continue to read, ""The secret of the Lord is with them that fear Him." Psalm 25:14. Abraham had honored God, and the Lord honored him, taking him into His counsels, and revealing to him His purposes…" On p. 170 we continue to read, "We must dwell as pilgrims and strangers here if we would gain "a better country, that is, an heavenly." Hebrews 11:16.

God has spoken, and His servant must obey; the happiest place on earth for him was the place where God would have him to be

Also, in chapter 18, "The Night of Wrestling," we read on pp. 202–203, "All who endeavor to excuse or conceal their sins, and permit them to remain upon the books of heaven, unconfessed and unforgiven, will be overcome by Satan… Jacob prevailed because he was persevering and determined. His experience testifies to the power of importunate prayer. It is now that we are to learn this lesson of prevailing prayer, of unyielding faith… They are those victories that are gained in the audience chamber with God, when earnest, agonizing faith lays hold upon the mighty arm of power. Those who are unwilling to forsake every sin and to seek earnestly for God's blessing, will not obtain it. But all who will lay hold of God's promises as did Jacob, and be as earnest and persevering as he was, will succeed as he succeeded."

Read in Sister White's book, *Last Day Events*, quotes from p. 55, "We cannot now step off the foundation that God has established. We cannot now enter into any new organization, for this would mean apostasy from the truth."

Also, on p. 62 we read, "The work is soon to close. The members of the church militant who have proved faithful will become the church triumphant."

On pp. 126–127 we read, "Those who are making an effort to change the Constitution and secure a law enforcing Sunday observance little realize what will be the result. A crisis is just upon us… As faithful watchmen you should see the sword coming and give the warning, that men and women may not pursue a course through ignorance that they would avoid if they knew the truth."

Also, p. 199 says, "The sins of Babylon will be laid open. The fearful results of enforcing the observances of the church by civil authority, the inroads of spiritualism, the stealthy but rapid progress of the papal power—all will be unmasked. By these solemn warnings the people will be stirred. Thousands upon thousands will listen who have never heard words like these."

Read pp. 212–214, "A good many do not see it now, to take their position, but these things are influencing their lives, and when the message goes with a loud voice they will be ready for it. They will not hesitate long; they will come out and take their position… More than one thousand will soon be converted in one day, most of whom will trace their first convictions to the reading of our publications… In a large degree through our publishing houses is to be accomplished the work of that other angel who comes down from heaven with great power and who lightens the earth with his glory." Revelation 18:1.

Page 227 reads, "The Lord has shown me clearly that the image of the beast will be formed before probation closes, for it is to be the great test for the people of God, by which their eternal destiny will be decided." Page 222 says, "Satan is now using every device in this sealing time to keep the minds of God's people from the present truth and to cause them to waver." Page 228 says, "Just before we entered it [the time of trouble], we all received the seal of the living God. Then I saw the four angels cease to hold the four winds. And I saw famine, pestilence and sword, nation rose against nation, and the whole world was in confusion."

Page 264 reads, "The people of God will not be free from suffering; but while persecuted and distressed, while they endure privation, and suffer for want of food, they will not be left to perish… Then will be the time for us to trust wholly in God, and He will sustain us." Also, on p. 270 we read, "The people of God—some in prison cells, some hidden in solitary retreats in the forests and the mountains—still plead for divine protection, … It is at midnight that God manifests His power for the deliverance of His people.… Prison walls are rent asunder, and God's people, who have been held in bondage for their faith, are set free."

On p. 373 in *The Great Controversy* by E.G. White, she writes: "Would that there were still with the professed people of God the same spirit of heart searching, the same earnest, determined faith… There is too little prayer, too little real conviction of sin, and the lack of living faith leaves many destitute of the grace so richly provided by our Redeemer."

Read also chapter 21, "A Warning Rejected," pp. 375–380; chapter 22, "Prophecies Fulfilled," pp. 391–408.

Read also on pp. 443–444, "It was apostasy that led the early church to seek the aid of the civil government, and this prepared the way for the development of the papacy—the beast. Said Paul: 'There' shall 'come a falling away, … and that man of sin be revealed.' 2 Thessalonians 2:3.

So apostasy in the church will prepare the way for the image to the beast... 2 Timothy 3:1–5, 12; 1 Timothy 4:1; 2 Thessalonians 2:9–11."

Read also, pp. 603–612, "The Final Warning," chapter 38. Revelation 18:1–5:

"As the teachings of spiritualism are accepted by the churches, the restraint imposed upon the carnal heart is removed, and the profession of religion will become a cloak to conceal the basest iniquity. A belief in spiritual manifestations opens the door to seducing spirits and doctrines of devils, and thus the influence of evil angels will be felt in the churches... Fearful is the issue to which the world is to be brought... All who refuse compliance will be visited with civil penalties... In every generation God has sent His servants to rebuke sin, both in the world and in the church. But the people desire smooth things spoken to them, and the pure, unvarnished truth is not acceptable... The words which the Lord gave them they uttered, fearless of consequences, and the people were compelled to hear the warning... As the time comes for it to be given with greatest power, the Lord will work through humble instruments, leading the minds of those who consecrate themselves to His service. The laborers will be qualified rather by the unction of His Spirit than by the training of literary institutions. Men of faith and prayer will be constrained to go forth with holy zeal, declaring the words which God gives them... As the movement for Sunday enforcement becomes more bold and decided, the law will be invoked against commandment keepers. They will be threatened with fines and imprisonment, and some will be offered positions of influence, and other rewards and advantages, as inducements to renounce their faith. But their steadfast answer is: "Show us from the word of God our error"—the same plea that was made by Luther under similar circumstances. Those who are arraigned before the courts make a strong vindication of the truth, and some who hear them are led to take their stand to keep all the commandments of God. Thus light will be brought before thousands who otherwise would know nothing of these truths... Conscientious obedience to the word of God will be treated as rebellion. Blinded by Satan, the parent will exercise harshness and severity toward the believing child; the master or mistress will oppress the commandment-keeping servant. Affection will be alienated; children will be disinherited and driven from home. The words of Paul will be literally fulfilled: "All that will live godly in Christ Jesus shall suffer persecution." 2 Timothy 3:12. As the defenders of truth refuse to honor the Sunday-sabbath, some of them will be thrust into prison, some will be exiled, some will be treated as slaves...

As the storm approaches, a large class who have professed faith in the third angel's message, but have not been sanctified through obedience to the truth, abandon their position and join the ranks of the opposition. By uniting with the world and partaking of its spirit, they have come to view matters in nearly the same light; and when the test is brought, they are prepared to choose the easy, popular side. Men of talent and pleasing address, who once rejoiced in the truth, employ their powers to deceive and mislead souls. They become the most bitter enemies of their former brethren. When Sabbathkeepers are brought before the courts to answer for their faith, these apostates are the most efficient agents of Satan to misrepresent and accuse them, and by false reports and insinuations to stir up the rulers against them. In this time of persecution the faith of the Lord's servants will be tried. They have faithfully given the warning, looking to God and to His word alone. God's Spirit, moving upon their hearts, has constrained them to speak… They remember that the words which they have spoken were not theirs, but His who bade them give the warning. God put the truth into their hearts, and they could not forbear to proclaim it.

The same trials have been experienced by men of God in ages past. Wycliffe, Huss, Luther, Tyndale, Baxter, Wesley, urged that all doctrines be brought to the test of the Bible and declared that they would renounce everything which it condemned. Against these men persecution raged with relentless fury; yet they ceased not to declare the truth… The Lord gives a special truth for the people in an emergency. Who dare refuse to publish it?… Servants of God, with their faces lighted up and shining with holy consecration, will hasten from place to place to proclaim the message from heaven. By thousands of voices, all over the earth, the warning will be given. Miracles will be wrought, the sick will be healed, and signs and wonders will follow the believers. Satan also works, with lying wonders, even bringing down fire from heaven in the sight of men. Revelation 13:13. Thus the inhabitants of the earth will be brought to take their stand."

On October 19, 2017, God gave me this dream: Quotes from E.G. White's book, *Education*, pp. 269–271, especially on p. 271, "With such an army of workers as our youth, rightly trained, might furnish, how soon the message of a crucified, risen, and soon–coming Saviour might be carried to the whole world! How soon might the end come—the end of suffering and sorrow and sin!" **Read** chapters 1–8 in *The Great Controversy* by E.G. White about the Reformation, and Maranatha by E. G. White, pp. 58, 60, 61, 66, 67, 224, 225.

"Acts 20:29, 30. God has not passed His people by and chosen one solitary man here and another there as the only ones worthy to be entrusted with His truth. He does not give one man new light contrary to the established faith of the body. In every reform men have arisen making this claim… The angels of God in their messages to men represent time as very short. Thus it has always been presented to me… The people of God must purify their souls through obedience to the truth, and be prepared to stand without fault before Him at His coming. Had Adventists, after the great disappointment in 1844, held fast their faith, and followed on unitedly in the opening providence of God, receiving the message of the third angel and in the power of the Holy Spirit proclaiming it to the world, …the Lord would have wrought mightily with their efforts, the work would have been completed, and Christ would have come ere this to receive His people to their reward. But in the period of doubt and uncertainty that followed the disappointment, many of the advent believers yielded their faith… Thus the work was hindered, and the world was left in darkness… For forty years did unbelief, murmuring, and rebellion shut out ancient Israel from the land of Canaan. The same sins have delayed the entrance of modern Israel into the heavenly Canaan. In neither case were the promises of God at fault. It is the unbelief, the worldliness, unconsecration, and strife among the Lord's professed people that have kept us in this world of sin and sorrow so many years.

The faith that strengthened Habakkuk and all the holy and the just in those days of deep trial was the same faith that sustains God's people today… Day by day, through faith in God, his hope and courage may be renewed…

We must cherish and cultivate the faith of which prophets and apostles have testified—the faith that lays hold on the promises of God and waits for deliverance in His appointed time and way…

Let us ever hold in remembrance the cheering message, 'The vision is yet for an appointed time, but at the end it shall speak, and not lie: though it tarry, wait for it; because it will surely come, it will not tarry.... Habakkuk 2:3… The just shall live by his faith.' Habakkuk 2:4.

There is coming rapidly and surely an almost universal guilt upon the inhabitants of the cities, because of the steady increase of determined wickedness. The corruption that prevails, is beyond the power of the human pen to describe. Every day brings fresh revelations of strife, bribery, and fraud; every day brings its heart–sickening record of violence and lawlessness, of indifference to human suffering, of brutal, fiendish destruction of human life…

The conditions prevailing in society, and especially in the great cities of the nations, proclaim in thunder tones that the hour of God's judgment is come and that the end of all things earthly is at hand

Our God is a God of mercy. With long–sufferance and tender compassion He deals with the transgressors of His law… The Lord bears long with men, and with cities, mercifully giving warnings to save them from divine wrath; but a time will come when pleadings for mercy will no longer be heard…

The conditions prevailing in society, and especially in the great cities of the nations, proclaim in thunder tones that the hour of God's judgment is come and that the end of all things earthly is at hand. We are standing on the threshold of the crisis of the ages. In quick succession the judgments of God will follow one another—fire, and flood, and earthquake, with war and bloodshed…

The storm of God's wrath is gathering; and those only will stand who respond to the invitations of mercy, … and become sanctified through obedience to the laws of the divine Ruler. The righteous alone will be hid with Christ in God till the desolation be overpast…

Appetite and passion, the love of the world and presumptuous sins, were the great branches of evil out of which every species of … corruption grew. Our lives may seem a tangle; but as we commit ourselves to the wise Master Worker, He will bring out the pattern of life and character that will be to His own glory. And that character which expresses the glory—character—of Christ, will be received into the Paradise of God. Everyone who by faith obeys God's commandments, will reach the condition of sinlessness in which Adam lived before his transgression…"

Read Jude 24, "Now unto him that is able to keep you from falling, and to present you faultless before the presence of his glory with exceeding joy."

"As we partake of the divine nature, hereditary and cultivated tendencies to wrong are cut away from the character, and we are made a living power for good."

Read on p. 214, *Maranatha*, we read, "The season of distress before God's people will call for a faith that will not falter… History will be repeated."

In *Desire of Ages* by E.G. White, on p. 324, she writes, "The only defense against evil is the indwelling of Christ in the heart through faith in His righteousness."

Read also, pp 335, 340, "It is in working to spread the good news of salvation that we are brought near to the Saviour… The two restored demoniacs were the first missionaries whom Christ sent to preach the gospel in the region of Decapolis… They could tell what they knew; what they themselves had seen, and heard, and felt of the power of Christ. This is what everyone can do whose heart has been touched by the grace of God… Though the Saviour Himself departed, the men whom He had healed remained as witnesses to His power…"

On p. 341 we read, "Satan's influence is constantly exerted upon men to distract the senses, control the mind for evil, and incite to violence and crime. He weakens the body, darkens the intellect, and debases the soul. Whenever men reject the Saviour's invitation, they are yielding themselves to Satan… The only safeguard against his power is found in the presence of Jesus. Before men and angels Satan has been revealed as man's enemy and destroyer; Christ, as man's friend and deliverer. His Spirit will develop in man all that will ennoble the character and dignify the nature… And souls that have been degraded into instruments of Satan are still through the power of Christ transformed into messengers of righteousness, and sent forth by the Son of God to tell what 'great things the Lord hath done for thee, and hath had compassion on thee.'"

Page 348 reads:

"The Lord works continually to benefit mankind. He is ever imparting His bounties. He raises up the sick from beds of languishing, He delivers men from peril which they do not see, He commissions heavenly angels to save them from calamity, to guard them from 'the pestilence that walketh in darkness" and "the destruction that wasteth at noonday' (Psalm 91:6); but their hearts are unimpressed. He has given all the riches of heaven to redeem them, and yet they are unmindful of His great love. By their ingratitude they close their hearts against the grace of God…

It is for our own benefit to keep every gift of God fresh in our memory. Thus faith is strengthened to claim and to receive more and more. There is greater encouragement for us in the least blessing we ourselves receive from God than in all the accounts we can read of the faith and experience of others. The soul that responds to the grace of God shall be like a watered garden. His health shall spring forth speedily; his light shall rise in obscurity, and the glory of the Lord shall be seen upon him. Let us then remember the loving–kindness of the Lord, and the multitude of His tender mercies. Like the people of Israel, let us set up our stones of witness, and inscribe upon them the precious story of what God has wrought for us. And as we review His dealings with us in our pilgrimage, let us, out of hearts melted with gratitude, declare, Psalm 116:12–14.'"

Continue reading on p. 371, "The means in our possession may not seem to be sufficient for the work; but if we will move forward in faith, believing in the all–sufficient power of God, abundant resources will open before us. If the work be of God, He Himself will provide the means for its accomplishment. He will reward honest, simple reliance upon Him. The little that is wisely and economically used in the service of the Lord of heaven will increase in the very act of imparting. In the hand of Christ the small supply of food remained undiminished until the famished multitude were satisfied. If we go to the Source of all strength, with our hands of faith outstretched to receive, we shall be sustained in our work, even under the most forbidding circumstances, and shall be enabled to give to others the bread of life."

It reminds me of the dream the Lord gave me on October 21, 2017. In my dream, I was saying, "Martin Luther wanted the people to know the truth, so he boldly and fearlessly nailed his 95 theses on the door of the Roman Catholic church. Today, we Seventh–day Adventists should be bold and fearless as we let the people know the truth, so they can take their stand on God's true 7th day Bible Sabbath and not go along with the Sunday Law when it is passed. We have a work to do for the Lord today, like Martin Luther did in his day. God is counting on us to use us like He used Martin Luther five hundred years ago to stand up for the Reformation. Even Martin Luther said, "The just shall live by faith." Martin Luther was the man for his time. God raised up His S.D.A. church for this time, and He has modern day Martin Luthers who will courageously stand and speak for the truth today! (Won't you be one?!) **Read** chapters 1–8 in *The Great Controversy* by E.G. White about Martin Luther of the Reformation.

It makes me think of the song Martin Luther wrote in 1529, "A Mighty Fortress is our God." Also, I think of the song, "Stand Up! Stand Up for Jesus!" This is what God's people will be doing today for Jesus and His truth!

On pp. 160–161 of The Great Controversy, we read what Sister White wrote of Martin Luther's stand before the Roman Catholic church:

> "Those who stubbornly closed their eyes to the light, and determined not to be convinced of the truth, were enraged at the power of Luther's words. As he ceased speaking, the spokesman of the Diet said angrily: 'You have not answered the question put to you… You are required to give a clear and precise answer… Will you, or will you not, retract?'
>
> The Reformer answered: 'Since your most serene majesty and your high mightinesses require from me a clear, simple, and precise answer, I will give you one, and it is this: I cannot submit my faith either to the pope or to the councils, because it is clear as the day that they have frequently erred and contradicted each other. Unless therefore I am convinced by the testimony of Scripture or by the clearest reasoning, unless I am persuaded by means of the passages I have quoted, and unless they thus render my conscience bound by the word of God, I cannot and I will not retract, for it is unsafe for a Christian to speak against his conscience. Here I stand, I can do no other; may God help me. Amen.'
>
> Luther's friend, who had with great joy listened to his noble defense, trembled at these words; but the doctor himself said calmly: 'May God be my helper, for I can retract nothing.'
>
> Thus stood this righteous man upon the sure foundation of the word of God. The light of heaven illuminated his countenance. His greatness and purity of character, his peace and joy of heart, were manifest to all as he testified against the power of error and witnessed to the superiority of that faith that overcomes the world."

On p. 164 we read, "There are many at the present day thus clinging to the customs and traditions of their fathers. When the Lord sends them additional light, they refuse to accept it, because, not having been granted to their fathers, it was not received by them... We shall not be approved of God in looking to the example of our fathers to determine our duty instead of searching the word of truth for ourselves... We are accountable for the light which they received, and which was handed down as an inheritance for us, and we are accountable also for the additional light which is now shining upon us from the word of God."

Continue reading on p. 165, "The people gazed upon him as if he were more than human. Even those who had no faith in his doctrines could not but admire that lofty integrity which led him to brave death rather than violate his conscience. Earnest efforts were made to obtain Luther's consent to a compromise with Rome... To this appeal Luther answered: "The gospel of Christ cannot be preached without offense.... Why then should the fear or apprehension of danger separate me from the Lord, and from that divine word which alone is truth? No; I would rather give up my body, my blood, and my life."

On p. 166, we read, "... The influence of this one man, who dared to think and act for himself in religious matters, was to affect the church and the world, not only in his own time, but in all future generations. His firmness and fidelity would strengthen all, to the close of time, who should pass through a similar experience. The power and majesty of God stood forth above the counsel of men, above the mighty power of Satan."

Continue reading on pp. 168–170, "God had provided a way of escape for His servant in this hour of peril... It was plain that Rome would be satisfied with nothing short of his death; only by concealment could he be preserved from the jaws of the lion. God gave wisdom to Frederick of Saxony to devise a plan for the Reformer's preservation... Upon his homeward journey he was seized, separated from his attendants, and hurriedly conveyed through the forest to the castle of Wartburg, an isolated mountain fortress... A host of tracts, issuing from his pen, circulated throughout Germany. He also performed a most important service for his countrymen by translating the New Testament into the German tongue. From his rocky Patmos he continued for nearly a whole year to proclaim the gospel and rebuke the sins and errors of the times... In the solitude and obscurity of his mountain retreat, Luther was removed from earthly supports and shut out from human praise. He was thus saved from the pride and self–confidence that are so often caused by success... Satan seeks to divert men's thoughts and affections from God, and to fix them upon human agencies; he leads them to honor the mere instrument and to ignore the Hand that directs all the events of providence. Too often religious leaders who are thus praised and reverenced lose sight of their dependence upon God and are led to trust in themselves. As a result they seek to control the minds and consciences of the people, who are disposed to look to them for guidance instead of looking to the word of God. The work of reform is often retarded because of this spirit indulged by its supporters. From this danger, God would guard the cause of the Reformation. He desired that work to receive, not the impress of man, but that of God. The

> *We are accountable for the light which they received, and which was handed down as an inheritance for us, and we are accountable also for the additional light which is now shining upon us from the word of God*

eyes of men had been turned to Luther as the expounder of the truth; he was removed that all eyes might be directed to the eternal Author of truth."

I once read these things that really impressed me, and so I added them to my book to be a blessing to others.

They are: "A Prayer for Today"; "I Refuse to Be Discouraged"; and "Footprints."

Here are some books that I recommend reading: The Spirit of prophecy books by E.G. White especially: *The Great Controversy*; *Maranatha*; *Last Day Events*; *Steps to Christ*; *Ministry of Healing*; *Desire of Ages*; *Patriarchs and Prophets*; *Counsels on Diet and Foods*; *Country Living*.

Read also my book: *Don't Be Trapped in the Cities!!! Get Out Now!*

Joe Crews' books: *Creeping Compromise and Reaping the Whirlwind*.

W.D. Frazee's books: *Coming Events and Crisis at the Close* (1979 edition) and *Another Ark to Build*.

Jere Franklin's book: *You Can Survive!*

Study your KJV Bible and the books of Daniel and Revelation.

2 Timothy 2:15: "Study to show thyself approved unto God, a workman that needeth not to be ashamed, rightly dividing the word of truth."

Read in *Patriarchs and Prophets* by E.G. White, chapter 13, pp. 145–155, "Test of Faith"; and chapter 14 "Destruction of Sodom," pp. 156–170, especially page 158, "It is little things that test the character."

Read in *Education* by E.G. White, "Faith and Prayer," pp. 253–261.

"A Prayer for Today"

This is the beginning of a new day. God has given me this day to use as I will. I can waste it – or use it for good, but what I do today is important, because I am exchanging a day of my life for it! When tomorrow comes, this day will be gone forever; leaving in its place something that I have traded for it. I want it to be gain, and not loss; good, and not evil; success, and not failure; in order that I shall not regret the price that I have paid for it."

> *This is the beginning of a new day. God has given me this day to use as I will. I can waste it – or use it for good, but what I do today is important, because I am exchanging a day of my life for it!*

The Just Shall Live by Faith | 21

A Mighty Fortress Is Our God

A might-y for-tress is our God, a bul-wark
Did we in our own strength con-fide, our striv-ing
And though this world, with dev-ils filled, should threat-en
That Word a-bove all earth-ly powers— no thanks to

nev-er fail-ing; our help-er he, a-mid the flood
would be los-ing, were not the right Man on our side,
to un-do us, we will not fear, for God has willed
them— a-bid-eth; the Spir-it and the gifts are ours

of mor-tal ills pre-vail-ing. For still our an-cient foe
the Man of God's own choos-ing. You ask who that may be?
his truth to tri-umph through us. The prince of dark-ness grim,
through him who with us sid-eth. Let goods and kin-dred go,

Text: Martin Luther, 1529; tr. Fredrick H. Hedge,
   1852; based on Psalm 46
Tune: Martin Luther, 1529, alt.; harm. Johann S.
   Bach. 1685-1750

87 87 66 66
EIN FESTE BURG
(isorhythmic
www.hymnary.org/text/a_mighty_fortress_is_our_god_a_bulwar

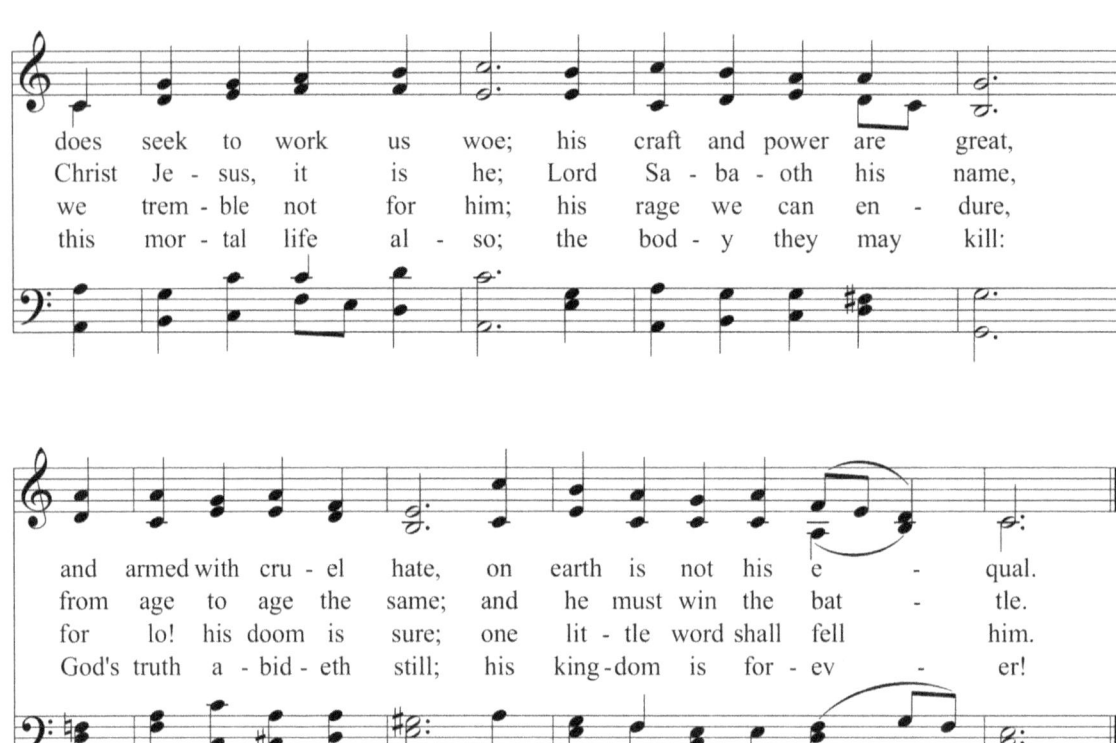

Stand Up, Stand Up for Jesus

1. Stand up, stand up for Jesus, Ye soldiers of the cross;
Lift high His royal banner, It must not suffer loss:
From vict'ry unto vict'ry His army shall He lead,
Till ev'ry foe is vanquished, And Christ is Lord indeed.

2. Stand up, stand up for Jesus, The trumpet call obey;
Forth to the mighty conflict, In this His glorious day:
Ye who are men, now serve Him Against unnumbered foes;
Let courage rise with danger, And strength to strength oppose.

3. Stand up, stand up for Jesus, Stand in His strength alone;
The arm of flesh will fail you, Ye dare not trust your own:
Put on the gospel armor, Each piece put on with pray'r;
Where duty calls, or danger, Be never wanting there.

4. Stand up, stand up for Jesus, The strife will not be long;
This day the noise of battle, The next, the victor's song:
To him who overcometh A crown of life shall be;
He, with the King of glory, Shall reign eternally.

Text: George Duffield, 1818-1888
Tune: Adam Geibel, 1855-1933

76 76D Refrain
GEIBEL
www.hymnary.org//text/stand_up_stand_up_for_jesus_duffield

This hymn is in the public domain. You may freely use this score for personal and congregational worship. If you reproduce the score, please credit *Hymnary.org* as the source.

24 | *The Just Shall Live by Faith*

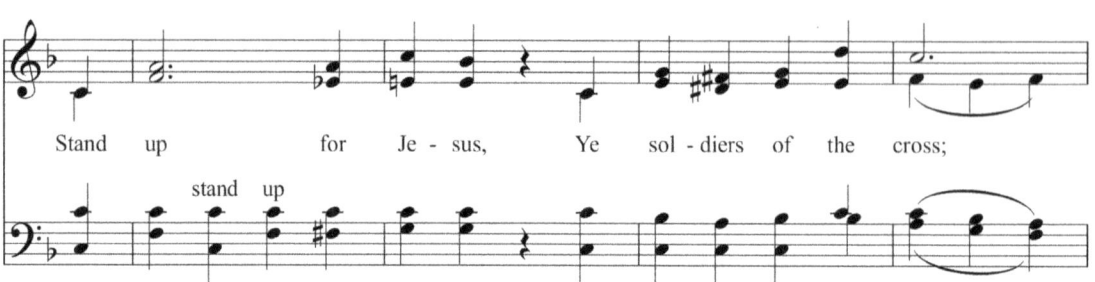

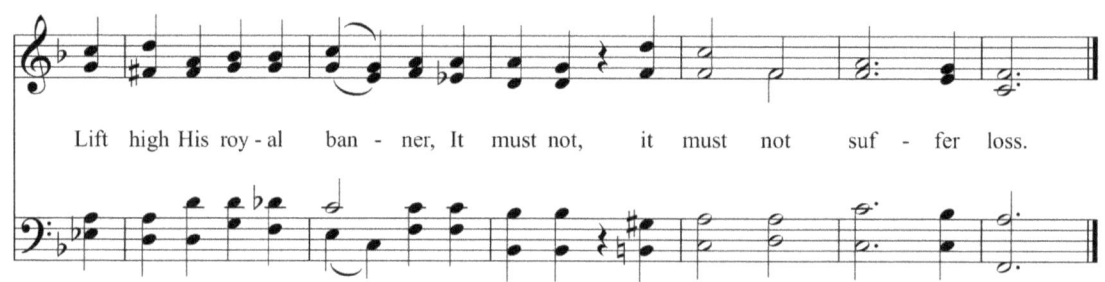

"God Is Always Right There!"
("… for he hath said, I will never leave thee, nor forsake thee." Hebrews 13:5)

Written August 19, 2016

The following is a terrible and terrifying experience the Lord brought us through! It strengthened our faith in God and His power to do anything!

Jonathan was having a problem with one of his medications and was wanting off of it because of the serious side effects it was causing him, and we needed to hurry him to the Emergency room because of it!

It was late and pouring down rain and so dark out! On the way to the Emergency room, the car overheated, but arrived safely to the Emergency room, thanks to the good Lord and a lot of prayer! Jonathan received the help he needed, and God had seen him through his crisis! Praise the Lord!

Now to face the problem with the car! On the way back home in the rain and the dark, the car kept overheating, and he had to pull over to the side of the road to let the car cool down. But before heading on home while still in Ottawa, two cops pulled up behind him to see what the problem was. They asked to see his driver's license, and David couldn't find his billfold! David said to the two cops, "It must have fallen out of my pocket in the Emergency room!" So, the two cops drove him in their cop car back to the Emergency room. David was praying all the way back to the Emergency room that his billfold would be there!

God had sent angels in the form of cops to help Dad in his time of trouble and distress, I'm sure

When they walked into the Emergency room, the nurses gathered around David and the two cops to see what was going on and sure enough, they had found his billfold and returned it to him! David was praising the Lord and thanked the nurses. The money was still in the billfold too!

Then, the two cops drove him back to his parked car and David thanked them for their help and kindness. They were strong and husky and friendly cops. God had sent angels in the form of cops to help Dad in his time of trouble and distress, I'm sure! God had been looking out for David by looking out for him sending those cops that could have been angels in disguise to help David get his lost billfold found before he left town! Praise the Lord!

David continued on his journey home in the dark and the rain pouring down. On his way home just out of Pomona, the car overheated and he pulled off the road again to let the car cool down. Before he even got out of the car, a police car pulled in behind him to see what the problem was. David explained to the policeman that his car keeps overheating and he's trying to make it home, but he has to keep stopping to let the car cool down.

David said the policeman was so nice and friendly, and he offered to help Daddy by going down a steep bank to a creek in the dark and rain and through the weeds and getting water in his shoes to get some water for Dad to put in the radiator. He was using Jonathan's urinal to get water. David thanked him for his help and kindness. He was so thankful and grateful for the policeman coming to his rescue! He offered him a "Great Controversy" book, but he refused it, and said, "Give it to someone else."

David said the cop's face and eyes were so kind–looking that he really looked like an angel as David talked to him. The cop was strong and husky and muscular and very intelligent looking. David was telling the cop how bad conditions were in the world and that the Lord is soon to come! The cop was very serious looking and he said, "Yes! I know!"

David mentioned to him about all these places buying up new modern armory and equipment like they're setting up for warfare and riots! And the cop with a serious and solemn expression on his face said, "Yes! I know!"

David shook the cop's hand and thanked him again for being so kind to help him out! The policeman went back to his police car and drove on back toward Ottawa. The two police in Ottawa must have called on their radio to this other cop to follow Dad and help him out on his journey home. Because as Daddy pulled off the road, the cop pulled right in behind him! Daddy didn't know a cop was following him looking out for him in his time of trouble! God was right there all the time! Praise God, He got the car safely home! We all just prayed and thanked the good Lord for getting Jonathan the help he needed and that he was doing okay! We praised and thanked the Lord for helping Dad find his lost billfold before he had gone all that way home! We were so grateful, too, that God had seen us all through this horrible nightmare experience and we safely home and praying and thanking the Lord for the angels in a policeman's garb to help us in our time of trouble! Truly, "The angel of the LORD encampeth round about them that fear him, and delivereth them." Psalm 34:7. **Read** Psalm 34:6–10, 15–19.

Through all this, I kept praying and claiming God's promises found in Mark 10:27 and Luke 1:37, "For with God nothing shall be impossible."

When we were safely home and going through all that had just happened and thanking God, I remarked about Joshua 1:5,9 how God will be there with us and not fail us or forsake us and for us to be strong and of a good courage and not to be afraid, nor dismayed, because God is with us wherever we go!

David remarked, "Don't you wonder why God allows all this to happen sometimes?"

I said, "So we'll develop faith and trust in God to make us strong to endure these trials we go through now, so we'll be ready for the crises ahead of us when the Sunday Law will be passed, and we will be true to God and His 7th day Sabbath and not give in or give up, but remain loyal no matter what happens, we have developed faith in God and can trust His promises to see us through it all!

Read, *Sons and Daughters of God* by Sister White, p. 195, "Will the Saviour ever turn away to leave you to struggle alone? No, never... Poverty is coming upon this world, and there will be a time of trouble such as never was since there was a nation... You may have to suffer distress; you may go hungry sometimes; but God will not forsake you in your suffering. He will test your faith... We are here to manifest Christ to the world, to represent Him and His power to mankind."

Also, read in *The Great Controversy* by Sister White, chapter 39, "The Time of Trouble." On p. 621, we read, "The season of distress and anguish before us will require a faith that can endure weariness, delay, and hunger—a faith that will not faint though severely tried. The period of probation is granted to all to prepare for that time..."

I said to David, "Also, our experiences God puts us through can be an encouragement to others that God will see them through their trying times and trials and troubles ahead of them, too! Just like we're praying to be among the 144,000 who'll be alive when Jesus comes and be giving the Loud Cry message calling people out of these fallen churches. We have no idea what we may have to go through and endure to be living on this earth when Jesus comes!" (**Read** chapter 37, "The Scriptures a Safeguard" in *The Great Controversy*).

Sister White writes in the *Review & Herald* (3/9/1905), "Let us strive with all the power God has given us to be among the 144,000." (Also, read *The Great Controversy* pp. 648–649).

It reminds me of the dream I had where God wrote me this poem in my dream:

"Through all the dangers ahead of me,

The pain and trials and troubles and all my sorrows—

I'll press on in faith and courage knowing that,

Jesus is in all my tomorrows!"

God is trying to toughen us up like strong soldiers, so we won't crumble when the pressures are put on us, but remain true and loyal to Jesus and His true 7th day Sabbath and all His Ten Commandments.

Like another dream God gave me that said that we're to train up like military soldiers. We're in like boot camp training right now to prepare us to be strong to stand through the crisis ahead of us. That's why we run and lift weights and do chin ups and push ups and sit ups and ride our bikes, so we can stay in shape physically and study and memorize our Bibles and the

> *We can stay in shape physically and study and memorize our Bibles and the promises and what we believe, so we can stand spiritually strong for Jesus when the majority will be shaken out of the church*

promises and what we believe, so we can stand spiritually strong for Jesus when the majority will be shaken out of the church.

God is trying, through all these experiences He's allowing us to go through to show us He can handle it and that nothing is too hard for God and that He'll always be there with us to see us through whatever happens! Like Psalm 46 and Psalm 91 and Psalm 121 and Psalm 55:22 and Psalm 50;15 says. Oh! Yes! God helped us to get $100.00 in the mail from my cousin, Nancy just when we needed it to fix our radiator problem. Praise God! God is always right there! Thank you Jesus!

"The Shaking!"
Written September 3, 2016

At around 8:00 a.m. on September 3, 2016, Sabbath morning, we were going to have our family worship, and I was standing in front of Jonathan, as he sat in his chair, and we were talking. He was getting upset with me about one of his drugs he wanted to take, and I was against him taking it.

All of a sudden, we felt an earthquake taking place! The house trailer shook, and the floor was shaking under my feet! The TV was off but making a funny noise, as it, too, was shaking! The curtains were shaking and the bowls on the refrigerator were rattling! I said to Jonathan, "We're having an earthquake!" Jonathan stopped arguing about his drug he wanted to take.

David had fallen asleep in his chair in his bedroom studying his Bible, and the earthquake shaking his chair woke him up! He came out to the front room where we were, and we both said together, "We're having an earthquake!"

Then, I said to David and Jonathan, "Jesus is trying to get our attention by giving us this earthquake to shake us up and let us know that He's getting ready to come, and we better shape up and examine ourselves as 2 Corinthians 13:5 says. We better stop sinning and be serious about our salvation. He's even at the door, as Matthew 24:32–44 and as Luke 21 and Mark 13 tells us of the signs of His coming, they mention earthquakes in divers places! Like right here in our place on the "Ark"!

The tremors we felt didn't last long, maybe a couple of minutes or so, and they were not real violent, just small tremors. Praise God! We were so thankful God protected us on the "Ark" from having a big serious and damaging earthquake that could have destroyed the "Ark" and us, too!

We immediately prayed and thanked the good Lord for sparing us and the "Ark." We then began to praise the Lord and thank Him, as we had our morning worship!

David said, "The Lord has sure been taking care of us and the "Ark" and watching over us so many times, through so many storms, truly the angel of the LORD is in this place, as Psalm 34 says!"

We had such a wonderful worship service that Sabbath morning, remarking about how soon the Lord is coming and trying to wake us up and shake us up, so we'll shape up and be more serious about getting rid of our sin and obeying the Lord in every area of our life and become perfect in Christ and be overcomers in the power of the Holy Spirit and develop a Christ–like character. 1 Corinthians 15:57–58. God wants to fill us with His Holy Spirit and place His seal on us so we can have a part in giving the Loud Cry message and be able to stand through the 7 last plagues!

We were reading in *Last Day Events* by E.G. White about "The Latter Rain" and "The Loud Cry." We were saying how much God loves us enough to personally help us to sense our true condition and get our attention to step fast and stop sinning by using this earthquake and let us know Jesus is coming <u>soon</u>! David then read a quote from *4T* 654–657, "Accountability to God." He said he had prayed and asked God that morning for God to help him find something God wanted him to read for his personal devotions, and that God led him to read this article by Sister White.

We were wondering if maybe there had been a bigger earthquake hit somewhere else, and we were just feeling the small tremors from that? We were talking about the shaking of the earthquake and how it made us think of the shaking that's going on in the church and how the sinners in Zion will be shaken out, especially when the Sunday Law is passed and the majority will go out because they won't stand true to God's 7th day Sabbath but go along with the Sunday Law, so they can keep buying and selling and be able to stay in the system and keep their jobs and have their utilities, and not be persecuted or fined or put into prison, etc. We read in *Last Day Events* about "The Shaking" and "The Sunday Laws" and "The Seal of God and the Mark of the Beast." Sister White says on p. 149 of the *Last Day Events* book, "If we are called to suffer for Christ's sake, we shall be able to go to prison trusting in Him as a little child trusts in its parents. Now is the time to cultivate faith in God."

DON'T LET SATAN SHAKE <u>YOU</u> OUT!!

Read: Joe Crews' book, *Reaping the Whirlwind*. This is a must–read book!

"A Red Bird Answers Our Prayer"
Written September 23, 2016

On August 21, 2016, I had a dream where I was trying to find places for people who were coming to the "Ark" for a place to flee to from the cities. I was trying to get them situated in different buildings we have on the "Ark." I was saying in my dream that I didn't want to put anyone in the dining hall to sleep, because we needed that big building for us all to meet in and eat. I was saying, "I need another building room for everyone who is coming for safety on the 'Ark' and we need room to put our things too." I was collecting our buckets we have for the people to use to potty in in the cabins. (end of dream)

Then on September 23, 2016, as we've been praying about another cabin for the "Ark," I was looking around on the "Ark" for just the right spot to place the new 12' x 20' cabin we ordered to use as a library and chapel. Our back porch leaks where we keep our books and dvds and videos, and we needed them in a safe dry place. We'd use this new 12' x 20' building as a library and chapel and take all the chairs out of the 10' x 16' building we're using as our chapel right now and put them in the 12' x 20' building we're getting and making the 10' x 16' chapel into a sleeping cabin for two, we'd make two bunk beds in it.

As I was walking around praying and asking the Lord where to place the new 12' x 20' building we'll use as our library and chapel, I saw a red bird fly by me in the spot where I was thinking would be a good spot to put the new 12' x 20' building. I thought, "Lord, are you trying to tell me this is the spot you want me to put the 12' x 20' building?" I went and looked at the other spots and then, I came back again to the spot where I saw the red bird fly by me. I was praying and asking the Lord if this is where He wanted the 12' x 20' library and chapel to be put? Then, I saw a red bird in the tree right next to where I was thinking of putting the 12' x 20' building. The red bird was just chirping away in the tree. I prayed, "Lord, if you want this 12' x 20' library and chapel building to be in this spot, then please let the red bird fly toward me." The red bird flew toward me, and then he flew right over my head! I knew then this was the spot God wanted the 12' x 20' library and chapel to be on the "Ark." I prayed and thanked the good Lord for directing me in this manner.

David and I have chosen the red bird to indicate God being near to us. We did this years ago and God has sent the red bird to answer our prayers many times. So, now, God used the red bird to answer our prayer to show us where He wanted us to place the 12' x 20' library and chapel building on the "Ark." Thank you Jesus! Praise the Lord! Psalm 32:8; Proverbs 3:5–8; Psalm 37:3–7.

When David would go canvassing, selling our S.D.A. literature and books, many times he'd ask the Lord to <u>please</u> send a red bird to direct him to where someone would buy a book, and each time the red bird would come and direct him to the right homes! Praise the Lord! The bird would fly just in front of him and go down a street and up another one, and then disappear at the house where the person was home and bought a book or two! God can do anything!

Read: Luke 1:37; Mark 10:27; Psalm 32:8; Matthew 21:22; Matthew 7:7; Jeremiah 33:3.

Thank You, Jesus!

<u>Psalm 32:8,</u> "I will instruct thee and teach thee in the way which thou shalt go: I will guide thee with mine eye."

"For with God Nothing Shall Be Impossible!"

Luke 1:37

Written October 26, 2016

We had been driving our old truck with the blown engine that could go out on us anywhere and at any time. The engine kept dying on us and the noises in the engine were making louder and louder sounds. One of the front tires had bolts that were stripped and kept coming loose and the tire kept coming loose and almost falling off, as you drove it. The bolts were wearing through the bolt holes and coming out ready to fall off and the tire wobbling. This was all we had to drive, because our old Honda car was in the shop with so much wrong with it and no one could figure out why it wouldn't start. We had put a new fuel pump and filter on it, and it still wouldn't start. So, we were down to just this junky dangerous truck to drive. We finally had to park it. It couldn't be driven any more with the tire falling off! Now we were down to no transportation at all to go get groceries, or pick up Jonathan's medicines or take him to his doctor appointments or to the Emergency room, if he had to go. We were stuck and couldn't go anywhere! What one friend suggested we should do was drive a horse and buggy with all the car problems we were having. (Ha). But really what were we going to do about this dilemma we were in?! We did what we always do! We took it to the Lord in prayer and claimed James 1:5; Philippians 4:19; Mark 10:27; Luke 1:37. We claimed the promise in *Ministry of Healing* on pp. 48–49.

Then, that same day, when we finally had to park our dangerous truck and couldn't drive it any more, we received two letters in the mail. One was from 3ABN, Danny Shelton, the CEO and President. 3ABN had received my bookmarker advertising my newly published book, *Don't Be Trapped in the Cities!! Get Out Now!* They were wanting to interview me and my book on 3ABN. They were asking me to send them my book so they could review it. I definitely didn't want to be on TV, but I desperately wanted my book to be interviewed on 3ABN and the warning message in my book to go around the world for God's people to prepare for what's coming! This was an answer to our prayers for God to use my book to go around the world and help people see the dangers of remaining in the big wicked cities any longer like Sister White says in her book, *Country Living* on p. 31, "Out of the cities; out of the cities!"—this is the message the Lord has been giving me. The earthquakes will come; the floods will come; and we are not to establish ourselves in the wicked cities, where the enemy is served in every way, and where God is so often forgotten."

Just recently I had had a dream where I saw pages 9 and 10 in Sister White's book, *Country Living*, where she urges this counsel, "In harmony with the light given me, I am urging people to come out from the great centers of population. Our cities are increasing in wickedness…

The time is fast coming when the controlling power of the labor unions will be very oppressive. Again and again the Lord has instructed that our people are to take their families away from the cities, into the country, where they can raise their own provisions; for in the future the problem of buying and selling will be a very serious one. We should now begin to heed the instruction given us over and over again: Get out of the cities into rural districts, where the houses are not crowded closely together, and where you will be free from the interference of enemies."

Again and again the Lord has instructed that our people are to take their families away from the cities, into the country, where they can raise their own provisions; for in the future the problem of buying and selling will be a very serious one

Well, there we stood reading 3ABN's letter for me to send my book to be reviewed and put on 3ABN, but we had no money, not a penny to our name to be able to send my copy of my book to 3ABN and no vehicle to take it to town to be mailed! We prayed to God about our situation and asked God what to do and left it in God's hands to help us with our problem! We claimed Philippians 4:19; Ephesians 3:17–21; Luke 1:37; Mark 10:27; James 1:5. We thought of *Ministry of Healing* pp. 48–49 and 248–249 and claimed that promise too! And *Desire of Ages* p. 667, "In every difficulty we are to see a call to prayer."

We, then, opened the other letter we had received in the mail that day, too. It was a letter from Cynthia, a very dear friend from New York. In her letter, she had sent us a $100.00 money order! God had just answered our prayers for money to be able to mail my book to 3ABN for them to review it and interview it on 3ABN around the world. We just praised the Lord for hearing and answering our prayers so quickly and thanked Him over and over again! We prayed and asked God to please bless Cynthia for her loving kindness shown to us, and for her listening to the Holy Spirit to send us money, just when we needed it most! I thought of that text in Isaiah 65:24, "And it shall come to pass, that before they call, I will answer; and while they are yet speaking, I will hear."

Now we had the money to send my book in the mail to 3ABN, but how were we to get it to the post office in town, a seven–mile round trip? We again prayed and asked God to please work out our problem for transportation, since we couldn't drive our junk, dangerous truck anymore and our car was still in the shop for repairs and trying to figure out why it wouldn't start. We were stranded with no transportation to go anywhere! I then said to David, I'll write a letter to 3ABN and put it in my book and wrap it up and put it in a plastic bag, and you can hang it on the handle bars of my old bicycle and ride it into town to the post office and mail it after you cash the $100 money order, from Cynthia, at our bank in town. It made me think of what God inspired Sister White to write, found in *Ministry of Healing*, pp. 478–482, "To be great in God's kingdom is to be as a little child in humility, in simplicity of faith, and in purity of love... Many are unable to make definite plans for the future. Their life is unsettled. They cannot discern the outcome of affairs, and this often fills them with anxiety and unrest. Let us remember that the life of God's children in this world is a pilgrim life. We have not wisdom to plan our own lives. It is not for us to shape our future. "By faith Abraham, when he was called to go out into a place which he should after receive for an inheritance, obeyed; and he went out, not knowing whither he went." Hebrews 11:8.

Christ in His life on earth made no plans for Himself. He accepted God's plans for Him, and day by day the Father unfolded His plans. So should we depend upon God, that our lives may be the simple outworking of His will. As we commit our ways to Him, He will direct our steps.

Too many, in planning for a brilliant future, make an utter failure. Let God plan for you... God never leads His children otherwise than they would choose to be led, if they could see the end from the beginning and discern the glory of the purpose which they are fulfilling as co–workers with Him...

Many who profess to be Christ's followers have an anxious, troubled heart because they are afraid to trust themselves with God. They do not make a complete surrender to Him, for they shrink from the consequences that such a surrender may involve. Unless they do make this surrender they cannot find peace... Worry is blind and cannot discern the future; but Jesus sees the end from the beginning. In every difficulty He has His way prepared to bring relief... Our heavenly Father has a thousand ways to provide for us of which we know nothing. Those who accept the one principle of making the service of God supreme, will find perplexities vanish and a plain path before their feet.

The faithful discharge of today's duties is the best preparation for tomorrow's trials... Let us be hopeful and courageous. Despondency in God's service is sinful and unreasonable. He knows our every necessity... He has means for the removal of every difficulty, that those who serve Him and respect the means He employs may be sustained... He watches over His children with a love that is measureless and everlasting. In the darkest days, when appearances seem most forbidding, have faith in God. He is working out His will, doing all things well in behalf of His people. The strength of those who love and serve Him will be renewed day by day. He is able and willing to bestow upon His servants all the help they need. He will give them the wisdom which their varied necessities demand. 2 Corinthians 12:9, 10."

So, we had prayer together before Dad left on my old bicycle to ride it into town to mail our book to 3ABN to go around the world to warn God's people to get out of these big wicked cities, while they still could before the Sunday Laws are passed!

Sister White warns on p. 11 of *Country Living*, "But erelong there will be such strife and confusion in the cities, that those who wish to leave them will not be able. We must be preparing for these issues. This is the light that is given me."

This could be like martial law, in a disaster, where they shut down the city and no one can go out and no one can come in! You're trapped!

Sister White also warns us in *Country Living* on pp. 7–8, "The same voice that warned Lot to leave Sodom bids us, 'Come out from among them, and be ye separate, ... and touch not the unclean.' Those who obey this warning will find a refuge. Let every man be wide awake for himself, and try to save his family. Let him gird himself for the work. God will reveal from point to point what to do next.

Hear the voice of God... The time is near when the large cities will be visited by the judgments of God. In a little while, these cities will be terribly shaken. No matter how large or how strong their buildings, no matter how many safeguards against fire may have been provided, let God touch these buildings, and in a few minutes or a few hours they are in ruins..."

(Makes me think of 9/11 in New York when the twin towers were destroyed! **Read** *Vol. 9 Testimonies for the Church* by E.G. White, pp. 11–18, "The Last Crisis.")

We know that on November 20, 2016, the pope has plans to close his door of mercy, and he says it will be severity for those who don't go along with him! He's got his Green sabbath planned to rest the land and with this inquisition planned with fines, imprisonment and indulgences. We know this opposition and persecution leading to no–buy–and–no–sell will end finally in the death decree. We know all this will lead to a Sunday Law passed and all this trouble will come upon God's people for staying true to God's 7th day Bible Sabbath and not go along with the Sunday sabbath. NOW is the time to prepare for these issues. Read in *The Great Controversy* by E.G. White, the chapter 38, "The Final Warning."

When David had gotten my book safely in the mail and riding on the bike, he noticed a nice-looking Lincoln car parked off in a yard close by the road, but it had no "For Sale" sign on it. He stopped his bike and walked up to the house, where the car was parked in the yard by the road and he knocked on the door. Two ladies came to the door. He asked if the car parked out by the road was for sale? The lady owner said, "Yes, it's for sale, but I just hadn't gotten around to putting the 'For Sale' sign on it yet." David explained to the lady the troubles he was having and the predicament he was in having no transportation to get around in. The lady owner spoke up and said, "You can have the car. But I'll need my new tires off the car that I just bought new." David said, "Okay. Thank you so much for the car! God bless you! Do you mind if I drive it?" She said, "Sure," and went and got him the keys. He gave her a 3ABN advertisement card that we pass out all over everywhere, like the leaves of autumn. He drove it home to show me what the Lord had just done for us to answer our prayers for help in our time of need for transportation! We prayed together and thanked the good Lord for hearing our prayer in such a miraculous way! We prayed God would richly bless this lady for her kindness shown to us in answer to our need of a car! I said to David, "Never underestimate the power of God to answer prayer, 'For with God nothing shall be impossible!' Luke 1:37."

When David drove the car back to the lady who owned the car, she spoke up and said to him, "You can have the new tires, too." David thanked her again for how she had answered our prayers for transportation we needed so badly and thanked her for the new tires, too! She had the title in her hands and asked David how he wanted it signed over to him. He said, "Put it in both my name and my wife's name." Then, she handed him the title and the keys to the car. She began to tell him all about the car, that it cost $40,000 new and that it only had 127,000 miles on it. She said that it was a specially–made car to go 150 mph and can out run a police car—it's so powerful an engine like a police car. She handed him some garden goods she had grown and David thanked her again for doing this for him! David told her and the other lady there about *The Great Controversy* book and *The National Sunday Law* book he wanted to give to them, but he had to go home to get them. They were both so excited about the books, as he explained what they were about! They were anxious to get the books! They both just wanted to talk and talk to him about all this he was telling them about these world events and what's happening and how these books explain what the pope is really out to do behind the scenes. He thanked them again for the car and what a blessing they had been to him!

When David came home driving the pretty white Lincoln Mark VIII car, we just thanked and praised the Lord for doing the impossible for us! David told me how excited the ladies were to get *The Great Controversy* book and *The National Sunday Law* book. I said, "You ought to give them your own personal copy, because it has two Amazing Facts free correspondence Bible Study cards in your *Great Controversy* book for them to send in and study their Bible." It was getting late and David was so hungry. He said that he'd take them the books tomorrow, he was too tired to go there that night. We just kept praising the Lord and thanking Him and saying, "For with God nothing shall be impossible!" Luke 1:37. We quoted Ephesians 3:19–21. We both agreed "God can do anything!"

Then, that night in a dream, God showed me two ladies all excited about taking a correspondence Bible Study course! I was saying to them, "It's like taking a college Bible Study course. There's so much valuable information in these 27 lessons."

The next day David took the ladies *The Great Controversy* book with the two free Bible Study correspondence cards in the book and *The National Sunday Law* book. I wrote them a "thank–you" note to the two ladies and encouraged them to read their books and send in for the free Bible Study correspondence course. I said to David, "They would make good SDAs." David agreed.

Then, when David gave them the books and mentioned the free correspondence Bible Study cards in *The Great Controversy* and for them to be sure and send the cards in and study their Bibles and that it was like taking a college Bible course and he said, "My wife dreamt about two ladies excited about taking this free Bible Study correspondence course!" The two ladies were excited about the books and the Bible Study lessons. They were happy with the "thank–you" note I wrote them and they said to David, "Where do you live? We want to come out and meet your wife." David gave them our address and directions how to get to our place. David thanked them again for the car and then left.

> *We truly feel God let David's path cross these two ladies' paths. We needed a transportation car and they needed the truth and eternal life*

We truly feel God let David's path cross these two ladies' paths. We needed a transportation car and they needed the truth and eternal life. This was no accident that God let David notice that car in the yard with no "For Sale" sign, but felt impressed to stop and inquire if it was for sale. God impressed them to give him the car and the new tires on it! God had orchestrated it all! This was truly a "Divine appointment"! God knows where His other sheep are out there in the world. John 10:16, "And other sheep I have, which are not of this fold: them also I must bring, and they shall hear my voice; and there shall be one fold, and one shepherd."

This experience God has put us through has made our faith in God all the stronger for in the time of trouble when we'll need to depend on God to supply all our needs as Philippians 4:19 promises, "But my God shall supply all your need according to his riches in glory by Christ Jesus." Also, Isaiah 33:15–16. Also, in *Desire of Ages* by E.G. White is the promise, pp. 121–122, "In the last great conflict of the controversy with Satan those who are loyal to God will see every earthly support cut off. Because they refuse to break His law in obedience to earthly powers, they will be forbidden to buy or sell. It will finally be decreed that they shall be put to death. See Revelation 13:11–17; Isaiah 33:16… By this promise the children of God will live."

A few days later in the mail, we received $100 from my cousin, Nancy. With hers and Cynthia's money, we were able to get the car tagged! Praise God! Genesis 18;14, "Is any thing too hard for the LORD?"

"Our Two New Friends"

Written December 19, 2016

Our two new friends are Lisa and Cindy from Pomona, Kansas. The following story is the sequel to the story, "For with God nothing shall be impossible," Luke 1:37. We've been asked, "Did you ever keep in touch with the two ladies that gave you the free Lincoln Mark VIII car?" At this time, we'd like to catch you up on what has transpired since then. One day an unknown vehicle drove up in our driveway. David went out to see who it was. We have people stop by here who are asking directions how to find a certain place or people. We thought it was someone seeking directions. When David went out to check it out, he found out it was the two ladies who had given us the free car. They had told David they wanted to come out sometime and meet me. I had written them a "thank–you" card for the car they had given us and how much we appreciated their love and kindness shown to us. Now, here they were in our driveway wanting to see me. David ran into the house and said, "Hurry out to meet the two ladies who gave us our free Lincoln Mark VIII car! They want to meet you!" I hurried out and we all enjoyed a long and wonderful visit and it was dark when they finally left and we had prayer with them and gave them hugs and thanked them for coming out to see us! Then, a couple weeks later we received the following letter from Lisa, one of the ladies who gave us the "free" car. The card said, "The earth is full of the goodness of the LORD," Psalm 33:5. Her letter said,

> Dear Linda,
>
> My writing is poor so I am trying to print this on lined paper because it's easier for me. It was WONDERFUL to meet you and I am writing because you and David both just make me feel good to be near, and I'm sure that Jonathan, though shy, would be the same. Linda, you and David possess a light(?) that shines and makes me feel good. I like being around you. I know that you two can't easily come to visit us, so I guess I'm asking if you would invite Cindy and I to come visit you sometime. If you tell me what to bring, I will try. I don't want to impose on you so I can either go shopping with you or give you money, not that I have much. I want friendship with good people. Please give my good thoughts and prayers to David and Jonathan.
>
> Love and prayers,
>
> Lisa

In Vol. 8 of *Testimonies for the Church*, p. 19 by Sister White, she says, "It is His purpose that every Christian shall be surrounded with a spiritual atmosphere of light and peace. There is no limit to the usefulness of the one who, putting self aside, makes room for the working of the Holy Spirit upon his heart and lives a life wholly consecrated to God."

Also, Matthew 5:16 says, "Let your light so shine before men, that they may see your good works, and glorify your Father which is in heaven."

We read, also, in Isaiah 60:1, "Arise, shine; for thy light is come, and the glory of the LORD is risen upon thee."

We had given them a *Great Controversy* book and a *National Sunday Law* book and two enrollment Bible Study cards to take a correspondence course from Amazing Facts. I answered their letter by writing a card back to them telling them we'll get together for a visit and a meal when the weather will change and we'll prepare them a vegetarian meal, since we're vegans. I let them know we were so happy the Lord brought us together, and we were so happy for our new friendship! We let them know we love them and pray for them and thanks for your prayers for us. I explained that Jonathan wasn't feeling good right now for a visit, that we just had gotten him from the Emergency room from him having a bad reaction from one of his drugs he was on and had to be changed over to another drug and try and get adjusted to a new medicine. I told them to keep in touch and we were looking forward to seeing them again and thanked them for being an answer to our prayers for the vehicle they gave us, when we were so in need of transportation! I asked God's blessings on them and let them know God was keeping the car running well for us! Praise God! May God continue to bless our friendship! (And in God's time may they become S.D.A.s for God's glory!)

> *I let them know we were so happy the Lord brought us together, and we were so happy for our new friendship*

On December 23, David stopped by to see Lisa and Cindy and to give them a *Ministry of Healing* book I had wrapped up as a Christmas gift for them and wrote a note in the book for them. They were so happy to see David and receive the book!

"Update on Our Two New Friends"
Written May 24, 2017

This is the sequel to the story, "Our Two New Friends." As you remember in the story, "For With God Nothing Shall be Impossible," Cindy and Lisa gave us a Lincoln Mark VIII free, when we had no transportation at all! We had corresponded with them and David had stopped by to see them and give them religious books and a little dish of food I had made them. They were so happy we had kept them in touch with us.

Then, several weeks had passed and we hadn't kept in touch with them. Then, Cindy drove up into our driveway and came in to visit with us, and to let us know that Lisa had moved out and moved back with her parents. Cindy was so heartbroken and stayed and talked to us until midnight and was crying. I gave her something to eat: sweet potatoes, and regular potatoes, salad and beans. She was so happy to fellowship with us. We had prayer with her before she left. I told her we love her and gave her a hug. I assured Cindy I'd write Lisa and let her know that Cindy would like to have her return. Cindy gave me Lisa's address.

The next day I wrote to Lisa and sent her some encouraging religious material. I told her Cindy had come out to visit with us and we gave her a meal. I let Lisa know we had missed seeing her and hoped she was doing okay. I told her how heartbroken Cindy was because Lisa had moved back home. I let her know we loved her and to keep in touch and that we were praying for her.

She wrote me back a beautiful letter and explained what happened between her and Cindy and she's not going to return back with Cindy. She sent me the beautiful poem, "Thinking of you." She said she'd keep in touch.

I wrote back to her and sent her some encouraging religious material. I thanked her for writing and explaining her side of the story. They both have their own story. I'm praying for both of them that they'll accept the truth and that God will work things out in both of their lives. God is in control of the situation and that He'll care for both of them. God's will be done.

I haven't seen Cindy since she left late that night. But there is another car parked in the driveway with hers. So, she must have someone else living with her and sharing expenses.

"Thinking of You"

Thoughts of you are welcome
Every moment of the day,
For you are someone special
Who means more than words can say.

You have the gift of sharing
God's goodness, love and grace,
And your simple acts of kindness
Make this world a better place.

I'm so thankful that I know you,
And I ask the Lord to bless
Your day with peaceful moments
And your life with happiness.

Unknown

"The Search"

Written November 10, 2016

God had provided us with a "free" pretty Lincoln Mark VIII car for us to have for transportation that we needed so badly. Then a few days later David had lost the one and only key we had to the car! What good is a car without a key to drive it! Now began the long hard search to find it! Though we prayed earnestly and searched diligently for the key, we could not find it! We finally said, "It's all in God's hands! He's in control of everything!" We claimed Romans 8:28. We said, "In every thing give thanks: for this is the will of God in Christ Jesus concerning you." 1 Thessalonians 5:18. David said, "But how can we give thanks for losing the only car key to our only source of transportation?" I said, "We don't always know why God does what He does, but we can trust His promises like Romans 8:28, 'And we know that all things work together for good to them that love God, to them who are the called according to his purpose.' For some reason, we may never know until heaven, why God allowed our car key to be lost. But we know He put the key out of our sight and in His own time and way He'll help us find it, if it's His will, so we can drive our car again. We must show faith in God to do the impossible and supply our need for our car key to be found." But we needed our car to pick up Jonathan's medicines he needed and to buy groceries and keep Jonathan's doctor appointment in a few days. We just had to trust God to hear our prayers to help us find the lost key when He was ready for it to be found. We had only one key to this car, so we couldn't make another one without the one that was lost. It costs $60 to buy another key to this car. We didn't have that much money, and now we don't have the key. For some reason, only God knew, He didn't want us going anywhere right now in the car. So, He let David lose the key and grounded us.

    We prayed and searched all over the yard, thinking maybe he had dropped the key getting out of the car, and he doesn't hear good and maybe the dog had grabbed the key on the chain and carried it off somewhere. But where on these 14 acres could the car key be?! We searched all over the house! Nothing! We prayed and claimed promises Matthew 7:7 and Matthew 21:22 but no key was found. David got up real early the next morning to search for the key in the full moonlight out in the yard, thinking the key and chain would shine in the moonlight, but nothing! We both searched again the next day and went over everything again where we thought the key could possibly be. We prayed God would please open our eyes to see where the key could be. I said, "God must want us to write another "faith" experience, so maybe that's why God is allowing this to happen to us? God wants our faith to grow in His power to do the impossible, like He promises in Luke 1:37, "For with God nothing shall be impossible," and Mark 10:27,

"And Jesus looking upon them saith, With men it is impossible, but not with God: for with God all things are possible." I said, "Surely the Lord wouldn't work a miracle to give us a "free" car for transportation, and then take the key away from us, so we can't get around and do all the things we have to do?! All we could do was to pray and claim promises and trust God to reveal to us where the key was and when He was ready for us to find it, as we continued to search and search and search diligently for it.

You always wonder and question why things are happening like they do when you're going through trials and hardships, and you wonder why God is testing you like this and what He's trying to teach you from this experience He's allowing you to go through? We read for our worship that morning in Vol. 6 of *Testimonies for the Church*, p. 363, "The company of believers may be few in number, (*there's just me and David and Jonathan in our little home church on the "Ark"*) but in God's sight they are very precious. By the cleaver of truth they have been taken as rough stones from the quarry of the world and have been brought into the workshop of God to be hewed and shaped. But even in the rough they are precious in the sight of God. The ax, the hammer, and the chisel of trial are in the hands of One who is skillful; they are used, not to destroy, but to work out the perfection of every soul. As precious stones, polished after the similitude of a palace, God designs us to find a place in the heavenly temple" (Psalm 144:12).

We remarked to each other how God is chiseling and hammering trying to make us into His image and prepared for the trials and hardships ahead of us and make us strong and trusting in Him and His power to see us through the crisis ahead of us

We remarked to each other how God is chiseling and hammering trying to make us into His image and prepared for the trials and hardships ahead of us and make us strong and trusting in Him and His power to see us through the crisis ahead of us when the Sunday Law will be passed, and we'll need faith and courage and strength to stand when we pass through fines, imprisonment, opposition, persecution, hunger and pain and taken to court, and the time of no–buy–no–sell and finally the death sentence. God must see we need an experience to go through to help us grow spiritually, learning to rely on God to see us through whatever the devil may throw at us. Also, that we may be an encouragement to others to see what God has done for us, and He'll do the same for them, and see them through their difficulties, too. Like Sister White writes on p. 154, *Last Day Events*, "Afflictions, crosses, temptations, adversity, and our varied trials are God's workmen to refine us, sanctify us, and fit us for the heavenly garner."

As I continued to search for the lost key and pray, I sang the song, "Open My Eyes that I May See." This searching diligently for our car key made me think of the promise in Jeremiah 29:11–14, especially verse 13, "And ye shall seek me, and find me, when ye shall search for me with all your heart."

Read in Sister White's book, *Thoughts From the Mount of Blessings*, pp. 130–134 on Matthew 7:7, "Ask, and it shall be given you; seek, and ye shall find; knock, and it shall be opened unto you." On pp. 132–134, we read these comforting words, "When we beseech the Lord to pity us in our distress, *(and distress is what we were sure feeling, not being able to find our one and only car key)* and to guide us by His Holy Spirit, He will never turn away our prayer… Every promise in the word of God furnishes us with subject matter for prayer, presenting the pledged word of Jehovah as our assurance… It is through the name of Jesus that every favor is received. God will honor that name, and will supply your necessities from the riches of His liberality… "Ask, and ye shall receive." John 16:24… Take God's promises as your own, plead them before Him as His own words, and you will receive fullness of joy." **Read** in *Last Day Events* by E.G. White, chapters 12–15, for a boost for the day.

I knew when it was God's time for us to find our car key, He could put it right where we could find it. We just have to show faith and wait patiently for His timing and trust Him and His promises and His power to do anything. God knows why He let the key get lost, and He'll return the key when He knows is best. In the meantime, we'll keep praying and asking God to please hear our prayers to remove all sin from our life, so our prayers will be heard and answered. Psalm 66:18 says, "If I regard iniquity in my heart, the Lord will not hear me." **Read** the chapter in *Steps to Christ*, "The Privilege of Prayer." The night David lost the key, and we had diligently searched for it and prayed we'd find it, but didn't find the key, I prayed and asked God that He would please put the key where we could find it or please give me a dream where it is at.

That night, in a dream, I saw David smiling and all excited and holding the key in his hand and bringing it to me to show me God had helped him find the lost key! But the next day we had searched all over again everything—the house and the yard, but no lost key was found, even though we prayed fervently to please find our only key to our car. I remembered my dream, that it was David that found the lost key, so I stopped looking and let him keep searching for the key he had lost. David had lost the key on a Thursday night and for two days we had prayed and searched but still no key was to be found. Then, on Saturday night, David was looking in his bedroom and going through his jeans, because he had on a pair of jeans when he had lost the car key. Then, as he reached into the pocket of one of his jeans, his hand felt the key in the pocket and his excitement knew no bounds! He was so happy and thankful and excited that God had helped him to find the lost key! He grabbed hold of the key in his hand and praised the Lord for answering our prayers to find our one and only key to our car! He hurried to show me the lost key and tell me where he found it! He was all smiles and so excited, as he dangled the lost key in my face! We both prayed and thanked the good Lord for doing this for us! We just praised the Lord! I said, "Don't you wonder why the Lord let us lose the key and search so long and hard for it and then, after two days find it? Don't you wonder what lesson God is trying to teach us in this experience? David said, "It's like I'm going to hang onto this car key for dear life and not lose it again and not be so careless and forgetful. It's like I don't want to lose Jesus either and hang onto Jesus for dear life and not let Him go!" What David said made me think of in *Desire of Ages* by Sister White, on p. 83 where she writes how Joseph and Mary lost sight of Jesus at the Passover visit when he was 12. He measures every trial. He watches the furnace fire that must test every soul."

Read in *Fundamentals of Christian Education* by E.G. White, p. 505, "Who, then, is to be regarded as the Ruler of the nations?—The Lord God Omnipotent. All kings, all rulers, all nations, are His under His rule and government." Read chapter 52 in *Desire of Ages* by E.G.

White, "The Divine Shepherd," especially pp. 479–480, 483, "Jesus knows us individually, and is touched with the feeling of our infirmities. He knows us all by name. He knows the very house in which we live, the name of each occupant. He has at times given directions to His servants to go to a certain street in a certain city, to such a house, to find one of His sheep... Every soul is as fully known to Jesus as if he were the only one for whom the Saviour died. The distress of every one touches His heart. The cry for aid reaches His ear. He came to draw all men unto Himself. He bids them, "Follow Me," and His Spirit moves upon their hearts to draw them to come to Him. Many refuse to be drawn. Jesus knows who they are. He also knows who gladly hear His call, and are ready to come under His pastoral care. He says, "My sheep hear My voice, and I know them, and they follow Me." He cares for each one as if there were not another on the face of the earth…

The soul that has given himself to Christ is more precious in His sight than the whole world. The Saviour would have passed through the agony of Calvary that one might be saved in His kingdom. He will never abandon one for whom He has died. Unless His followers choose to leave Him, He will hold them fast. Through all our trials we have a never–failing Helper. He does not leave us alone to struggle with temptation, to battle with evil, and be finally crushed with burdens and sorrow. Though now He is hidden from mortal sight, the ear of faith can hear His voice saying, Fear not; I am with you… I know your tears; I also have wept. The griefs that lie too deep to be breathed into any human ear, I know. Think not that you are desolate and forsaken. Though your pain touch no responsive chord in any heart on earth, look unto Me, and live… Because we are the gift of His Father, and the reward of His work, Jesus loves us. He loves us as His children. Reader, He loves you… Therefore trust."

What's so amazing about finding the car key in David's jean pocket, is that we had already gone through all his jeans pockets and there was no car key! Now, here it was! **Read** *9T* pp. 273, 286–287.

"Lost"

Written November 14, 2016

David had to make a trip into the BIG city of Lawrence, Kansas where there is a BIG university and heavy traffic, and he was trying to find his way to the junk yard, and there was so much construction going on all through the city and detours and roads closed and so many one way streets and everything was in a mess, with streets torn up from construction, that he just couldn't find his way to the junk yard! He got all twisted and turned around and lost and confused and couldn't find his way in all the maze. He kept praying that God would please help him to get out of this mess he was in! He asked so many people directions to the junk yard and he tried to follow their directions through all the detours and construction throughout the city to get to the junk yard, and he became more and more lost and mixed up and tangled up in all the roads closed and detours. He kept handing out 3ABN advertising cards to everyone he asked directions from. Finally, in desperation, he stopped at a house and told the lady his predicament and that he was lost and turned all around and couldn't find his way in all this construction and one way streets and detours, and he had no idea where to go to get to the junk yard he was looking for. The lady said, "I'll drive my car and you can follow me, and I'll show you how to get out of this mess and to the junk yard, just follow me."

David was so grateful and thankful for the lady's help and kindness to take her time and drive him through all the construction mess! He thanked her and gave her a 3ABN advertisement card. She then drove him all over the place to get him though all the construction mess and took him right to the junk yard, where he wanted to go! When he told me about it, when he got home, we thanked the Lord for doing this for him in his time of need for help to find someone to help him find his way out of the mess he was in and so lost and turned around! We asked the Lord to please bless this kind lady and may she be helped and blessed by watching 3ABN, and all the others he had given 3ABN cards to, too. He said he had passed out a lot of 3ABN cards all over the city! I said, "Maybe God was using this experience you went through to spread the light of truth all over that area? Acts 13:49, "And the word of the Lord was published throughout all the region."

This experience David went through made me think of all the people out there in the world who are lost and all turned around and twisted in their thinking and don't know what is truth and which way to turn to find their way through all the falsehood and errors and don't know who to trust and what is truth? Then, some true Seventh–day Adventist, like David, comes along with the truth found in a *National Sunday Law* book or a *Great Controversy* book, or a 3ABN advertisement card to lead and guide and direct them through all the errors and falsehoods out there in the world, to the truth in God's word. God wants to use us as His witnesses to help Him find His lost sheep out there, struggling and searching to know the truth. (Read John 10; Vol. 9 *Testimonies for the Church*, the chapter, "Called to Be Witnesses," by E.G. White). God wants to use our voice, our hands, our feet, our ears, our money and our time and our talents to be His witnesses. John 20:21–22; Isaiah 6:5–10; Isaiah 55.

David was sowing seeds all over the rich section of that big city, as he asked directions of so very many people and gave them a 3ABN card. May God bless the harvest of all these seeds sown. Praise God! Sometimes God has to lead us through trials and hardships to use us as His witness to win souls. Look what Paul went through to be a witness for Jesus and the other apostles and the early reformers and our early pioneers of our church and Jesus Himself, what He went through to save this lost world!

Read the *Desire of Ages* on the life of Christ and the *Acts of the Apostles* book by E.G. White, and *The Great Controversy* book by Sister White. Study the lives of these people, because history will be repeated and we'll learn from them what we're to do when we go through the crisis ahead of us when the Sunday Law will be forced upon us. May God help us, because Sister White says in *Last Day Events*, p. 134, "History will be repeated." **Read** in *Prophets and Kings*, chapter 43, "The Unseen Watcher" pp. 535–538 and 709.

"The Fall"

Written December 1, 2016

We have a Border Collie/Australian Shepherd mix dog and for several nights in a row, she would bark and bark and bark keeping me awake. She was barking at something trying to make its way up from the valley and creek below that has a path coming up to our home on top of the hill. In the dark we can never see what kind of animal it is that's irritating her and in turn, barking irritating us. She has caught opossums, rabbits, woodchucks and chased deer and raccoons away from our garden and our place. She's a good hunter and watchdog. She likes chasing cars out on the gravel road, too. But for some reason she had barked at something, but we couldn't tell what. I don't sleep good at night anyway, and her barking night after night was keeping me awake each night and wearing me out. Daddy would try and rub my back and feet to help me relax so I could get some sleep. Well, after about four nights of this barking, he decided to put his shoes and coat and hat on and go check it out, so I could get some sleep.

He grabbed his flashlight and turned on the outside light and he and our dog, "Tippy," headed down the dark path to the valley and creek below. Across our creek, there's a concrete slab and we put concrete blocks on the concrete slab to step on to cross the creek to the other side without getting our feet wet. As he jumped onto these concrete blocks to get to the other side of the creek to try and see in the woods what might be out there irritating the dog and us, he lost his balance on the blocks and in the dark, he fell off the blocks and fell over the edge of the concrete slab about two feet down into the rocky creek below banging his shins on the edge of the concrete slab and splashing into the creek and landing hard on the big rocks in the creek. Picking himself up and dripping wet, he thanked the good Lord he was okay and didn't break a bone or hit his head on the big rocks when he fell, or didn't get killed from this dangerous fall! Wet, cold and shivering in the 30-degree temperature, he made his way back up the hill to the house, never finding out what kind of varmit was out there causing all this trouble! When he told me what he had done and how he fell into the creek and onto the big rocks, we prayed and thanked the Lord for sparing his life, taking a terrible fall like that at his age of 75. The next few days his back and bottom were sore and his

> *Picking himself up and dripping wet, he thanked the good Lord he was okay and didn't break a bone or hit his head on the big rocks when he fell, or didn't get killed from this dangerous fall*

shins all cut and bruised, but he was alive and mending okay. Praise the Lord! Everything healed up okay with no complications! Thank you Jesus! (Psalm 34).

This terrible fall Daddy took reminds me of another terrible fall that happened to Satan in heaven when he rebelled against God and was cast out of heaven to this earth. (Luke 10:18; Isaiah 14:12–14). **Read** about it in *Early Writings* by E.G. White on pp. 145–147, "The Fall of Satan." There was another terrible fall that took place and that was the "Fall of Man"—it's recorded in *Early Writings* pp. 147–149. Also, on pp. 149–153, Sister White tells of "The Plan of Salvation." On p. 153 she was shown Satan as he once was, a happy exalted angel. Then she was shown Satan as he now is… She writes, "As I beheld him, his chin was resting upon his left hand. He appeared to be in deep thought. A smile was upon his countenance, which made me tremble, it was so full of evil and satanic slyness. This smile is the one he wears just before he makes sure of his victim, and as he fastens the victim in his snare, this smile grows horrible."

Let's be determined to stay out of his traps and snares. Read the description Sister White gives of Satan as the "conductor" of a train of cars and that it seemed that the whole world was on board, except for a little company travelling a narrow pathway, all seemed to be firmly united, bound together by the truth, pp. 88–89, *Early Writings*.

Read in *The Great Controversy* by E.G. White the chapter 32, "Snares of Satan." **Read**, also, my book, *Don't Be Trapped in the Cities!! Get Out <u>NOW</u>!* Don't fall into Satan's trap by remaining in the cities!

"God to the Rescue"
Written December 12, 2016

Have you ever made a big mistake and then had to ask God to help you out of the big problem you were in? Well, that's what happened to me, and God had to come to my rescue! Here's how it happened. The weather radio was forecasting freezing temperatures in the 20s and snow and rain coming in! We thought we better get to town and buy up some food to hold us over, in case we got stranded out here in the country and couldn't make it into town for several days. The snow plow takes care of the city roads first and the country roads are cleared last. We knew we were needing groceries anyway, so we made up our grocery list and took the last of what money we had and bought up the groceries we needed, plus extra beans and things just in case we got stranded in the ice and snow storm coming and couldn't make it into town for supplies for who knows how long.

After we got our groceries bought and safely home before the winter storm hit, the realization hit me, that we had just spent our electric bill money! I had forgotten to set aside our electric bill money when figuring our bills, and I thought this was money we had. Then, the startling thought hit me, "How am I going to pay our electric bill that's due in a few days and no money to pay it?!" I had no money and no idea where I was going to get that much money in just a few days, and we don't get our social security check for several weeks! The only thing I could do was to turn to the Lord to come to my rescue as I earnestly prayed for help out of my terrible situation I was in, because of my terrible mistake I had made and put me in this terrible, stressful condition as to how I was going to be able to pay my electric bill! I prayed, "Lord, please forgive me for my negligence! I have no way to come up with that much money to pay our electrical bill, but I know You've promised in Philippians 4:19 to supply all our needs. Also, You've said in *Ministry of Healing* on pp 481–482, "Worry is blind and cannot discern the future; but Jesus sees the end from the beginning. In every difficulty He has His way prepared to bring relief. "No good thing will He withhold from them that walk uprightly." Matthew 11:30; Psalm 84:11. Our heavenly Father has a thousand ways to provide for us of which we know nothing. Those who accept the one principle of making the service of God supreme, will find perplexities vanish and a plain path before their feet…

Let us be hopeful and courageous. Despondency in God's service is sinful and unreasonable. He knows our every necessity… He has means for the removal of every difficulty, that those who serve Him and respect the means He employs may be sustained… He watches over His children with a love that is measureless and everlasting.

In the darkest days, when appearances seem most forbidding, have faith in God. He is working out His will, doing all things well in behalf of His people… He is able and willing to bestow upon His servants all the help they need."

Thank you Lord, for your promises. I believe them, and I claim them and thank you for hearing my prayer for help!

Then a Christmas card came in the mail from my cousin, Nancy, in Florida, and she had sent money for our Christmas, that would help pay our electric bill! We also received in the mail some truck insurance money we received from dropping the insurance on our truck that had a blown engine and had to be junked out. Between these two checks, we had received enough to pay our electrical bill! Praise the Lord! God had used my dear cousin, Nancy, to answer our prayers for help and also, the truck insurance money coming in the mail at just the right time! Thank you Jesus and thank you Nancy! God had come to our rescue! What a wonderful God we serve! Even before we had the problem of spending our electric bill money and needing money to be able to pay our bill, God was providing a way out of our predicament by impressing Nancy to send us the amount of money she did for our Christmas gift. And, also, letting our cancelled truck insurance refund money to arrive in the mail when God knew we'd need it right at that time! God is always working for our good, as Romans 8:28 promises and working behind the scenes to orchestrate things to happen as He wants them to! He's always right there, when we need Him the most, to see us through whatever our trial or trouble may be! Have faith in God! Hebrews 11; Luke 1:37, "For with God nothing shall be impossible."

"A Walk of Faith and Works"

Written December 13, 2016

Read Hebrews 11 and James 2:14–26. In 2001, while my husband, David, was still working, the Lord heard our prayers to help us find and purchase our 14 acres, the "Ark," with a live creek and producing walnut trees and producing berries and paw paw grove and in the forest with lots of trees for firewood. We had a well dug that runs on electricity to the mobile home we purchased, and also we had a well dug for a hand pump. We had a small cellar dug. We put in a septic tank and a propane tank. We had a gravel driveway put in and we planted lots of fruit trees of all kinds like: peach, cherry, plums, apricot, persimmon, apple, prune and pear. We have really good soil for a garden. We planted asparagus and grapes. Through the years, we purchased little cabins for people to stay in and furnished them with electricity and woodstove and stove and refrigerator and furniture. There was no water to the cabins. We, also, through the years, built some buildings ourselves for storage and tool shed and cabins. Also, through the years of building the "Ark," we've purchased buildings for a dining hall and chapel and a classroom and treatment room and a library. At the present, we have a greenhouse under construction. We have pretty flowers and flower bushes growing, making the place look pretty and pretty trees.

One time when we were having Bible studies at our place with two of our SDA friends and Jonathan and David and I, one of the ladies remarked about our place, "You should call this place, 'Heavenly Places.' It's so pretty and peaceful out here in the country, and you can feel the Holy Spirit in this place!" It made me think of Ephesians 1:3, 20 and Ephesians 2:6 talking about sitting together in heavenly places and hath blessed us with all spiritual blessings in heavenly places in Christ Jesus. We kept praying and asking the Lord what to name our 14 acres we were building for God's people to come to as a refuge to go through the small time of trouble, when the Sunday Laws would be passed, and there'll be no buy and no sell for those who are true and loyal to God's 7th day Sabbath and all His Ten Commandments, and we'd need to grow our own gardens to eat from to survive when we'll lose all our utilities and are taken out of the system. We read the story of Noah and how God impressed him to build the Ark to go through the Flood. We read Hebrews 11:7 and decided that's what we'd name our place, the "Ark." It's been a walk of faith and works, as we have put all our time and energy and money into building the "Ark" and trusting the Lord and His promises to supply all our needs to see us through all we're doing. Philippians 4:13, 19; James 1:5.

We have prayed in faith for God's help and guidance in building the "Ark" for His people. Sister White says in her book *Education*, p. 257–258, "Prayer and faith are closely allied, and they need to be studied together. In the prayer of faith there is a divine science; it is a science that everyone who would make his lifework a success must understand. Christ says, 'What things soever ye desire, when ye pray, believe that ye receive them, and ye shall have them.' Mark 11:24. He makes it plain that our asking must be according to God's will; we must ask for the things that He has promised, and whatever we receive must be used in doing His will. The conditions met, the promise is unequivocal."

> *We know it's been the Lord helping us and supplying all our needs and necessities as we have prayed in faith and claimed His promises and received His wisdom and guidance and help*

My husband, David, and I have acknowledged our inability to do all we have done to build the "Ark," and we know it's been the Lord helping us and supplying all our needs and necessities as we have prayed in faith and claimed His promises and received His wisdom and guidance and help as James 1:5–6 says, "If any of you lack wisdom, let him ask of God, that giveth to all men liberally, and upbraideth not; and it shall be given him. But let him ask in faith, nothing wavering. For he that wavereth is like a wave of the sea driven with the wind and tossed." So many times, as we were building or working on the "Ark," and we couldn't figure something out and we needed help, we'd pause and pray and ask God for wisdom and knowledge and claim James 1:5. We are not carpenters, but He's the "Master Builder." In Vol. 7 *Testimonies for the Church*, p. 213 by E.G. White, she writes, "Just as soon as we realize our inability to do God's work and submit to be guided by His wisdom, the Lord can work with us. If we will empty the soul of self, He will supply all our necessities."

In the book *Life Sketches*, p. 196, Sister White tells us, "We have nothing to fear for the future, except as we shall forget the way the Lord has led us, and His teaching in our past history." What God has done for us in helping us financially and physically in building our 14 acres into the "Ark," He's willing and able to do for others who will step out in faith and let the Lord lead and guide and direct in their decision to leave the big cities and find a retreat in the country. Sister White says in *Country Living* p. 5, "Instead of the crowded city, seek some retired situation where your children will be, so far as possible, shielded from temptation, and there train and educate them for usefulness." She also writes on p. 21, "The Protestant world have set up an idol Sabbath in the place where God's Sabbath should be, and they are treading in the footsteps of the Papacy. For this reason I see the necessity of the people of God moving out of the cities into retired country places, where they may cultivate the land and raise their own produce. Thus they may bring their children up with simple, healthful habits. I see the necessity of making haste to get all things ready for the crisis."

Every home should be a place of refuge, a little "Ark of safety" for the members of our family and friends to prepare to go to heaven and to endure the crisis ahead of us all when we'll need a place to survive during the Sunday Law and the no–buy–no–sell time and every earthly support cut off, as *Desire of Ages* p. 121–122 by Sister White says. Sister White tells us on p. 17 in her *Country Living* book, "Get out of the cities as soon as possible, and purchase a little piece of land, where you can have a garden, where your children can watch the flowers growing, and learn from them lessons of simplicity… Much depends upon laying our plans according to the Word of the Lord, and with persevering energy carrying them out." This is what we did to find and purchase our 14 acres. We prayed and fasted and claimed God's promises like James 1:5; Psalm 32:8; Psalm 37:3–5; Proverbs 3:5–8. What He's done for us, He'll do for you as you have faith in God. It's a walk of faith and works as James 2:14–26 says and Hebrews 11 tells us. Let your faith in God grow now through the experiences He's allowing you to go through and it will be strong when it will be tested when the Sunday Law will be passed. Prepare now for the storm coming and have your little "Ark" all prepared to stand true to God when the majority go out and forsake us. In *Last Day Events* Sister White tells us on p. 180, "Soon God's people will be tested by fiery trials, and the great proportion of those who now appear to be genuine and true will prove to be base metal… To stand in defense of truth and righteousness when the majority forsake us, to fight the battles of the Lord when champions are few—this will be our test."

We read Sister White's counsel on pp. 26–28 in *Country Living*, "To every man was given his work according to his several ability. Then let him not move hesitatingly, but firmly, and yet humbly trusting in God… Let there be much praying done, and even with fasting, that not one shall move in darkness, but move in the light as God is in the light… We cannot have a weak faith now; we cannot be safe in a listless, indolent, slothful attitude. Every jot of ability is to be used, and sharp, calm, deep thinking is to be done. The wisdom of any human agent is not sufficient for the planning and devising in this time. Spread every plan before God with fasting, and with the humbling of the soul before the Lord Jesus, and commit thy ways unto the Lord. The sure promise is, He will direct thy paths."

God gave me an experience that helped my faith to grow in God's ability to hear our prayers and answer them like Matthew 21:22 says, "And all things, whatsoever ye shall ask in prayer, believing, ye shall receive." (Also, read Sister White's counsel in *Selected Messages Vol. 2*, pp. 142, 354–359, *8T* p. 28, *6T* p. 407, 195.) (God gave me a dream of *2SM* 142 and *8T* 28).

My experience: I had lost my glasses and couldn't find them, even though I had prayed and asked God to please help me to find them. I looked and looked all through the house praying and searching, but still I couldn't find my glasses. I knelt down again and prayed, "Lord, please open my eyes to see where my glasses are. You know I can't read or see to write without them, and I know Satan doesn't like what I'm writing and he's trying to stop me and hide my glasses from me. But, Lord, I know you can do anything and with you all things are possible, as you promised in Luke 1:37, "For with God nothing shall be impossible." Thank you, Lord, for hearing my prayer to find my glasses." When I opened my eyes, my eyes fell on my glasses, hid under the blood pressure cuff. When I had checked our blood pressures that morning, I had put my glasses away with the blood pressure machine and had forgotten about them. When I saw and found my glasses, I was so happy and excited, I shouted out loud, "Praise the Lord! Jesus had helped me find my lost glasses!"

I was wondering, as I was looking all over for my lost glasses, what lesson Jesus is trying to teach me in this experience He is allowing me to go through right now, losing my glasses? I thought, "If He never let us go through these trying experiences of having to show faith in God to hear our prayers for help in our time of need, then He couldn't teach us faith in His power to answer our prayers and to teach us to turn to Him in prayer for help, as naturally as the flower turns to the sun. God knows we all are going to need our faith in Him to grow, and we need to go through things that will help our faith to grow. We'll need faith in God and His promises to get us through the time of trouble ahead of us all, when we'll be living by faith for the Lord to take care of us and supply all our needs as Philippians 4:19 promises, "But my God shall supply all your need according to his riches in glory by Christ Jesus." And when every earthly support will be cut off during the Sunday Law crisis, as *Desire of Ages* by Sister White says on pp. 121–122. Also, we'll need faith in God during the great time of trouble when we'll have to flee and leave everything behind and be totally dependent on God to supply our bread and water as Isaiah 33:15–17 promises, and also to protect us while the plagues are falling like Psalm 46 and Psalm 91 and Psalm 121 promises and read Psalm 34 and Psalm 50:15. We need to now let our faith grow in Christ through our troubles and trials we're having right now, so we'll be in the habit of trusting in Jesus and His promises and have faith to know God will take care of us no matter what happens, and we need not fear the storm coming upon us when the Sunday Laws will be forced upon us, Psalm 56:3, and we'll have to decide which side we'll choose to be on—Sabbath or Sunday, Christ or Satan, Christ's Ten Commandments or man–made commandments?!

We'll need to have faith in God and His promises that He'll see us through it all and not crumble and give in when the pressures are put upon us through fines, imprisonment, inducements and no–buy and no–sell, and finally the death decree. **Read** *The Great Controversy* by E.G. White, pp. 603–610, "The Final Warning" and chapter 39 "The Time of Trouble," pp. 613–634 (especially p. 618).

So, let's let Jesus mold and make us into His character now as we allow Him to have complete control of our lives and the experiences we're going through right now

In *Last Day Events* by E.G. White, she tells what Satan will say on p. 149, "Satan says … 'For fear of wanting food and clothing they will join with the world in transgressing God's law. The earth will be wholly under my dominion…'" [Sister White says]: "If we are called to suffer for Christ's sake, we shall be able to go to prison trusting in Him as a little child trusts in its parents. Now is the time to cultivate faith in God." So, let's let Jesus mold and make us into His character now as we allow Him to have complete control of our lives and the experiences we're going through right now. Job said in Job 13:15, "Though he slay me, yet will I trust in him: but I will maintain mine own ways before him." We're like soldiers in boot camp training, being made into strong soldiers for Christ and His cause making it possible for us to be able to stand strong and true when the battle rages hot, and people are giving in and giving up their faith and trust in God and His word and turning against us. Jesus knows the future of each one of us, and He knows what we each have to go through to prepare us for the crisis that is soon to break upon us, and everyone's faith will be tested and tried and what experiences we need to go through to make us strong and our faith strong when the Sunday Law is passed. [1 Corinthians 10:13]. Sister White in *Last Day Events* on p. 154 writes, "Afflictions, crosses, temptations, adversity, and our varied trials are God's workmen to refine us, sanctify us, and fit us for the heavenly garner." Sister White continues to write on p. 180–181, "The church may appear as about to fall, but it does not fall. It remains, while the sinners in Zion will be sifted out—the chaff separated from the precious wheat. This is a terrible ordeal, but nevertheless it must take place. As the storm approaches, a large class who have professed faith in the third angel's message, but have not been sanctified through obedience to the truth, abandon their position and join the ranks of the opposition."

Be sure and let God plan for you, as you make your plans to prepare your place of refuge to go through the crisis before us. When the crisis hits, you'll be so glad you did God's will. Praise God we're free of debt! Sister White says to "shun debt as leprosy" in *Counsels on Stewardship*, pp. 257, 272.

We studied our Bible and the Spirit of Prophecy books by Sister White like *Country Living* to help us know how to prepare our "Ark" for the crisis ahead of us. As we prayed, we also read books like *Another Ark to Build* by W.D. Frazee and also his other book *Coming Events and Crisis at the Close*. We also read Jere Franklin's book, *You Can Survive!* God helped me to write a book to help God's people to see the dangers of city living and how to prepare for the coming crisis ahead, *Don't Be Trapped in the Cities!! Get Out NOW!* by Linda Clore.

Just recently, God gave me a dream. In my dream, we were looking for something to study. I said, "I don't study the Sabbath School Quarterly from the church." I went and picked up my book by W.D. Frazee called *Coming Events and Crisis at the Close* and we began studying Frazee's book and were so helped and blessed! I recommend that book and his other book, *Another Ark to Build*.

There was a S.D.A. who lives about 50 miles from here, who years ago, had a dream, too, about Elder Frazee's book *Coming Events and Crisis at the Close*. She said, "I had a dream and I saw an angel hand me Frazee's book and said, 'You need to read and study this book!'"

Another walk of faith and works have been from 2013–2015 while writing my book, *Don't Be Trapped in the Cities!! Get Out NOW!* I literally wrote that book on my knees. I would want a quote from the Spirit of Prophecy, and I couldn't find it. I have no computer or internet, so I'd kneel down on my knees and pray that God would please help me to find that quote I wanted, and while still on my knees, the Lord would put it in my mind where the reference was found! Like I wanted the quote, "Worry is blind and cannot discern the future; but Jesus sees the end from the beginning. In every difficulty He has His way prepared to bring relief… Our heavenly Father has a thousand ways to provide for us of which we know nothing." Then, the Lord put it in my mind, *Ministry of Healing* p. 481. Truly, as I wrote my book God would put things in my mind He wanted me to write about. Read the chapter in *Ministry of Healing*, "Help for Daily Living"—there's a lot of quotes to help you!

God bless you in your "walk of faith and works!"

Have faith in God! He's working all things for your good! Romans 8:28.

Read: *Desire of Ages*: pp. 172–173, 322–327, 380–382, 428–431; chapter 69, this chapter is based on Matthew 24; Mark 13; Luke 21. *Testimonies for the Church, Vol. 6*, pp. 128–129, 140, 324, "Preparation for the Final Crises," pp. 404–410, 441. *Testimonies for the Church, Vol. 5*, pp. 132–146, 206–216, 217–235. *Sons and Daughters of God*, pp. 32–37, 290. *Evangelism*, pp. 566–568. *Gospel Workers*, pp. 160–162, 505–519. *Selected Messages Vol. 2*, chapter 12, pp. 100–118.

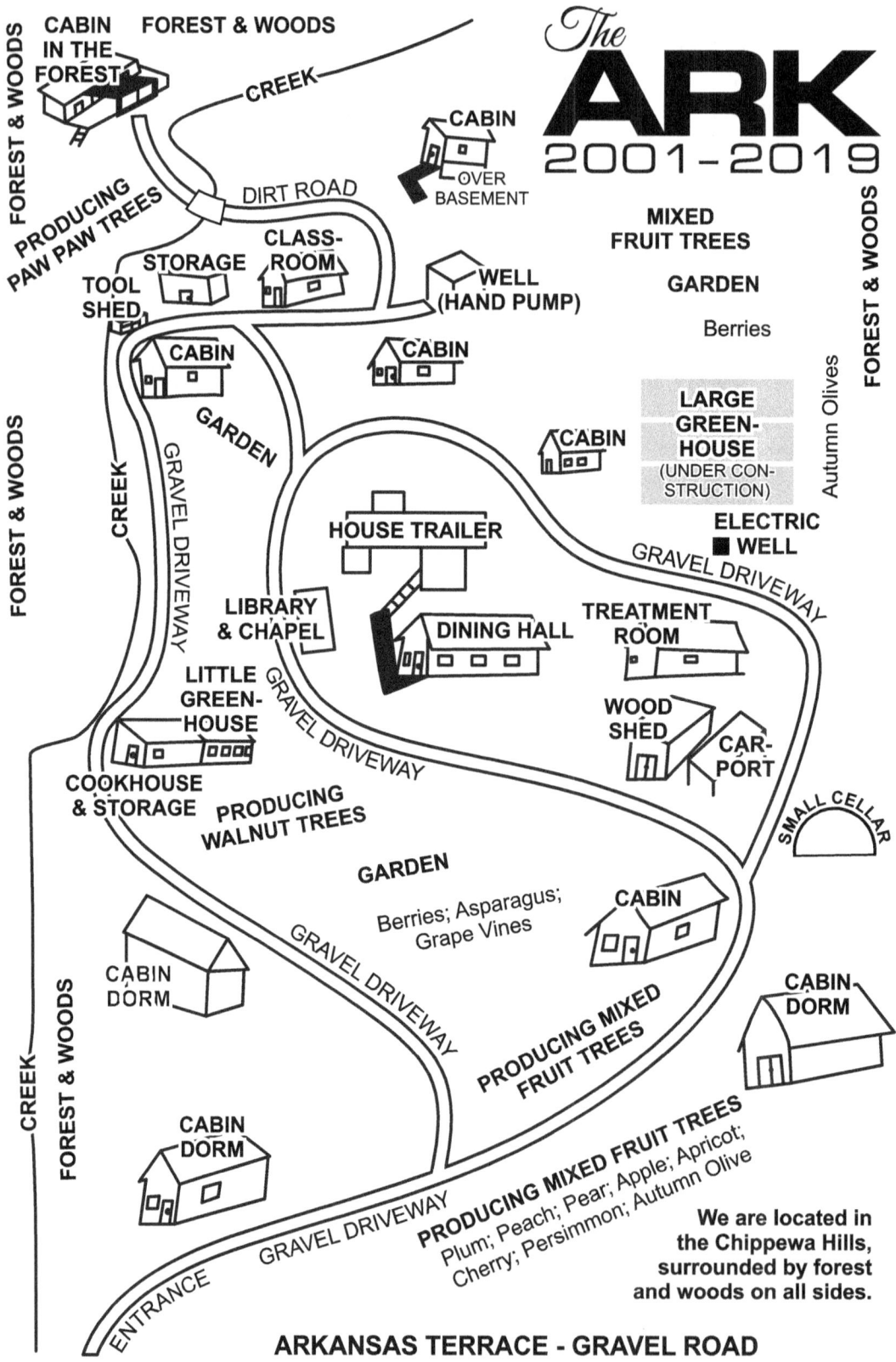

"God Hears the Prayers of Faith"
(Hebrews 11, the faith chapter, especially verses 5–6)
Written January 2, 2017

Jonathan had lost his ear piece off his glasses, and we looked all over for it, and we just couldn't find it! Jonathan said, "Lets pray!" So, we prayed and God opened my eyes to see the ear piece off his glasses. Praise the Lord! Thank you Jesus! We, then, prayed and thanked Jesus for hearing our prayer of faith, knowing Jesus would answer our prayer to find his lost ear piece from off his glasses. Jonathan is legally blind, 20/400 without his glasses, and 20/200 with his glasses. He really needed his glasses badly! I was so proud of Jonathan to know he knew the right source to turn to for help, and he had faith in Jesus to know to pray and for God to hear his prayers for help! He's learning to trust in God for himself and as his source of help in his time of need and knows that God can do anything! Luke 1:37; Mark 10:27; Matthew 21:22; Matthew 7:7. Thank you Jesus for this encouraging experience, as we keep claiming Proverbs 22:6 for our son, Jonathan.

Another experience we had in praying in faith and God heard and answered our prayer, was when Dad and I were putting the electricity in the walls of our 12' x 20' cabin we had just bought, David got stumped and didn't know what to do and I said, "Lets pray and claim James 1:5–6." So, we prayed in faith and claimed James 1:5–6, and God put it in my mind how to figure out our problem and what we needed to do to finish getting the electricity hooked up right and safe! Praise the Lord! Thank you Jesus! God helped Daddy to get the job done and finished! There's power in prayer! We know where our source of help and strength and wisdom and knowledge is found, and it's in faith in Jesus and the power of prayer and claiming God's promises. This is what I'm hoping and praying God will do with my book, *Don't Be Trapped in the Cities!! Get Out NOW!* And also the new book I'm working on right now.

I hope, as God's people read our experiences and stories of faith, that it will strengthen their faith and trust in Jesus to hear their sincere prayers for help and guidance in their plans and decisions as to what Jesus wants them to be doing right now in leaving these large wicked cities and move to the country and prepare their lives and homes for the crisis soon to break upon us as an overwhelming surprise! *2SM* 142; *8T* 28; *6T* 407; Jeremiah 33:3; Psalm 32:8.

I had an interesting experience happen to me. David and Jonathan and I were watching a sermon on a DVD, and I went to use the bathroom and while in the bathroom, I heard someone with a low-pitched voice humming the song, "I Sing the Mighty Power of God." When I came out of the bathroom, I asked David and Jonathan, who was humming the song, "I Sing the Mighty Power of God?" Neither one of them had been humming the song, nor had they heard it. David said to me, "What are you hearing?" I said, "I must be hearing 'Heavenly Music'." By faith we still keep praying and claiming Proverbs 22:6 for our son Jonathan, too. **Read** in *Steps to Christ* by E.G. White, the chapter, "The Privilege of Prayer," especially pp. 65–70, 72:

> "The darkness of the evil one encloses those who neglect to pray… Why should the sons and daughters of God be reluctant to pray, when prayer is the key in the hand of faith to unlock heaven's storehouse, where are treasured the boundless resources of Omnipotence?... When we do not receive the very things we asked for, at the time we ask, we are still to believe that the Lord hears and that He will answer our prayers… Then do not fear to trust Him, even though you do not see the immediate answer to your prayers. Rely upon His sure promise, 'Ask, and it shall be given you.' Matthew 7:7… By calm, simple faith the soul holds communion with God and gathers to itself rays of divine light to strengthen and sustain it in the conflict with Satan. God is our tower of strength… Keep your wants, your joys, your sorrows, your cares, and your fears before God. You cannot burden Him; you cannot weary Him. He who numbers the hairs of your head is not indifferent to the wants of His children… Take to Him everything that perplexes the mind. Nothing is too great for Him to bear, for He holds up worlds, He rules over all the affairs of the universe. Nothing that in any way concerns our peace is too small for Him to notice. There is no chapter in our experience too dark for Him to read; there is no perplexity too difficult for Him to unravel. No calamity can befall the least of His children, no anxiety harass the soul, no joy cheer, no sincere prayer escape the lips, of which our heavenly Father is unobservant, or in which He takes no immediate interest. 'He healeth the broken in heart, and bindeth up their wounds.' Psalm 147:3. The relations between God and each soul are as distinct and full as though there were not another soul upon the earth to share His watchcare, not another soul for whom He gave His beloved Son… We should keep in our thoughts every blessing we receive from God, and when we realize His great love we should be willing to trust everything to the hand that was nailed to the cross for us."

Read Sister White's book, *Ministry of Healing*. On. p. 482, she writes, "In the darkest days, when appearances seem most forbidding, have faith in God. He is working out His will, doing all things well in behalf of His people. The strength of those who love and serve Him will be renewed day by day. He is able and willing to bestow upon His servants all the help they need. He will give them the wisdom which their varied necessities demand." **Read** 2 Corinthians 12:9–10. Also, on p. 509, she continues to write, "We, too, must have times set apart for meditation and prayer and for receiving spiritual refreshing. We do not value the power and efficacy of prayer as we should. Prayer and faith will do what no power on earth can accomplish… Christ is ever sending messages to those who listen for His voice."

I recently had a dream. In my dream, a few of us were at a hospital singing to the patients. In one particular room, the nurses asked us to go sing to this patient who was dying and needed power to get well. She was needing prayer for healing and so after we had sung the song to her, "I Sing the Mighty Power of God," and then we had prayer for her and when prayer had been offered for her, the word "POWER" lighted up and flashed and showed up on her computer screen on her life support machine, keeping her alive, that she was hooked up to. The two nurses and all of us in the room saw the word "POWER" on the screen, and we all saw and felt the power of God and knew that God was hearing the sincere prayer of faith offered for this patient! The nurses thanked us for coming! It felt so good to be used of God to be a help and blessing to others and to make a difference in someone's life! That's what life is all about like Isaiah 58 says.

(End of dream).

I remember hearing of an experiment that was made on patients in the I.C.U. in the hospital. They found that the patients being prayed for did better than the patients not prayed for. There's power in prayer! We saw the power of prayer, when we prayed for Jonathan the times he was in the hospital! God saw him through his crises! Praise God! God hears the prayers of faith! Sister White says in *Ministry of Healing* on pp. 48–49, "The providence of God had placed Jesus where He was, and He depended on His heavenly Father for means to relieve the necessity. When we are brought into strait places, we are to depend on God. In every emergency we are to seek help from Him who has infinite resources at His command." So many times when we've been in need of money to keep working on the "Ark," God will use someone to feel impressed by the Holy Spirit to send us money in the mail, just when we're in a strait place, and we're praying earnestly for God to please supply our needs as Philippians 4:19 promises, "But my God shall supply all your need according to his riches in glory by Christ Jesus." We praise and thank God for always being there to help us and hear our prayers of faith! God has been with us in the building of the "Ark." God has been with us in hearing our many prayers of faith for our son, Jonathan, who has gone through so many troubles and times of sickness, etc. Sister White says in *Steps to Christ*, pp. 102, "We need to praise God more 'for His goodness, and for His wonderful works to the children of men.' Psalm 107:8… We are the constant recipients of God's mercies, and yet how little gratitude we express, how little we praise Him for what He has done for us."

Read in *The Great Controversy*, by E.G. White, chapter 38, "The Final Warning," pp. 603–612. Especially on p. 608 we read, "In this time of persecution the faith of the Lord's servants will be tried. They have faithfully given the warning, looking to God and to His word alone. God's Spirit, moving upon their hearts, has constrained them to speak."

I Sing the Almighty Power of God

1. I sing the mighty power of God that made the mountians rise,
that spread the flowing seas abroad and built the lofty skies.
I sing the wisdom that ordained the sun to rule the day;
the moon shines full at his command and all the stars obey.

2. I sing the goodness of the Lord that filled the earth with food;
he formed the creatures with his word and then pronounced them good.
Lord, how your wonders are displayed where'er I turn my eye,
if I survey the ground I tread or gaze upon the sky!

3. There's not a plant or flower below but makes your glories known,
and clouds arise and tempests blow by order from your throne;
while all that borrows life from you is ever in your care,
and everywhere that we can be, you, God, are present there.

Text: Isaac Watts (1674-1748)
Tune: *Gesangbuch der H. W. K. Hofkapelle*, 1784

CMD
ELLACOMBE
www.hymnary.org/text/i_sing_the_mighty_power_of_god

This hymn is in the public domain. You may freely use this score for personal and congregational worship. If you reproduce the score, please credit Hymnary.org as the source.

"When We All Have to Decide!"
Written January 10, 2017

Times are becoming more and more serious, and people are going to have to decide what they're going to do about getting out of the big, wicked cities, while they still can, before God's judgment falls upon the big wicked city they're in. Sister White says in *Last Day Events*, pp. 110–111, "The cities of today are fast becoming like Sodom and Gomorrah… Light has been given me that the cities will be filled with confusion, violence, and crime, and that these things will increase till the end of this earth's history… The world over, cities are becoming hotbeds of vice. On every hand are the sights and sounds of evil… The end is near and every city is to be turned upside down every way… O that God's people had a sense of the impending destruction of thousands of cities, now almost given to idolatry… The time is near when large cities will be swept away, and all should be warned of these coming judgments." Sister White goes on to say on p. 115, "I am bidden to declare the message that cities full of transgression, and sinful in the extreme, will be destroyed by earthquakes, by fire, by flood."

In *Country Living* by E.G. White on pp. 7–9, we read, "The same voice that warned Lot to leave Sodom bids us, 'Come out from among them, and be ye separate, ... and touch not the unclean.' Those who obey this warning will find a refuge. Let every man be wide awake for himself, and try to save his family. Let him gird himself for the work. God will reveal from point to point what to do next… Hear the voice of God through the apostle Paul: 'Work out your own salvation with fear and trembling. For it is God which worketh in you both to will and to do of His good pleasure.' Lot trod the plain with unwilling and tardy steps… The time is near when the large cities will be visited by the judgments of God. In a little while, these cities will be terribly shaken… The ungodly cities of our world are to be swept away by the besom of destruction…

Calamities will come—calamities most awful, most unexpected; and these destructions will follow one after another…" (Sister White relates a view of destruction she saw on p. 8). "Last Friday morning, just before I awoke, a very impressive scene was presented before me. I seemed to awake from sleep, but was not in my home. From the windows I could behold a terrible conflagration. Great balls of fire were falling upon houses, and from these balls fiery arrows were flying in every direction. It was impossible to check the fires that were kindled, and many places were being destroyed. The terror of the people was indescribable." (This could be like an atomic bomb she saw? Also, in Joel 2:30, this could be describing an atomic bomb, like pillars of smoke, "And I will show wonders in the heavens and in the earth, blood, and fire, and pillars of smoke.") On pp. 9–11, Sister White continues to say:

"In harmony with the light given me, I am urging people to come out from the great centers of population. Our cities are increasing in wickedness, and it is becoming more and more evident that those who remain in them unnecessarily do so at the peril of their soul's salvation… The time is fast coming when the controlling power of the labor unions will be very oppressive. Again and again the Lord has instructed that our people are to take their families away from the cities, into the country, where they can raise their own provisions; for in the future the problem of buying and selling will be a very serious one. We should now begin to heed the instruction given us over and over again: Get out of the cities into rural districts, where the houses are not crowded closely together, and where you will be free from the interference of enemies… The trades unions will be one of the agencies that will bring upon this earth a time of trouble such as has not been since the world began… The work of the people of God is to prepare for the events of the future, which will soon come upon them with blinding force… Trades unions will be formed, and those who refuse to join these unions will be marked men… The trades unions and confederacies of the world are a snare. Keep out of them, and away from them, brethren. Have nothing to do with them. Because of these unions and confederacies, it will soon be very difficult for our institutions to carry on their work in the cities. My warning is: Keep out of the cities. Build no sanitariums in the cities. Educate our people to get out of the cities into the country, where they can obtain a small piece of land, and make a home for themselves and their children... But erelong there will be such strife and confusion in the cities, that those who wish to leave them will not be able. We must be preparing for these issues. This is the light that is given me."

Read in *Last Day Events* by E.G. White, the chapters 7, "Country Living"; 8, "The Cities"; 9 "Sunday Laws"; 10 "The Little Time of Trouble"; 11 "Satan's Last Day Deceptions"; 12 "The Shaking."

Read also in *Country Living* by E.G. White, pp. 20–21, "Preparing for the Sunday Law Crisis" – "There are troublous times before us," p. 20. Also, on p. 21, Sister White writes, "The Protestant world have set up an idol Sabbath in the place where God's Sabbath should be, and they are treading in the footsteps of the Papacy. For this reason I see the necessity of the people of God moving out of the cities into retired country [places,] where they may cultivate the land and raise their own produce. Thus they may bring their children up with simple, healthful habits. I see the necessity of making haste to get all things ready for the crisis."

A friend of ours was telling us about the new book put out by the E.G. White estate. It's the last of her manuscripts that hadn't been published yet, until now. But in this new book, she tells of the big ball of fire she saw fall on Nashville, Tennessee! This friend of ours has written a small booklet called, "From Nineveh to Nashville." It's a warning message to them in Nashville for them to repent and hopefully divert the disaster. This author was saying how wicked the Grand Ole Opry is and what a terribly wicked place! He said that hundreds of SDAs are just waiting to distribute his booklet out around Nashville to call them to repentance before it's too late! That's why I wrote my book, *Don't Be Trapped in the Cities!! Get Out <u>NOW</u>!* God inspired me to write my book, to warn the people of God to get out of the cities while they still can, before it's too late! I don't want the people's blood on my hands like Ezekiel chapters 3 and 33, and Joel chapters 2 and 3 say. We all need to take our individual case before the Lord and let Him direct our steps! The promises in Psalm 32:8 and Matthew 7:7; Psalm 37:3–5; Proverbs 3:5–6; James 1:5–6 are some we can claim and ask God to please help us know what He would have you do at this time to prepare for the crises ahead of each of us with the Sunday Law to soon be enforced.

The Pope's door of mercy closed November 20, 2016 and he's up to no good! God's door of mercy is soon to close, too, and none know how soon it will close on them, too, if they should die or how soon it will close on these big wicked cities like Nashville, and God's judgments fall on them, like in the days of Noah and Lot. These are very serious and solemn times we're living in! God is trying to wake His people up to the dangers they're in in these big wicked cities and to get out of them as soon as possible. Joshua 24:14–15 says, "Now therefore fear the LORD, and serve him in sincerity and in truth: and put away the gods which your fathers served on the other side of the flood, and in Egypt; and serve ye the LORD. And if it seem evil unto you to serve the LORD, choose you this day whom ye will serve; whether the gods which your fathers served that were on the other side of the flood, or the gods of the Amorites, in whose land ye dwell: but as for me and my house, we will serve the LORD."

> *We all need to take our individual case before the Lord and let Him direct our steps*

It's decision time! The decisions we're making <u>now</u> will determine our destiny <u>then</u>, when the Sunday Laws will be passed. Don't put it off. Time is running out. No one knows what tomorrow holds. <u>NOW</u> is the time to prepare for the crisis, both spiritually and physically! **Read** and **study** Sister White's books, *Country Living*, *Last Day Events*, and *The Great Controversy*, and my book *Don't Be Trapped in the Cities!! Get Out <u>NOW</u>*!

Read *5T* by E.G. White, pp. 62–84, "The Testimonies Slighted." On p. 81, she writes, "The time is not far distant when the test will come to every soul. The mark of the beast will be urged upon us." (I dreamt this p. 81 some time back.)

"Coming to a Town Near You!"
Written January 14, 2017

On January 14, 2017, I had a dream and a voice in my dream was saying these words to me, "Coming to a town near you. Write something, so when it comes to the town nearest you, you'll be ready for it and separate from their fellowship." Then, I heard the words quoted by the voice, from the book, *Country Living* by E.G. White on p. 32, "Preparatory for leaving the smaller ones for retired homes in secluded places among the mountains." Sister White writes in *Maranatha* on p. 270:

> "I saw the saints leaving the cities and villages, and associating together in companies, and living in the most solitary places. Angels provided them food and water, [Isaiah 33:15–16] while the wicked were suffering from hunger and thirst. During the night a very impressive scene passed before me. There seemed to be great confusion and the conflict of armies. A messenger from the Lord stood before me, and said, 'Call your household. I will lead you; follow me.' He led me down a dark passage, through a forest, then through the clefts of mountains, and said, 'Here you are safe.' There were others who had been led to this retreat. [The dictionary defines "retreat" – an act or process of withdrawing especially from what is difficult, dangerous, or disagreeable]. The heavenly messenger said. 'The time of trouble has come as a thief in the night, as the Lord warned you it would come.' In the time of trouble just before the coming of Christ, the righteous will be preserved through the ministration of heavenly angels; but there will be no security for the transgressor of God's law. Angels cannot then protect those who are disregarding one of the divine precepts. In the closing period of earth's history the Lord will work mightily in behalf of those who stand steadfastly for the right.... In the midst of the time of trouble—trouble such as has not been since there was a nation—His chosen ones will stand unmoved. Satan with all the hosts of evil cannot destroy the weakest of God's saints. Angels that excel in strength will protect them, and in their behalf Jehovah will reveal Himself as a "God of gods," able to save to the uttermost those who have put their trust in Him… In the day of fierce trial He [Christ] will say, 'Come, my people, enter thou into thy chambers, and shut thy doors about thee: hide thyself as it were for a little moment, until the indignation be over–past.' Isaiah 26:20. What are the chambers in which they are to hide? They are the protection of Christ and holy angels. The people of God are not at this time all in one place. They are in different companies, and in all parts of the earth."

The voice I heard speaking to me in my dream continued to quote p. 32 in *Country Living* by E.G. White, "It is no time now for God's people to be fixing their affections or laying up their treasure in the world. The time is not far distant, when, like the early disciples, we shall be forced to seek a refuge in desolate and solitary places. As the siege of Jerusalem by the Roman armies was the signal for flight to the Judean Christians, so the assumption of power on the part of our nation, in the decree enforcing the papal Sabbath, will be a warning to us. It will then be time to leave the large cities, preparatory to leaving the smaller ones for retired homes in secluded places among the mountains. And now, instead of seeking expensive dwellings here, we should be preparing to move to a better country, even a heavenly. Instead of spending our means in self–gratification, we should be studying to economize."

In my dream as I listened to the voice quote Sister White, I was thinking, now he's saying, "preparatory to leaving the small ones for retired homes in secluded places among the mountains." In my dream I was thinking, I've also written about God's people to get out of the large cities as soon as possible. In my book *Don't Be Trapped in the Cities! Get out NOW*! like E.G. White says on p. 17 in her *Country Living* book, "In a little while they will have to leave the cities. These cities are filled with wickedness of every kind,—with strikes and murders and suicides. Satan is in them, controlling men in their work of destruction. Under his influence they kill for the sake of killing, and this they will do more and more... If we place ourselves under objectionable influences, can we expect God to work a miracle to undo the results of our wrong course?—No, indeed. Get out of the cities as soon as possible, and purchase a little piece of land, where you can have a garden, where your children can watch the flowers growing, and learn from them lessons of simplicity and purity." Also, on p. 12, *Country Living*, Sister White warns, "Before the overflowing scourge shall come upon the dwellers of the earth, the Lord calls upon all who are Israelites indeed to prepare for that event. To parents He sends the warning cry, Gather your children into your own houses; gather them away from those who are disregarding the commandments of God, who are teaching and practicing evil. Get out of the large cities as fast as possible. Establish church schools. Give your children the Word of God as the foundation of all their education... I am instructed by the Lord to warn our people not to flock to the cities to find homes for their families. To fathers and to mothers I am instructed to say, Fail not to keep your children within your own premises."

The Sunday Law is the final call given to leave the large cities. On p. 19, Sister White tells us in her *Country Living* book that, "Believers who are now living in the cities will have to move to the country, that they may save their children from ruin… If the poor now crowded into the cities could find homes upon the land, they might not only earn a livelihood, but find health and happiness now unknown to them. Hard work, simple fare, close economy, often hardship and privation, would be their lot. But what a blessing would be theirs in leaving the city, with its enticements to evil, its turmoil and crime, misery and foulness, for the country's quiet and peace and purity. To many of those living in the cities who have not a spot of green grass to set their feet upon, who year after year have looked out upon filthy courts and narrow alleys, brick walls and pavements, and skies clouded with dust and smoke,—if these could be taken to some farming district, surrounded with the green fields, the woods and hills and brooks, the clear skies and the fresh, pure air of the country, it would seem almost like heaven. Cut off to a great degree from contact with and dependence upon men, and separated from the world's corrupting maxims and customs and excitements, they would come nearer to the heart of nature. God's presence would be more real to them. Many would learn the lesson of dependence upon Him. Through nature they would hear His voice speaking to their hearts of His peace and love, and mind and soul and body would respond to the healing, life–giving power."

Now, in my dream of January 14, 2017, I'm saying to myself, "Now this voice is telling me to write for the people to be preparing to leave the smaller ones for retired homes in secluded places among the mountains." This is what I quoted on p. 32 of *Country Living*, what the voice I heard said to write. According to Sister White on p. 270 of *Maranatha*, this will be at the close of probation, when the death decree is passed, and we flee to solitary places and angels provide us with food and water. Now's the time to be leaving the large cities where all the calamities and judgments are falling. The Sunday Law, when it's passed, will be the final call to leave the large cities, preparatory to leaving the small ones, (at the close of probation) for retired homes in secluded places among the mountains, where the angels of the Lord will lead us to safety, while the saints are leaving the cities and villages and associating together in companies and living in the most solitary places, refers to *Maranatha* p. 270. Sister White writes of the calamities and God's judgments soon to fall and in *Country Living* on pp 7–8, "Lot had too much of a lingering spirit. Let us not be like him. The same voice that warned Lot to leave Sodom bids us, 'Come out from among them, and be ye separate, ... and touch not the unclean.' Those who obey this warning will find a refuge. Let every man be wide awake for himself, and try to save his family. Let him gird himself for the work. God will reveal from point to point what to do next. Hear the voice of God through the apostle Paul: 'Work out your own salvation with fear and trembling. For it is God which worketh in you both to will and to do of His good pleasure.' Lot trod the plain with unwilling and tardy steps. He had so long associated with evil workers that he could not see his peril until his wife stood on the plain a pillar of salt forever."

Country Living says on p. 30, "As God's commandment–keeping people, we must leave the cities. As did Enoch, we must work in the cities but not dwell in them. When iniquity abounds in a nation, there is always to be heard some voice giving warning and instruction, as the voice of Lot was heard in Sodom… Yet Lot could have preserved his family from many evils, had he not made his home in this wicked, polluted city. All that Lot and his family did in Sodom could have been done by them, even if they had lived in a place some distance away from the city. Enoch walked with God, and yet he did not live in the midst of any city, polluted with every kind of violence and wickedness, as did Lot in Sodom." Continuing to quote again on pp.7–8 of the *Country Living* book, "The time is near when the large cities will be visited by the judgments of God. In a little while, these cities will be terribly shaken… The ungodly cities of our world are to be swept away by the besom of destruction… I am bidden to declare the message that cities full of transgression, and sinful in the extreme, will be destroyed by earthquakes, by fire, by flood… His unseen agencies will cause destruction, devastation, and death… Calamities will come—calamities most awful, most unexpected; and these destructions will follow one after another… There are reasons why we should not build in

> *The time is near when the large cities will be visited by the judgments of God. In a little while, these cities will be terribly shaken*

the cities. On these cities, God's judgments are soon to fall… The time is near when large cities will be swept away, and all should be warned of these coming judgments…

O that God's people had a sense of the impending destruction of thousands of cities, now almost given to idolatry."

Read the following references: *Country Living* pp. 5, 16, 20–21; *Early Writings* by E.G. White, pp. 282–285; *The Great Controversy*, pp. 626, 627, 629; *Last Day Events*, p. 173; Vol. 7 *SDA Bible Commentary*, pp. 975–977 "Sunday Law & Probation Closes"; *Fundamentals of Christian Education*, p. 526; *Vol. 5 Testimonies for the Church*, p. 523; Matthew 24; Mark 13; Luke 21.

God is trying to tell the world something! But who sees it? At the same time the horrors came to Japan and Indonesia, the Munich Reinsurance Company reported the busy activities of the devil and his army in a single year.

January 1—a 6.9 earthquake hits Argentina. The same day, a 5.2 earthquake hits China.

January 2—a 7.1 earthquake hits Chile. The same day, more than 1,000 dead birds fall from the sky in Arkansas. The same day, dead fish cover a 20–mile section of the Arkansas River.

January 3—a 7.0 earthquake hits Argentina. The same day, thousands of birds fall dead in Manitoba.

January 4—100 tons of dead fish wash up in Brazil.

January 5—millions of dead fish wash up in Maryland and New Zealand.

January 6—40,000 crabs wash up on England's beaches.

February 4—thousands of marine animals dead in the Amazon.

February 21—a 6.3 earthquake shakes New Zealand. In March, millions of fish wash up in Redondo Beach, CA.

March 11—a 9.0 earthquake and a tsunami devastates Japan.

March 16—a 40-foot section of California highway falls into the Pacific Ocean.

March 17—a 3.5 earthquake shakes northern California. The same day, a 6.5 earthquake hits Vanuatu.

March 23—a 7.0 earthquake strikes Burma. The same day, a 6.8 earthquake hits Thailand.

March 25—a 6.4 earthquake hits Japan. The same day, thousands of fish wash up in Florida.

April 1—a 5.4 earthquake hits the Sandwich Islands.

April 3—a 6.4 earthquake hits Fiji. The same day a 6.7 earthquake hits Java.

April 4 & 5—46 tornadoes sweep through 10 U.S. states.

April 7—a 6.5 earthquake hits Veracruz, Mexico. The same day, a 7.4 earthquake hits Japan.

April 8 to 11—59 tornadoes hit 9 U.S. states.

April 11—a 6.5 earthquake hits Japan, and dead fish wash up in 36 lakes in Connecticut.

April 14 to 16—160 tornadoes hit 10 states.

April 16—deadly tornadoes hit North Carolina and Virginia killing 47.

April 25 to 30—more than 300 tornadoes cause 321 deaths in the U.S. with 240 dead in Alabama alone.

April 20—thousands of fish wash up in New York. That month, 137 tornadoes kill over 180 people in Alabama.

April 27—more than 300 tornadoes kill 321 in the U.S.

"Destruction Is Coming to These Cities!"

Written January 25, 2017

Read p. 8 *Country Living* by E.G. White, "O that God's people had a sense of the impending destruction of thousands of cities, now almost given to idolatry."

On January 21, 2017, I dreamt I was saying in my dream, "Destruction is coming to these cities!" (Three different times, in the same night, I dreamt this).

On January 25, 2017, I dreamt, "Church and state are uniting more and more!

People will be thinking everything is going along okay, but on p. 142 in Book 2 *Selected Messages* by Sister White, she writes: "The trades unions will be one of the agencies that will bring upon this earth a time of trouble such as has not been since the world began… The work of the people of God is to prepare for the events of the future, which will soon come upon them with blinding force." On p. 143, she continues to write, "These unions are one of the signs of the last days. Men are binding up in bundles ready to be burned. They may be church members, but while they belong to these unions, they cannot possibly keep the commandments of God; for to belong to these unions means to disregard the entire Decalogue." Again, on p. 144, Sister White continues to warn us, "Those who claim to be the children of God are in no case to bind up with the labor unions that are formed or that shall be formed. This the Lord forbids. Cannot those who study the prophecies see and understand what is before us?" We read the startling quote of Sister White in Vol. 8 *Testimonies for the Church*, p. 28, "Transgression has almost reached its limit. Confusion fills the world, and a great terror is soon to come upon human beings. The end is very near. We who know the truth should be preparing for what is soon to break upon the world as an overwhelming surprise."

In *Early Writings*, Sister White tells us on pp. 43–44, "Satan is now using every device in this sealing time to keep the minds of God's people from the present truth and to cause them to waver. I saw a covering that God was drawing over His people to protect them in the time of trouble; and every soul that was decided on the truth and was pure in heart was to be covered with the covering of the Almighty… I saw that Satan was working through agents in a number of ways. He was at work through ministers who have rejected the truth and are given over to strong delusions to believe a lie that they might be damned… Oh, that all could get a view of it as God revealed it to me, that they might know more of the wiles of Satan and be on their guard! I saw that Satan was at work in these ways to distract, deceive, and draw away God's people, just now in this sealing time. I saw some who were not standing stiffly for present truth. Their knees were trembling, and their feet sliding, because they were not firmly planted on the truth, and the covering of Almighty God could not be drawn over them while they were thus trembling.

Satan was trying his every art to hold them where they were, until the sealing was past, until the covering was drawn over God's people, and they left without a shelter from the burning wrath of God, in the seven last plagues. God has begun to draw this covering over His people, and it will soon be drawn over all who are to have a shelter in the day of slaughter. God will work in power for His people; and Satan will be permitted to work also…" On p. 45, we read, "I saw that the mysterious signs and wonders and false reformations would increase and spread. The reformations that were shown me were not reformations from error to truth." Continuing to read on p. 256, "Many saw the perfect chain of truth in the angels' messages, and gladly received them in their order, and followed Jesus by faith into the heavenly sanctuary. These messages were represented to me as an anchor to the people of God. Those who understand and receive them will be kept from being swept away by the many delusions of Satan…"

Sister White again on pp. 258–259 says, "I saw a company who stood well guarded and firm, giving no countenance to those who would unsettle the established faith of the body. God looked upon them with approbation. I was shown three steps—the first, second, and third angels' messages. Said my accompanying angel, 'Woe to him who shall move a block or stir a pin of these messages. The true understanding of these messages is of vital importance. The destiny of souls hangs upon the manner in which they are received.' God had led them along step by step, until He had placed them upon a solid, immovable platform." Reading on p. 261 in *Early Writings*, Sister White makes this statement, "Satan deceives some with Spiritualism. He also comes as an angel of light and spreads his influence over the land by means of false reformations. The churches are elated, and consider that God is working marvelously for them, when it is the work of another spirit. The excitement will die away and leave the world and the church in a worse condition than before.

I saw that God has honest children among the nominal Adventists and the fallen churches, and before the plagues shall be poured out, ministers and people will be called out from these churches and will gladly receive the truth. Satan knows this; and before the loud cry of the third angel is given, he raises an excitement in these religious bodies, that those who have rejected the truth may think that God is with them. He hopes to deceive the honest and lead them to think that God is still working for the churches. But the light will shine, and all who are honest will leave the fallen churches, and take their stand with the remnant." On the chapter on "Spiritualism," on p. 262, Sister White writes, "I saw that the saints must have a thorough understanding of present truth, which they will be obliged to maintain from the Scriptures. They must understand the state of the dead."

Read: *Early Writings* on pp. 270–295; *The Great Controversy* by E.G. White, the chapter 32, "Snares of Satan"; *6T* pp. 126–140, "Education"; *Last Day Events* by E.G. White, chapters 1–6, pp. 11–93, also, pp. 111, 115–118, 126, 142, 186.

On p. 186 of *Last Day Events*, we read, "Before the final visitation of God's judgments upon the earth there will be among the people of the Lord such a revival of primitive godliness as has not been witnessed since apostolic times. The Spirit and power of God will be poured out upon His children… The work will be similar to that of the Day of Pentecost… At that time the "latter rain," or refreshing from the presence of the Lord, will come, to give power to the loud voice of the third angel, and prepare the saints to stand in the period when the seven last plagues shall be poured out. I heard those clothed with the armor speak forth the truth with great power. It had effect.... I asked what had made this great change. An angel answered, 'It is the latter rain, the refreshing from the presence of the Lord, the loud cry of the third angel.'"

The following information is my book *Don't Be Trapped in the Cities!! Get Out NOW!* pp. 72–82. The Lord showed me these pages in a dream:

God is testing our faith and trust in Him. He's the only all wise counselor we can depend on. Man will only fail us, but Jesus never fails. He's always there to help and strengthen and guide us as we learn to depend and rely on Him and not weak sinful man. We need to keep our eyes on Jesus and not the problems of life, like Ps. 121 says.

In my letters to people who had children or grand- children, I tried to encourage them to stay faithful to Jesus and keep Him as their pattern and not follow the crowd or give in to peer pressures. I mentioned how our son, Jonathan, started on the downward road in church school, when he wanted to be liked and accepted and not feel different. But there was so much peer pressure, so he got in with the wrong crowd, which was the popular kids doing the wrong things and he'd follow along instead of standing up for Jesus, and doing what he knew was right. As he got older and out on his own, one step down led to others and others until he was doing and saying things he thought he would never do or say. We now have our son living at home with us, so we can help him get well and come back to Jesus again with all his heart and encourage him to turn his life over to Jesus and find the peace and joy and happiness that comes from living to please Jesus and obey and follow Him with all his heart. We need to spend time with Jesus through prayer and Bible study and pattern our life after Jesus and not the people of the world. We must guard the avenues of our soul, seeing, hearing, smelling, touching, tasting. Sister White admonishes us in *Messages to Young People*, p. 285, "Those who would not fall a pray to Satan's devices must guard well the avenues of the soul; they must avoid reading, seeing, or hearing that which will suggest impure thoughts."

Also, in my letters I've mentioned to people about listening to Hal Mayer's CD on, "The Sunday Movements Gain Momentum." I, also, mentioned to people I've written to about hearing from a good source about our economy situation and they were saying by December 2014 we were supposed to change over to a new currency and the money we now use won't have the value it now has. God in His love and mercy has been holding this off. Praise God! Sister White says in *Evangelism*, p. 63, "Money will soon depreciate in value very suddenly when the reality of eternal scenes opens to the senses of man."

My dear cousins in Florida, Nancy and her sister Diane and her husband, Larry, have written and encouraged us to keep writing on my book, ***Don't Be Trapped in the Cities!! Get Out <u>Now!</u>*** and keep building on the "ARK." Also, a dear friend, Cynthia, from New York writes and encourages us to keep building on the "ARK." We hear how people are blessed by the DVDs of my book that Bill and Mary are making for me. Now is our time to be praying for the outpouring of the Holy Spirit and receive the latter rain to be able to stand during the time of trouble and give the Loud Cry message. We need to keep our records straight in heaven.

Step Fast!

"Said the angel, 'Deny self; ye must step fast.'" *Early Writings* p. 67. I had been having dreams saying, "HURRY! URGENT! Get Ready! Get Ready! Get Ready! 'What thou doest do Quickly!'"

I had a dream that showed a clock with its hand showing just minutes before midnight. My husband, that same night, had dreamed all night seeing a clock in his dreams! Then my husband and I had both dreamed in the same night the words, "The Midnight Cry." Then I dreamed on another night these words, "The Midnight Cry! Give the trumpet a certain sound!" My husband dreamed the words: "Lift up the Trumpet!" My husband and I on the same night dreamed the same dream: "Come out of her my people!" Rev. 18:4 (Read about it in *The Great Controversy*, the chapter on, "Prophecies Fulfilled—The Midnight Cry.")

One time, David, during the night had had a dream that I had had a dream that very night about the NEARNESS of Christ's SOON coming and that things are almost over. He couldn't remember the dream but he said it was startling! I had been fasting and praying that day and had skipped a meal because there were so many things I had been praying about and I wanted answered. Some of the things I had been praying about was the salvation of our son, Jonathan, and praying for the outpouring of the Holy Spirit in my life and to overcome my sins and I was claiming Bible promises like Matt. 21:22, "And all things whatsoever ye shall ask in prayer, believing, ye shall receive."

After David told me about him dreaming that I had had a frightening dream that night, we prayed that God would please give me the dream He wanted me to have that night. I prayed myself back to sleep that night asking God to please give me a dream about His soon coming and the urgency of getting ready! During that very night God gave me this dream: I saw charts showing the signs of the times of Christ's soon coming!

It said, "STEP FAST!" ("We should study the great way marks that point out the times in which we are living." *Last Day Events*, p. 14, by E. G. White). The next morning when I told my dream to my husband that God had given me that night he said, "You need to write this in your book you're writing that you've entitled, **Don't Be Trapped in the Cities!! Get Out Now!** The people need to be warned to get ready before it's too late! They need to STEP FAST! There's no time to lose in getting ourselves ready and others ready for Christ's soon coming and things are wrapping up FAST! People need to be in earnest in getting out of these big wicked cities as FAST as they can before it will be too late for them to leave and will be TRAPPED! They need to be studying and learning their Bibles and the Spirit of Prophecy books like: *The Great Controversy, Country Living, Last Day Events, Maranatha* by E. G. White and books like: *You Can Survive* by Jere Franklin; and *Another Ark to Build* by W. D. Frazee and also, W. D. Frazee's book, *Coming Events and Crisis at the Close*. Everything is so Urgent! Time is Running Out!"

We both agreed and knelt down and prayed and thanked the Lord for the dream and prayed for us and God's people that their eyes and ours would be opened to the events happening in quick succession and all the signs pointing to the nearness of Christ's soon return! God is trying to wake up His people! "We are standing on the threshold of the crisis of the ages. In quick succession the judgments of God will follow one another—fire, and flood, and earthquake, with war, and bloodshed." *Last Day Events*, p. 12, by E. G. White.

Matt. 24:42 and 44: "Watch therefore: for ye know not what hour your Lord doth come…. Therefore be ye also ready: for in such an hour as ye think not the Son of man cometh." (Read Matt. 24; Mark 13; Luke 21; Matt 25).

Mark 13:29: "So ye in like manner, when ye shall see these things come to pass, know that it is nigh, even at the door."

Just recently I had this quote of E. G. White in my dream: *Selected Messages*, book 2, p. 142: "The work of the people of God is to prepare for the events of the future, which will soon come upon them with blinding force." Also read, *Testimonies for the Church*, vol. 8, p. 28: "Transgression has almost reached its limit. Confusion fills the world, and a great terror is soon to come upon human beings. The end is very near. We who know the truth should be preparing for what is soon to break upon the world as an overwhelming surprise."

Testimonies for the Church, vol. 6, p. 407: "The judgments of God are about to fall upon the world, and we need to be preparing for that great day."

Testimonies for the Church, vol. 5, p. 452: "God has revealed what is to take place in the last days, that His people may be prepared to stand against the tempest of opposition and wrath. Those who have been warned of the events before them are not to sit in calm expectation of the coming storm, comforting themselves that the Lord will shelter His faithful ones in the day of trouble."

Early Writings, p. 119: "I saw that the remnant were not prepared for what is coming upon the earth. Stupidity like lethargy, seemed to hang upon the minds of most of those who profess to believe that we are having the last message. My accompanying angel cried out with awful solemnity, GET READY! GET READY! GET READY! for the fierce anger of the Lord is soon to come. His wrath is to be poured out, unmixed with mercy, and ye are not ready."

Messages to Young People, pp. 99, 100: "Remember, that you will never reach a higher standard than you yourself set. Then set your mark high, and step by step, even though it be by painful effort, by self-denial and sacrifice, ascend the whole length of the ladder of progress. Let nothing hinder you."

Welfare Ministry, p. 136: "I heard someone say, 'We knew that the judgments of God were coming upon the earth, but we did not know that they would come so soon.' Others said, 'You knew? Why then did you not tell us? We did not know.' On every side I heard such words spoken… The prophecies of the eleventh of Daniel have almost reached their final fulfillment."

Early Writings, p. 58: "…Some are looking too far off for the coming of the Lord. Time has continued a few years longer than they expected, therefore they think it may continue a few years more, and in this way their minds are being led from present truth, out after the world… I saw that the time for Jesus to be in the most holy place was nearly finished and that time can last but a very little longer… Live and act wholly in reference to the coming of the Son of man. The sealing time is very short, and will soon be over. Now is the time, while the four angels are holding the four winds, to make our calling and election sure."

Testimonies for the Church, vol. 3, p. 380: "Will you heed the voice of warning which tells you that destruction lies in the path of those who are at ease in the hour of danger? God's patience will not always wait for you, poor, trifling souls. He who holds our destinies in His hands will not always be trifled with… It shall be more tolerable for Sodom and Gomorrah in the day of judgment than for those who have had the privileges and the great light which shines in our day, but who have neglected to follow the light and to give their hearts fully to God."

Testimonies for the Church, vol. 1, p. 187: "Individuals are tested and proved a length of time to see if they will sacrifice their idols and heed the counsel of the True Witness… Those who come up to every point, and stand every test, and overcome, be the price what it may, have heeded the counsel of the True Witness, and they will receive the latter rain, and thus be fitted for translation."

Country Living, p. 31: "Out of the cities; out of the cities!'—this is the message the Lord has been giving me. The earthquakes will come; the floods will come; and we are not to establish ourselves in the wicked cities, where the enemy is served in every way, and where God is so often forgotten."

Country Living, p. 21: "The Protestant world have set up an idol sabbath in place where God's Sabbath should be, and they are treading in the footsteps of the Papacy. For this reason I see the necessity of the people of God moving out of the cities, into retired country places, where they may cultivate the land and raise their own produce. Thus they may bring their children up with simple, healthful habits. I see the necessity of making haste to get all things ready for the crisis."

Country Living, p. 17: "If we place ourselves under objectionable influences, can we expect God to work a miracle to undo the results of our wrong course? No, indeed. Get out of the cities as soon as possible, and purchase a little piece of land, where you can have a garden…"

Country Living, p. 27: "Let there be much praying done, and even with fasting, that not one shall move in darkness, but move in the light as God is in the light."

I recommend the book, *Country Living* by E. G. White for everyone to read and study and pray and fast over, so the Lord can direct your paths. Claim God's promises in Prov. 3:5, 6; and Ps. 37:3–5; Ps. 32:8; Remember, Jesus loves you and He has plans for you! Jer. 29:11–13; Jer. 33:3; "Remember Lot's wife." Luke 17:32; Great changes are soon to take place in our world, and the final movements will be rapid ones." *Testimonies for the Church*, vol. 9, p. 11

God's People, Wake Up!

At 3:15 AM, 7-29-14, I awoke with this impressive dream on my mind: I was telling someone of the fallout destruction in Kansas City. (There's a big underground nuclear arsenal there.) Continuing on in the dream, some of us were together seeing what it would be like if we were experiencing a disaster and what we needed to do in case of going through one and how one needed to prepare for it. We could see we weren't ready like we should be. I was telling someone of the dream God gave me that we should be using our money to get ready for what's coming and have what things we'll need for such a time ahead of us and be prepared and ready for it. One thing I remember in my dream, "Have your clothes ready." In *Prophets and Kings*, p. 184, Sister White quotes Satan speaking, saying "…Human laws will be made so stringent that men and women will not dare to observe the seventh-day Sabbath. For fear of wanting food and clothing, they will join with the world in transgressing God's law. The earth will be wholly under my dominion." Read the whole chapter 14, pp. 177–189, "In the Spirit and Power of Elias." (I looked up in the dictionary the word, "fallout." It said, "The falling to earth of radioactive particles after a nuclear explosion.")

I, also, looked up in the dictionary the word, "nuclear," it said, "Having to do with a nucleus or nuclei…involving or using the nuclei of atoms… or involving atomic bombs or other nuclear weapons like nuclear warfare."

It won't only be BIG Kansas City involved in terrible disasters, but Sister White says in *Country Living*, p. 8, "O that God's people had a sense of the impending destruction of thousands of cities, now almost given to idolatry."

Also, in *Country Living*, p. 6, Sister White says, "I could not sleep past two o'clock this morning. During the night season I was in council. I was pleading with some families to avail themselves of God's appointed means and get away from the cities to save their children. Some were loitering, making no determined efforts."

On page 8 of *Country Living*, Sister White continues to warn God's people by saying, "There are reasons why we should not build in the cities, on these cities, God's judgments are soon to fall… The time is near when large cities will be swept away, and all should be warned of these coming judgments."

Sister White relates one of her very impressive scenes she had. *Country Living*, p. 8, she relates the dream: "Last Friday morning, just before I awoke, a very impressive scene was presented before me. I seemed to awake from sleep, but was not in my home. From the windows I could behold a terrible conflagration. Great balls of fire were falling upon houses, and from these balls fiery arrows were flying in every direction. It was impossible to check the fires that were kindled, and many places were being destroyed. The terror of the people was indescribable."

Country Living, p. 9, Sister White urges God's people to heed her warning, when she says, "In harmony with the light given me, I am urging people to come out from the great centers of population. Our cities are increasing in wickedness, and it is becoming more and more evident that those who remain in them unnecessarily do so at the peril of their soul's salvation." Sister White, in *Country Living*, pp. 9, 10, 11, and 12, tells of the future problem of buying and selling. "The time is fast coming when the controlling power of the labor unions will be very oppressive. Again and again the Lord has instructed that our people are to take their families away from the cities, into the country, where they can raise their own provisions, for in the future the problem of buying and selling will be a very serious one. We should now begin to heed this instruction given us over and over again: Get out of the cities into rural districts, where the houses are not crowded closely together, and where you will be free from the interference of enemies…

The trades unions will be one of the agencies that will bring upon this earth a time of trouble such as has not been since the world began… The work of the people of God is to prepare for the events of the future, which will soon come upon them with blinding force… But erelong there will be such strife and confusion in the cities, that those who wish to leave them will not be able. We must be preparing for these issues. This is the light that is given me." (This could be like Martial Law passed on cities.) Also, Sister White, referring to the Sunday Law, tells us this, "Before the overflowing scourge shall come upon the dwellers of the earth, the Lord calls upon all who are Israelites indeed to prepare for that event. To the parents He sends the warning cry, gather your children into your own houses, gather them away from those who are disregarding the commandments of God, who are teaching and practicing evil. Get out of the large cities as fast as possible." On pp. 13 and 14, Sister White, in her book, *Country Living* goes on to give this counsel…, "…Fathers and mothers, how do you regard the souls of your children? Are you preparing the members of your families for translation into the heavenly courts?… How will ease, comfort, convenience, compare with the value of the souls of your children?… We cannot fail to see that the end of the world is soon to come. Satan is working upon the minds of men and women, and many seem filled with a desire for amusement and excitement. As it was in the day of Noah, every kind of evil is on the increase. Divorce and marriage is the order of the time. At such a time as this, the people who are seeking to keep the commandments of God should look for retired places away from the cities… Who will be warned? We say again, Out of the Cities. Do not consider it a great deprivation that you must go into the hills and mountains, but seek for that retirement where you can be alone with God,to learn His will and way… I urge our people to make it their life work to seek for spirituality. Christ is at the door."

Why Didn't Someone Warn Us?!

There's a dream my husband, David, had that just makes him shudder to think about it! He said he was up high in the sky. He wasn't in an airplane, he said. But it was at night and he could look down and see fires all over in different places and different size fires. It was cities being burned up and destroyed. Some were little fires on the small cities and some were medium size fires on medium size cities, and there were real BIG fires destroying BIG cities. He remembers hearing the shrieks and screams and cry of the terrified people calling out to one another and arguing with one another and moaning and groaning and wailing and screaming out, "Why didn't someone warn us of these judgments coming?!!"

They were turning on each other and blaming each other for not warning them of this terrible destruction they were suffering. Read in *Country Living*, p. 6–8, by E. G. White of the destruction of these cities! David's dream reminded me of the dream God gave me, the words spoken were, "Blow the trumpet! Sound an alarm! Warn my people!" This made me realize I must write my book and warn the people like God says or their blood will be on my hands as Ez. 33 and Joel 2 says and also, Ez. 3.

Read *Testimonies for the Church*, vol. 6, pp. 60–62, the chapter entitled, "The Last Warning" where Sister White says, "The trumpet is to give a certain sound… Lift up the standard—the commandments of God and the faith of Jesus… Our warfare is aggressive. Tremendous issues are before us, yea, and right upon us. Let our prayers ascend to God that the four angels may still hold the four winds, that they may not blow to injure or destroy until the last warning has been given to the world. Then let us work in harmony with our prayers. Let nothing lessen the force of the truth for this time. The present truth is to be our burden. The third angels' message must do its work of separating from the churches a people who will take their stand on the platform of eternal truth. Our message is a life and death message, and we must let it appear as it is, the great power of God. We are to present it in all its telling force. Then the Lord will make it effectual… The perils of the last days are upon us, and in our work we are to warn the people of the danger they are in. Let not the solemn scenes which prophecy has revealed be left untouched. If our people were half awake, if they realized the nearness of the events portrayed in the Revelation, a reformation would be wrought in our churches, and many would believe the message. We have no time to lose; God calls upon us to watch for souls as they must give an account… Let Daniel speak, let the Revelation speak, and tell what is truth. But whatever phase of the subjects presented, uplift Jesus as the center of all hope, the root and offspring of David, and the bright morning star.'" Rev. 22:16.

This is why I'm so earnest to get my book, **Don't Be Trapped in the Cities!! Get Out <u>Now!</u>** written. To warn the people of the dangers of remaining unnecessarily in these cities, like Sister White says in her book, *Country Living*, p. 9, "In harmony with the light given me, I am urging people to come out from the great centers of population. Our cities are increasing in wickedness, and it is becoming more and more evident that those who remain in them unnecessarily do so at the peril of their soul's salvation."

This is why I want to encourage people to look to Jesus and His promises in faith, trusting Jesus to see them through the trying experiences they will pass through in the crisis ahead, when we'll all have to face the Sunday Law issue soon to break upon us! The choices and decisions we're making now will decide our destiny then! We need to be drawing closer and closer to Jesus and learning to depend more and more on Him and less and less on man. If we're crumbling now under the pressures of life, how will we expect to stand true to God and His seventh-day Sabbath when the real pressures will be brought against us during the Sunday Laws enforced upon us? Like it says in Jer. 12:5, "If thou hast run with the footmen, and they have wearied thee, then how canst thou contend with horses? And if in the land of peace, wherein thou trustedst they wearied thee, then how wilt thou do in the swelling of Jordon?"

"In every period of this earth's history, God has had His men of opportunity, to whom He has said, 'Ye are my witnesses.' In every age there have been devout men, who gathered up the rays of light as they flashed upon their pathway, and spoke to the people the words of God. Enoch, Noah, and Moses, Daniel, and the long roll of patriarchs and prophets,—these were ministers of righteousness. They were not infallible, they were weak, erring men; but the Lord wrought through them as they gave themselves to His service." *Gospel Workers*, (1915), p. 13.

These faithful witnesses gave the warning message for their time and I think of how God has used Ellen G. White to warn us, for our time we're living in today, to prepare us for the days of trial before us! May we, too, each one, choose to be God's faithful witness and be used of God to let our light shine in this dark sinful world so God can say of each of us, "Ye are my witnesses, saith the Lord, and my servant whom I have chosen: that ye may know and believe me, and understand that I am he; before me there was no God formed, neither shall there be after me." Isa. 43:10.

"The cities are to be worked from outposts. Said the Messenger of God, 'Shall not the cities be warned? Yes; not by God's people living in them, but by their visiting them, to warn them of what is coming upon the earth." *Country Living*, p. 30.

"As God's commandment-keeping people, we must leave the cities. As did Enoch, we must work in the cities but not dwell in them." *Country Living*, p. 30.

"Through the working of trusts, and the results of labor unions and strikes the conditions of life in the city are constantly becoming more and more difficult. Serious troubles are before us; and for many families' removal from the cities will become a necessity. The physical surroundings in the cities are often a peril to health. The constant liability to contact with disease, the prevalence of foul air, impure water, impure food, the crowded, dark, unhealthful dwellings are some of the many evils to be met. It was not God's purpose that people should be crowded into cities, huddled together in terraces and tenements. In the beginning He placed our first parents amidst the beautiful sights and sounds He desires us to rejoice in today. The more nearly we come into harmony with God's original plan, the more favorable will be our position to secure health of body, and mind, and soul." *Country Living*, p. 6.

"The angels of mercy hurried Lot and his wife and daughters by taking hold of their hands. Had Lot hastened as the Lord desired him to, his wife would not have become a pillar of salt. Lot had too much of a lingering spirit. Let us not be like him. The same voice that warned Lot to leave Sodom bids us, 'Come out from among them, and be ye separate… and touch not the unclean.' Those who obey this warning will find a refuge. Let every man be wide awake for himself, and try to save his family. Let him gird himself for the work. God will reveal from point to point what to do next… Lot trod the plain with unwilling and tardy steps. He had so long associated with evil workers that he could not see his peril until his wife stood on the plain a pillar of salt forever." *Country Living*, pp. 6, 7. "Remember Lot's wife." Luke 17:32.

"The time is near when the large cities will be visited by the judgments of God. In a little while, these cities will be terribly shaken. No matter how large or how strong their buildings, no matter how many safeguards against fire may have been provided, let God touch these building, and in a few minutes or a few hours they are in ruins." *Country Living*, p. 7.

It makes me think of what Sister White wrote in *Testimonies for the Church*, vol. 9, p. 11–18, the chapter entitled, "The Last Crisis." In this article she brings out about the description of the two towers that was destroyed in New York City on Sept. 11, 2001. This terrible destruction that happened should be a wakeup call to us to get ready for these disasters and calamities that warn us of His soon coming!

"I am bidden to declare the message that cities full of transgression & sinful in extreme, will be destroyed by earthquakes, by fires, by floods… Calamities will come—calamities most awful, most unexpected, and these destructions will follow one after another. If there will be a heeding of the warnings that God has given, and if churches will repent, returning to their allegiance, then other cities may be spared for a time. But if men who have been deceived continue in the same way in which they have been walking, disregarding the law of God and presenting falsehoods before the people, God allows them to suffer calamity, that their senses may be awakened… There are reasons why we should not build in the cities. On these cities, God's judgments are soon to fall. The time is near when large cities will be swept away, and all should be warned of these coming judgments. O that God's people had a sense of the impending destruction of thousands of cities, now almost given to idolatry." *Country Living,* pp. 7, 8.

Urgent!

I was dreaming I had written an article entitled, "URGENT!" and it was 15 and 16 pages long and I was giving this article to someone to publish for me and to get it out to the people as soon as possible, and they were anxious to get it out to the public for me! I prayed and asked God to please help me write this article. This dream made me think of Bill and Mary publishing my book, ***Don't Be Trapped in the Cities!! Get Out Now!*** They've been putting my material on DVD's and getting it out to the people to help them realize the urgency of getting ready spiritually and physically for the crisis ahead of us when the Sunday Laws will be passed and we won't be able to buy or sell. We'll need to have our little ARKS of safety ready and set up for this time and have wells, trees, and our gardens and fruit trees and berry bushes producing so we can survive this time ahead of us. We'll also need to know our Bibles and what we believe and have our faith and trust in Jesus firmly established. We need to know Jesus and His power to save and have faith in His promises to us to care for us and protect us during the little time of trouble and then the great time of trouble when the plagues will be falling. Now is the time to be developing a Christ-like character. Now is the time to be obeying Jesus and all His requirements so we can have reform in our lives, which is the early rain and receive the Holy Spirit in the Latter rain so we can give the Loud Cry message of the third angel, because we have received the seal of God because we keep God's seventh day Sabbath holy and are true to all God's ten commandments. Revival and reformation is what we now need and the outpouring of the Holy Spirit power.

Sister White says, "A revival of true godliness among us is the greatest and most urgent of all our needs. To seek this should be our first work. There must be earnest effort to obtain the blessing of the Lord, not because God is not willing to bestow His blessing upon us, but because we are unprepared to receive it. Our heavenly Father is more willing to give His Holy Spirit to them that ask Him than are earthly parents to give good gifts to their children. But it is our work, by confession, humiliation, repentance, and earnest prayer, to fulfill the conditions upon which God has promised to grant us His blessing. A revival need be expected only in answer to prayer… I tell you that there must be a thorough revival among us. There must be a converted ministry. There must be confessions, repentances, and conversions. Many who are preaching the Word need the transforming grace of Christ in their hearts. They should let nothing stand in the way of their making thorough work before it shall be forever too late… A revival and a reformation must take place, under the ministration of the Holy Spirit. Revival and reformation are two different things. Revival signifies a renewal of spiritual life, a quickening of the powers of mind and heart, a resurrection from spiritual death. Reformation signifies a reorganization, a change of ideas and theories, habits, and practices. Reformation will not bring forth the good fruit of righteousness unless it is connected with the revival of the spirit. Revival and reformation are to do their appointed work, and in doing this work they must blend." *Last Day Events*, pp. 189, 190.

Also, on page 186 of *Last Day Events* Sister White says, "Before the final visitation of God's judgments upon the earth there will be among the people of the Lord such a revival of primitive godliness as has not been witnessed since apostolic times. The Spirit and power of God will be poured out upon His children… The work will be similar to that of the Day of Pentecost. As the former rain was given in the outpouring of the Holy Spirit at the opening of the gospel, to cause the upspringing of the precious seed, so the 'latter rain' will be given at its close for the ripening of the harvest… At that time the 'latter rain' or refreshing from the presence of the Lord, will come to give power to the loud voice of the third angel and prepare the saints to stand in the period when the seven last plagues shall be poured out."

This chapter in *Ministry of Healing*, pp. 161–169, makes me think of the experiences Jonathan and his dad and I are going through helping Jonathan to get well and off his addictions and coming back to Jesus. Sister White says on pp. 164, 165, "Mark how all through the Word of God there is manifest the spirit of urgency of imploring men and women to come to Christ. We must seize upon every opportunity, in private and in public, presenting every argument urging every motive of infinite weight, to draw men to the Saviour. With all our power we must urge them to look unto Jesus and to accept His life of self-denial and sacrifice. We must show that we expect them to give joy to the heart of Christ by using every one of His gifts in honoring His name."

It makes me think of my dream I had 4-17-13, "Only two years." There's an urgency here making us realize we must be about our Father's business. Here it is May 2014, and none of us are sure what may be in our future. Time is running out! This is not a date set for Jesus to come but to hurry and get ready. In two years, God helped me write my book, from 2013-2015, and ready for publication! Praise God! Also, a lot has happened making history in 2015 to let us know, time is running out!

This is why Sister White says in *Testimonies for the Church*, vol. 6, p. 61, 62, talking about "The Last Warning," "The Lord bids us: 'Show My people their transgression, and the house of Jacob their sins,' Isa. 58:1 The trumpet is to give a certain sound… Lift up the standard—the commandments of God and the faith of Jesus make this the important theme. Then, by your strong arguments, make it of still greater force. Dwell more on Revelation. Read, explain, and enforce its teachings. Our warfare is aggressive. Tremendous issues are before us, yea, and right upon us. Let our prayers ascend to God that the four angels may still hold the four winds, that they may not blow to injure or destroy until the last warning has been given to the world. Then let us work in harmony with our prayers. Let nothing lessen the force of the truth for this time. The present truth is to be our burden. The third angel's message must do its work of separating from the churches a people who will take their stand on the platform of eternal truth. Our message is a life-and-death message, and we must let it appear as it is, the great power of God. We are to present it in all its telling force! Then the Lord will make it effectual. It is our privilege to expect large things, even the demonstration of the Spirit of God. This is the power that will convict and convert the soul… The perils of the last days are upon us, and in our work we are to warn the people of the danger they are in. Let not the solemn scenes which prophecy has revealed be left untouched. If our people were half awake, if they realized the nearness of the events portrayed in the Revelation, a reformation would be wrought in our churches, and many more would believe the message. We have no time to lose; God calls upon us to watch for souls as they that must give an account… There will be times when we must stand still and see the salvation of God. Let Daniel speak, let the Revelation speak, and tell what is truth. But whatever phase of the subject is presented, uplift Jesus as the center of all hope, 'the root and the offspring of David, and the bright and morning Star.'" Rev. 22:16.

In *Last Day Events*, pp. 15–17, Sister White says, "There is need of a much closer study of the Word of God; especially should Daniel and the Revelation have attention as never before… The light received from God was given especially for these last days… Let us read and study the 12th chapter of Daniel. It is a warning that we shall all need to understand before the time of the end… The unfulfilled predictions of the book of Revelation are soon to be fulfilled. This prophecy is now to be studied with diligence by the people of God and should be clearly understood. It does not conceal the truth, it clearly forewarns, telling us what will be in the future… The solemn messages that have been given in their order in the Revelation are to occupy the first place in the minds of God's people… Let the watchmen now lift up their voices and give the message which is present truth for this time. Let us show the people where we are in prophetic history… There is a day that God hath appointed for the close of this world's history: 'This gospel of the kingdom shall be preached in all the world for a witness unto all nations; and then shall the end come.' Prophecy is fast fulfilling. More, much more, should be said about these tremendously important subjects. The day is at hand when the destiny of souls will be fixed forever… Great pains should be taken to keep this subject before the people. The solemn fact is to be kept not only before the people of the world but before our own churches also, that the day of the Lord will come suddenly, unexpectedly. The fearful warning of the prophecy is addressed to every soul. Let no one feel that he is secure from danger of being surprised.

Let no one's interpretation of prophecy rob you of the conviction of the knowledge of events which show that this great event is near at hand."

I have had dreams saying, "Hurry!" "Step Fast!" "URGENT!" "Get Ready! Get Ready! Get Ready!" "What thou doest, Do Quickly!" "Get Busy!" "Be in earnest to get things done!"

I have dreamed I saw charts showing the signs of the time of Christ soon coming and it said, "Step Fast!" David, my husband, has dreamed about the nearness of Christ's soon coming, and that things are almost over!

We are living in serious and solemn times in this world's history! God's prophet, E. G. White, for our day in which we are living NOW, said in *Testimonies for the Church*, vol. 5, p. 452, "God has revealed what is to take place in the last days, that His people may be prepared to stand against the tempest of opposition and wrath. Those who have been warned of the events before them are not to sit in calm expectation of the coming storm, comforting themselves that the Lord will shelter His faithful ones in the day of trouble. We are to be as men waiting for their Lord, not in idle expectancy, but in earnest work, with unwavering faith. It is no time now to allow our minds to be engrossed with things of minor importance. While men are sleeping, Satan is actively arranging matters so that the Lord's people may not have mercy or justice. The Sunday movement is now making its way in darkness." Read the whole chapter, "The Coming Crisis" *Testimonies for the Church*, vol. 5, pp. 449–454. Sister White says in *Country Living*, p. 21, "I see the necessity of making haste to get all things ready for the crisis."

I have had dreams of Sister White's quotes like the one in *Selected Messages*, book 2, p. 142, "The work of the people of God is to prepare for the events of the future, which will soon come upon them with blinding force," and *Testimonies for the Church*, vol. 8, p. 28, "Transgression has almost reached its limit. Confusion fills the world, and a great terror is soon to come upon human beings. The end is very near. We who know the truth should be preparing for what is soon to break upon the world as an overwhelming surprise."

In *Last Day Events*, p. 72, Sister White tells us, "We have nothing to fear for the future, except as we shall forget the way the Lord has led us, and His teachings in our past history." She goes on to say in *Last Day Events*, p. 72 and 73, "If there ever was a time when serious reflection becomes everyone who fears God, it is now, when personal piety is essential. The inquiry should be made, 'What am I, and what is my work and mission in this time? On which side am I working—Christ's side or the enemy's side?' Let every soul now humble himself or herself before God, for now we are surely living in the great Day of Atonement. The cases even now of many are passing in review before God, for they are to sleep in their graves a little season. Your profession of faith is not your guarantee in that day, but the state of your affections. Is the soul-temple cleansed of its defilement? Are my sins confessed and am I repenting of them before God that they may be blotted out? Do I esteem myself too lightly? Am I willing to make any and every sacrifice for the excellency of the knowledge of Jesus Christ? Do I feel every moment I am not my own, but Christ's property, that my service belongs to God, whose I am?... We should ask ourselves, "For what are we living, and working? And what will be the outcome of it all?... I have questioned in my mind, as I have seen the people in our cities hurrying to and fro with business, whether they ever thought of the day of God that is just upon us. Every one of us should be living with reference to the great day which is soon to come upon us… We cannot afford to live with no reference to the day of judgment; for though long delayed, it is now near, even at the door, and hasteth greatly. The trumpet of the Archangel will soon startle the living and wake the dead."

Sister White tells us in *Counsels to Parents, Teachers, and Students*, p. 249, "It should be the determination of every soul, not so much to seek to understand all about the conditions that will prevail in the future state, as to know what the Lord requires of him in this life. It is the will of God that each professing Christian shall perfect a character after the divine similitude. By studying the character of Christ revealed in the Bible, by practicing His virtues, the believer will be changed into the same likeness of goodness and mercy. Christ's work of self-denial and sacrifice brought into the daily life will develop the faith that works by love and purifies the soul. There are many who wish to evade the cross-bearing part, but the Lord speaks to all when He says, "If any man will come after me, let him deny himself, and take up his cross, and follow me. Matt. 16:24."

The Lord instructed Sister White to write these words found in *Fundamentals of Christian Education*, pp. 526, 527, "In the night season these words were spoken to me: 'Charge the teachers in our schools to prepare the students for what is coming upon the world….' Bear in mind that the Lord will accept as teachers only those who will be gospel teachers. A great responsibility rests upon those who attempt to teach the last gospel message. They are to be laborers together with God in the training of human minds. The teacher who fails to keep the Bible standard always before him, misses an opportunity of being a laborer together with God in giving to the mind the mold that is essential for a place in the heavenly courts."

Satan is Wroth!

Rev. 12:17, "And the dragon was wroth with the woman, and went to make war with the remnant of her seed, which keep the commandments of God, and have the testimony of Jesus Christ."

The Great Controversy, p. 36, Sister White says, "We cannot know how much we owe to Christ for the peace and protection which we enjoy. It is the restraining power of God that prevents mankind from passing fully under the control of Satan." Also, in *The Great Controversy*, p. 623, Sister White continues to tell us of the wrath of Satan, "Woe to the inhabitants of the earth and of the sea! for the devil is come down unto you, having great wrath, because he knoweth that he hath but a short time," Rev. 12:12. Fearful are the scenes which call forth this exclamation from the heavenly voice. The wrath of Satan increases as his time grows short, and his work of deceit and destruction will reach its culmination in the time of trouble."

As we've been trying to get God's last day message out to the world, to prepare for the soon coming crisis, by writing these articles for my book, **Don't Be Trapped in the Cities!! Get Out <u>Now!</u>** The devil has been trying in every way to get to us and try and stop us from warning God's people to prepare for the crisis and be ready! Satan has had our car break down so many times and overheat. Satan almost destroyed our car and us, when we were coming home late at night and a BIG deer walked right in front of our car and David slammed on the brakes and God removed the deer in time so we didn't ram into him at 60 miles per hour. How we praised the Lord! We always pray, for God's protection, when we get into the car. God was certainly there to spare our lives and our car! The Devil has had our son, Jonathan end up in emergency room several times and admitted to the hospital. Satan is trying to take his life! God has protected us from dangerous storms and our garden and our place, when Satan was out to destroy everything! Satan has tried to get us stung with wasps so many times, and even one time he had a wasp sting David, my husband, right beside his eye, but God kept it from stinging him right in the eyeball. Praise God! We all are feeling the attacks of Satan as we reach out to work for Jesus and to save souls. We know Satan is the destroyer like John 10:10 says, "The thief cometh not, but for to steal, and kill, and to destroy; I am come that they might have life, and that they might have it more abundantly." Praise God! Jesus is the restorer! Jesus is stronger than Satan and Jesus keeps watching over us!

In *The Great Controversy*, p. 560–562, Sister White writes "Because thou hast kept the word of my patience, I also will keep thee" (Rev. 3:10), is the Saviour's promise. He would sooner send every angel out of heaven to protect His people than leave one soul that trusts in Him to be overcome by Satan… Satan has long been preparing for his final effort to deceive the world… Little by little he has prepared the way for his masterpiece of deception in the development of spiritualism… Except those who are kept by the power of God, through faith in His Word, the whole world will be swept into the ranks of this delusion."

In *The Great Controversy*, p. 624, by Sister White, we are warned, "As the crowning act in the great drama of deception, Satan himself will personate Christ… Now the great deceiver will make it appear that Christ has come… The shout of triumph rings out upon the air 'Christ has come! Christ has come!' … In gentle, compassionate tones he presents some of the same gracious, heavenly truths which the Savior uttered; he heals the disease of the people, and then, in his assumed character of Christ, he claims to have changed the Sabbath to Sunday, and commands all to hallow the day which he has blessed. He declares that those who persist in keeping holy the seventh day are blaspheming his name by refusing to listen to his angels sent to them with light and truth. This is the strong, almost overmastering delusion." On p. 625 of *The Great Controversy*, Sister White goes on to say, "But the people of God will not be misled… To all the testing time will come… Are the people of God now so firmly established upon His word that they would not yield to the evidences of their senses? Would they, in such a crisis, cling to the Bible and the Bible only? Satan will, if possible, prevent them from obtaining a preparation to stand in that day. He will so arrange affairs as to hedge up their way, entangle them with earthly treasures, cause them to carry a heavy, wearisome burden, that their hearts may be overcharged with the cares of this life and the day of trial may come upon them as a thief."

On pp. 632–634 of *The Great Controversy*, Sister White writes, "In the hour of peril and distress 'the angel of the Lord encampeth round about them that fear Him, and delivereth them.' Ps. 34:7… The precious Saviour will send help just when we need it… The eye of God, looking down the ages, was fixed upon the crisis which His people are to meet, when earthly powers shall be arrayed against them… But the Holy One who divided the Red Sea before Israel, will manifest His mighty power and turn their captivity" … In the time of trouble He shall hide me in His pavilion; in the secret of His tabernacle shall He hide me." Ps. 27:5. In *The Great Controversy*, p. 621, Sister White says, "While Satan seeks to destroy this class, God will send His angels to comfort and protect them in the time of peril. The assaults of Satan are fierce and determined, his delusions are terrible; but the Lord's eye is upon His people, and His ear listens to their cries. Their affliction is great, the flames of the furnace seem about to consume them; but the Refiner will bring them forth as gold tried in the fire… The season of distress and anguish before us will require a faith that can endure weariness, delay, and hunger—a faith that will not faint through severely tried. The period of probation is granted to all to prepare for that time." On p. 622 of *The Great Controversy*, we read, "Those who exercise but little faith now, are in the greatest danger of falling under the power of satanic delusions and the decree to compel the conscience… We should now acquaint ourselves with God by proving His promises… We should rather dispense with selfish gratifications than neglect communion with God… We must take time to pray."

I recently had a dream that said, "Like everything else we have got to do, we have got to PRAY!" Sister White goes on to say in *The Great Controversy*, p. 622, "If we allow our minds to be absorbed by worldly interests, the Lord may give us time by removing from us our idols of gold, of houses, or of fertile lands… The 'time of trouble, such as never was,' is soon to open upon us; and we shall need an experience which we do not now possess and which many are too indolent to obtain."

Also, in *The Great Controversy*, p. 623, Sister White tells us that, "Now, while our Great High Priest is making the atonement for us, we should seek to become perfect in Christ… Satan finds in human hearts some point where he can gain a foothold; some sinful desire is cherished, by means of which his temptations assert their power… Satan could find nothing in the Son of God that would enable him to gain the victory. He had kept His Father's commandments, and there was no sin in Him that Satan could use to his advantage. This is the condition in which those must be found who shall stand in the time of trouble. It is in this life that we are to separate sin from us, through faith in the atoning blood of Christ. Our precious Saviour invites us to join ourselves to Him, to unite our weakness to his strength, our ignorance to His wisdom, our unworthiness to His merits."

In *The Great Controversy*, p. 619 it says, "Satan endeavors to terrify them with the thought that their cases are hopeless, that the stain of their defilement will never be washed away. He hopes so to destroy their faith that they will yield to his temptations and turn from their allegiance to God."

In *The Great Controversy*, p. 586, we read, "Now that Satan can no longer keep the world under his control by withholding the Scriptures, he resorts to other means to accomplish the same object. To destroy faith in the Bible serves his purpose as well as to destroy the Bible itself." We read of something else Satan will do in *The Great Controversy*, p. 560,

"Many will be confronted by the spirits of devils personating beloved relatives or friends and declaring the most dangerous heresies." On p. 612 of *The Great Controversy* it says, "Satan also works with lying wonders, even bringing down fire from heaven in the sight of men. (Rev. 13:13) Thus the inhabitants of the earth will be brought to take their stand… The publications distributed by missionary workers have exerted their influence, yet many whose minds were impressed have been prevented from fully comprehending the truth or from yielding obedience. Now the rays of light penetrate everywhere the truth is seen in its clearness, and the honest children of God sever the bands which have held them. Family connections, church relations, are powerless to stay them now. Truth is more precious than all besides. Notwithstanding the agencies combined against the truth a large number take their stand upon the Lord's side."

In the book *Country Living*, p. 32, Sister White warns, "It is no time now for God's people to be fixing their affections or laying up their treasures in the world. The time is not far distant, when, like the early disciples, we shall be forced to seek a refuge in desolate and solitary places. As the siege of Jerusalem by the Roman armies was the signal for flight to the Judean Christians, so the assumption of power on the part of our nation, in the decree enforcing the papal Sabbath, will be a warning to us. It will then be time to leave the large cities, preparatory to leaving the smaller ones for retired homes in secluded places among the mountain. And now, instead of seeking expensive dwellings here, we should be preparing to move to a better country, even a heavenly. Instead of spending our means in self-gratification, we should be studying to economize."

In *The Great Controversy*, pp. 35–38, Sister White writes, "By stubborn rejection of divine love and mercy, the Jews had caused the protection of God to be with- drawn from them, and Satan was permitted to rule them according to his will. The horrible cruelties enacted in the destruction of Jerusalem are a demonstration of Satan's vindictive power over those who yield to his control. We cannot know how much we owe to Christ for the peace and protection which we enjoy. It is the restraining power of God that prevents mankind from passing fully under the control of Satan…

Let men beware lest they neglect the lesson conveyed to them in the words of Christ. As He warned His disciples of Jerusalem's destruction, giving them a sign of the approaching ruin, that they might make their escape; so He has warned the world of the day of final destruction and has given them tokens of its approach, that all who will may flee from the wrath to come. Jesus declares: 'There shall be signs in the sun, and in the moon, and in the stars; and upon the earth distress of nations.' Luke 21:25; Matt. 24:29; Mark 13: 24–26; Rev. 6:12–17. Those who behold these harbingers of His coming are to 'know that it is near, even at the doors.' Matt. 24:33. 'Watch ye therefore,' are His words of admonition. Mark 13:35. They that heed the warning shall not be left in darkness, that that day should overtake them unawares. But to them that will not watch, 'the day of the Lord so cometh as a thief in the night.' 1 Thess. 5:2–5. The world is no more ready to credit the message for this time than were the Jews to receive the Saviour's warning concerning Jerusalem. Come when it may, the day of God will come unawares to the ungodly. When life is going on in its unvarying round; when men are absorbed in pleasure, in business, in traffic, in money-making; when religious leaders are magnifying the world's progress and enlightenment, and the people are lulled in a false security—then as the midnight thief steals within the unguarded dwelling, so shall sudden destruction come upon the careless and ungodly, 'and they shall not escape.'" 1 Thess. 5:3.

"A Call to Leave the Cities!"

Part One

Written February 3, 2017

On January 30, 2017, I had a dream this was happening: All these calamities and judgments were falling on all these different places, and I was writing it out to warn the people of their danger of remaining in these cities and to get out of these wicked cities while they still could! In my dream, I was quoting Sister White's quotes from *Country Living* book and Spirit of Prophecy. One quote I remember was taken from *Country Living* p. 5, "Few realize the importance of shunning, so far as possible, all associations unfriendly to religious life. In choosing their surroundings, few make their spiritual prosperity the first consideration… The world over, cities are becoming hotbeds of vice. On every hand are the sights and sounds of evil. Everywhere are enticements to sensuality and dissipation. The tide of corruption and crime is continually swelling. Every day brings the record of violence,—robberies, murders, suicides, and crimes unnamable." (**Read** all p. 5) Also, I was quoting on p. 12, "Get out of the large cities as fast as possible…" p. 17, "Get out of the cities as soon as possible, and purchase a little piece of land, where you can have a garden, where your children can watch the flowers growing, and learn from them lessons of simplicity and purity." I was, also, quoting p. 7, "The time is near when the large cities will be visited by the judgments of God. In a little while, these cities will be terribly shaken… The ungodly cities of our world are to be swept away by the besom of destruction…

I am bidden to declare the message that cities full of transgression, and sinful in the extreme, will be destroyed by earthquakes, by fire, by flood… Calamities will come—calamities most awful, most unexpected; and these destructions will follow one after another." I was quoting quotes of Sister White all through her book, *Country Living*. Take time to read the whole book. Also, in my dream, I was entitling my article I was writing, "A CALL TO LEAVE THE CITIES!" Some other Spirit of Prophecy quotes to **read** are: *Fundamentals of Christian Education* pp. 98 and 475; *1T* p. 466; *2T* p. 337; *5T* 62–84, 331; *6T* p. 126; *Prophets and Kings* p. 224; *Education* pp. 45–50; *Last Day Events* pp. 204–205; *The Great Controversy* chapters, 35–38; *Testimonies to Ministers and Gospel Workers* p. 114; Vol 3, *Selected Messages* p. 388; *Early Writings* pp. 71, 271; Romans 13:11; Matthew 13; Isaiah 28:8–9; 1 Corinthians 2:11–14. (**End of dream.**)

Also, on January 25, 2017, in my dream I was thinking, "Church and State are uniting more and more!" (**Read** chapter 25 in *The Great Controversy* by E.G. White, especially pp 438–450.)

Then, on January 26, 2017, in my dream I saw my husband, David, hurrying with two bags of ground up cornmeal clutched in his arms, and he was looking behind him, over his shoulder, as if he was running fast, like something was coming, and he was hurrying to beat it! When I had this dream on January 26, 2017, I asked the Lord to please show me in a dream what's coming, and what this dream could mean? On that same night, in another dream God gave me, a voice said to me, "It would be too hard for you." On that very same night, January 26, 2017, the Lord gave me another dream, and the voice said to me, "A storm is coming!" There was more to the dream, but this is all I remember, because David had gotten up and was making noise in the front room and this woke me up, so I don't know what kind of a storm was coming? We need to be preparing for the storm both physically and spiritually. **Read** *Last Day Events* by E.G. White chapter 12, "The Shaking," especially pp. 174–182. On p. 180, Sister White says, "Soon God's people will be tested by fiery trials, and the great proportion of those who now appear to be genuine and true will prove to be base metal… The church may appear as about to fall, but it does not fall. It remains, while the sinners in Zion will be sifted out—the chaff separated from the precious wheat. This is a terrible ordeal, but nevertheless it must take place… As the storm approaches, a large class who have professed faith in the third angel's message, but have not been sanctified through obedience to the truth, abandon their position and join the ranks of the opposition." On pp. 20, 21, 28, 29 of *Country Living*, Sister White writes:

> *I asked the Lord to please show me in a dream what's coming, and what this dream could mean? On that same night, in another dream God gave me, a voice said to me, It would be too hard for you*

> "We are not to locate ourselves where we will be forced into close relations with those who do not honor God… A crisis is soon to come in regard to the observance of Sunday… The Sunday party is strengthening itself in its false claims, and this will mean oppression to those who determine to keep the Sabbath of the Lord… And we are to be careful not to place ourselves where it will be hard for ourselves and our children to keep the Sabbath… If in the providence of God we can secure places away from the cities, the Lord would have us do this. There are troublous times before us… The Protestant world have set up an idol Sabbath in the place where God's Sabbath should be, and they are treading in the footsteps of the Papacy. For this reason I see the necessity of the people of God moving out of the cities into retired country places, where they may cultivate the land and raise their own produce. Thus they may bring their children up with simple, healthful habits. I see the necessity of making haste to get all things ready for the crisis… We cannot have a weak faith now; we cannot be safe in a listless, indolent, slothful attitude. Every jot of ability is to be used, and sharp, calm, deep thinking is to be done. The wisdom of any human agent is not sufficient for the planning and devising in this time. Spread every plan before God with fasting, and with the humbling of the soul before the Lord Jesus, and commit thy ways unto the Lord. The sure promise is, He will direct thy paths. He is infinite in resources… The instruction is still being given, Move out of the cities. Establish your sanitariums, your schools, and offices away from the centers of population. Many now will plead to remain in

the cities, but the time will come erelong when all who wish to avoid the sights and sounds of evil will move into the country; for wickedness and corruption will increase to such a degree that the very atmosphere of the cities will seem to be polluted… God means that we shall not locate in the cities; for there are very stormy times before us… Men will arise speaking perverse things, to counterwork the very movements that the Lord is leading His servants to make... Conditions are arising in the cities that will make it very hard for those of our faith to remain in them."

We know the storm clouds are coming, may Jesus hold them back!

On January 28, 2017, I was looking over my different dreams that I had had and reading the material on them, and I fell asleep long enough to have this following dream, and then I woke right up!

In my dream I was saying, "GOD'S PEOPLE WAKE UP! Church and State are uniting more and more! Get ready for what's soon to come!" Then, I had some of my articles I had written taken from my book, *Don't Be Trapped in the Cities!! Get Out NOW!* These were repeated to me in my dream, pp. 72–82.

Listen to Hal Mayer's CD for February 2017. Also, **read** in *The Great Controversy* by E.G. White, chapter 32, "Snares of Satan" and chapter 35, "Liberty of Conscience Threatened." **Read** also, *Fundamentals of Christian Education* by E.G. White, p. 475. On p. 407 in *Vol. 3 Selected Messages* by E.G. White, she says, "As we near the close of this earth's history, we advance more and more rapidly in Christian growth, or we retrograde just as decidedly." On p. 452, Vol. 5 of *Testimonies for the Church*, by E.G. White, she writes, "God has revealed what is to take place in the last days, that His people may be prepared to stand against the tempest of opposition and wrath. Those who have been warned of the events before them are not to sit in calm expectation of the coming storm, comforting themselves that the Lord will shelter His faithful ones in the day of trouble." **Read** also, *Early Writings* p. 119 by E.G. White.

"A Call to Leave the Cities!"

Part 2

Written February 9, 2017

I had been praying that God would please help me know what He wanted me to write about and on February 9, 2017, I dreamt I saw this title that I had written about already called, "A Call to Leave the Cities!" God was drawing my attention to this article I had written and sent out to God's people, so I decided to write a "Part 2" to this article. Read pp. 11–18 in Vol. 9 of *Testimonies for the Church* by Sister White entitled, "The Last Crisis," … "We are living in the time of the end." **Read** pages 5–9 from *Country Living* by E.G. White (found at the end of this chapter) about "A Call to Leave the Cities."

On February 10, 2017, I heard these words spoken to me in the night, two different times, in two different dreams: "Before the overflowing scourge…" This was taken from p. 12 in *Country Living* by E.G. White, "Before the overflowing scourge (*Sunday Laws*) shall come upon the dwellers of the earth, the Lord calls upon all who are Israelites indeed to prepare for that event. To parents He sends the warning cry, Gather your children into your own houses; gather them away from those who are disregarding the commandments of God, who are teaching and practicing evil. Get out of the large cities as fast as possible."

This quote was also given to me in a dream in my article I wrote on February 7, 2017, "Preparing for the Issue!"

In *Country Living* by E.G. White, she lets us know on p. 24, "The time has come, when, as God opens the way, families should move out of the cities… Parents can secure small homes in the country, with land for cultivation, where they can have orchards and where they can raise vegetables and small fruits to take the place of flesh meat, which is so corrupting to the life blood coursing through the veins. On such places the children will not be surrounded with the corrupting influences of city life. God will help His people to find such homes outside the cities… More and more, as time advances, our people will have to leave the cities." Also, on p. 28, Sister White continues to say, "Spread every plan before God with fasting, and with the humbling of the soul before the Lord Jesus, and commit thy ways unto the Lord. The sure promise is, He will direct thy paths. He is infinite in resources." On p. 29, she writes, "God means that we shall not locate in the cities; for there are very stormy times before us." Again on p. 31, Sister White's counsel is: ""Out of the cities; out of the cities!"—this is the message the Lord has been giving me. The earthquakes will come; the floods will come; and we are not to establish ourselves in the wicked cities, where the enemy is served in every way, and where God is so often forgotten."

Read in E.G. White's book, *My Life Today*, p. 308, "Revelation 7:2, 3—Four mighty angels are still holding the four winds of the earth. Terrible destruction is forbidden to come in full. The accidents by land and by sea; the loss of life, steadily increasing, by storm, by tempest, by railroad disaster, by conflagration; the terrible floods, the earthquakes, and the winds will be the stirring up of the nations to one deadly combat, while the angels hold the four winds, forbidding the terrible power of Satan to be exercised in its fury until the servants of God are sealed in their foreheads… A terrible conflict is before us. We are nearing the battle of the great day of God Almighty."

Read in Vol. 7 *Testimonies for the Church* by E.G. White, pp. 80–88, "Out of the Cities" and "In the Country." On p. 49 in *Early Writings*, Sister White warns us, "The angel said, 'Destruction is coming like a mighty whirlwind.'"

Read in *The Great Controversy* by E.G. White, pp. 582–592, "The Impending Conflict"; *Prophets and Kings*, p. 265–278, "Nineveh, That Great City," by E.G. White; *5T*, pp. 467–476, 571–580; *Last Day Events* by E.G. White, pp. 94–142.

Country Living, pp. 5–9

Chapter 1—A Call to Leave the Cities
The Perils of the Cities

Few realize the importance of shunning, so far as possible, all associations unfriendly to religious life. In choosing their surroundings, few make their spiritual prosperity the first consideration.

Parents flock with their families to the cities, because they fancy it easier to obtain a livelihood there than in the country. The children, having nothing to do when not in school, obtain a street education. From evil associates, they acquire habits of vice and dissipation. The parents see all this, but it will require a sacrifice to correct their error, and they stay where they are, until Satan gains full control of their children.

Better sacrifice any and every worldly consideration than to imperil the precious souls committed to your care. They will be assailed by temptations, and should be taught to meet them; but it is your duty to cut off every influence, to break up every habit, to sunder every tie, that keeps you from the most free, open, and hearty committal of yourselves and your family to God.

Instead of the crowded city, seek some retired situation where your children will be, so far as possible, shielded from temptation, and there train and educate them for usefulness. The prophet Ezekiel thus enumerates the causes that led to Sodom's sin and destruction: "Pride, fullness of bread, and abundance of idleness was in her and in her daughters; neither did she strengthen the hands of the poor and needy." All who would escape the doom of Sodom, must shun the course that brought God's judgments upon that wicked city.

City Living Not God's Plan

The world over, cities are becoming hotbeds of vice. On every hand are the sights and sounds of evil. Everywhere are enticements to sensuality and dissipation. The tide of corruption and crime is continually swelling. Every day brings the record of violence,—robberies, murders, suicides, and crimes unnamable.

Life in the cities is false and artificial. The intense passion for money getting, the whirl of excitement and pleasure seeking, the thirst for display, the luxury and extravagance, all are forces that, with the great masses of mankind, are turning the mind from life's true purpose. They are opening the door to a thousand evils. Upon the youth they have almost irresistible power.

One of the most subtle and dangerous temptations that assails the children and youth in the cities is the love of pleasure. Holidays are numerous; games and horse racing draw thousands, and the whirl of excitement and pleasure attracts them away from the sober duties of life. Money that should have been saved for better uses is frittered away for amusements.

> *One of the most subtle and dangerous temptations that assails the children and youth in the cities is the love of pleasure*

Through the working of trusts, and the results of labor unions and strikes the conditions of life in the city are constantly becoming more and more difficult. Serious troubles are before us; and for many families removal from the cities will become a necessity.

The physical surroundings in the cities are often a peril to health. The constant liability to contact with disease, the prevalence of foul air, impure water, impure food, the crowded, dark, unhealthful dwellings, are some of the many evils to be met.

It was not God's purpose that people should be crowded into cities, huddled together in terraces and tenements. In the beginning He placed our first parents amidst the beautiful sights and sounds He desires us to rejoice in today. The more nearly we come into harmony with God's original plan, the more favorable will be our position to secure health of body, and mind, and soul.

A Loitering Spirit

I could not sleep past two o'clock this morning. During the night season I was in council. I was pleading with some families to avail themselves of God's appointed means, and get away from the cities to save their children. Some were loitering, making no determined efforts.

The angels of mercy hurried Lot and his wife and daughters by taking hold of their hands. Had Lot hastened as the Lord desired him to, his wife would not have become a pillar of salt. Lot had too much of a lingering spirit. Let us not be like him. The same voice that warned Lot to leave Sodom bids us, 'Come out from among them, and be ye separate, ... and touch not the unclean.' Those who obey this warning will find a refuge. Let every man be wide awake for himself, and try to save his family. Let him gird himself for the work. God will reveal from point to point what to do next.

Hear the voice of God through the apostle Paul: 'Work out your own salvation with fear and trembling. For it is God which worketh in you both to will and to do of His good pleasure.' Lot trod the plain with unwilling and tardy steps. He had so long associated with evil workers that he could not see his peril until his wife stood on the plain a pillar of salt forever.

Cities to Be Visited by God's Judgments

The time is near when the large cities will be visited by the judgments of God. In a little while, these cities will be terribly shaken. No matter how large or how strong their buildings, no matter how many safeguards against fire may have been provided, let God touch these buildings, and in a few minutes or a few hours they are in ruins.

The ungodly cities of our world are to be swept away by the besom of destruction. In the calamities that are now befalling immense buildings and large portions of cities, God is showing us what will come upon the whole earth.

Results of Unheeded Warnings

I am bidden to declare the message that cities full of transgression, and sinful in the extreme, will be destroyed by earthquakes, by fire, by flood. All the world will be warned that there is a God who will display His authority as God. His unseen agencies will cause destruction, devastation, and death. All the accumulated riches will be as nothingness....

Calamities will come—calamities most awful, most unexpected; and these destructions will follow one after another. If there will be a heeding of the warnings that God has given, and if churches will repent, returning to their allegiance, then other cities may be spared for a time. But if men who have been deceived continue in the same way in which they have been walking, disregarding the law of God, and presenting falsehoods before the people, God allows them to suffer calamity, that their senses may be awakened.

The Lord will not suddenly cast off all transgressors, or destroy entire nations; but He will punish cities and places where men have given themselves up to the possession of Satanic agencies. Strictly will the cities of the nations be dealt with, and yet they will not be visited in the extreme of God's indignation, because some souls will yet break away from the delusions of the enemy, and will repent and be converted, while the mass will be treasuring up wrath against the day of wrath.

Imminence of God's Judgments

There are reasons why we should not build in the cities. On these cities, God's judgments are soon to fall.

The time is near when large cities will be swept away, and all should be warned of these coming judgments.

O that God's people had a sense of the impending destruction of thousands of cities, now almost given to idolatry.

A View of Great Destruction

Last Friday morning, just before I awoke, a very impressive scene was presented before me. I seemed to awake from sleep, but was not in my home. From the windows I could behold a terrible conflagration. Great balls of fire were falling upon houses, and from these balls fiery arrows were flying in every direction. It was impossible to check the fires that were kindled, and many places were being destroyed. The terror of the people was indescribable.

God's Efforts to Arouse the People

While at Loma Linda, Calif., April 16, 1906, there passed before me a most wonderful representation. During a vision of the night, I stood on an eminence, from which I could see houses shaken like a reed in the wind. Buildings, great and small, were falling to the ground. Pleasure resorts, theaters, hotels, and the homes of the wealthy were shaken and shattered. Many lives were blotted out of existence, and the air was filled with the shrieks of the injured and the terrified.

The destroying angels of God were at work. One touch, and buildings so thoroughly constructed that men regarded them as secure against every danger, quickly became heaps of rubbish. There was no assurance of safety in any place. I did not feel in any special peril, but the awfulness of the scenes that passed before me I cannot find words to describe. It seemed that the forbearance of God was exhausted, and that the judgment day had come.

The angel that stood at my side then instructed me that but few have any conception of the wickedness existing in our world today, and especially the wickedness in the large cities. He declared that the Lord has appointed a time when He will visit transgressors in wrath for persistent disregard of His law.

Terrible as was the representation that passed before me, that which impressed itself most vividly upon my mind was the instruction given in connection with it. The angel that stood by my side declared that God's supreme rulership, and the sacredness of His law, must be revealed to those who persistently refuse to render obedience to the King of kings. Those who choose to remain disloyal, must be visited in mercy with judgments, in order that, if possible, they may be aroused to a realization of the sinfulness of their course.

Peril to Those Who Remain Unnecessarily

In harmony with the light given me, I am urging people to come out from the great centers of population. Our cities are increasing in wickedness, and it is becoming more and more evident that those who remain in them unnecessarily do so at the peril of their soul's salvation.

Country Living, pp. 9, 10

Chapter 2—Avoiding Labor Conflicts
Withdraw to the Freedom of Rural Areas

"The time is fast coming when the controlling power of the labor unions will be very oppressive. Again and again the Lord has instructed that our people are to take their families away from the cities, into the country, where they can raise their own provisions; for in the future the problem of buying and selling will be a very serious one. We should now begin to heed the instruction given us over and over again: Get out of the cities into rural districts, where the houses are not crowded closely together, and where you will be free from the interference of enemies."

"Preparing for the Issue!"
(A Warning Cry Message!)
Written February 7, 2017

On February 7, 2017, during the night, I had the first dream: I was quoting to the people of God, pp. 9–10 in the *Country Living* book, by E.G. White. Then, I quoted p. 7. One quote in particular I was quoting was, "The ungodly cities of our world are to be swept away by the besom of destruction…"

Then, on the same night, February 7, 2017, God gave me this dream: I was giving this "warning cry" message to the people of God found on pp. 12–17 from *Country Living*, "An Appeal to Parents." On p. 12, I saw this quote:

> "Before the overflowing scourge shall come upon the dwellers of the earth, the Lord calls upon all who are Israelites indeed to prepare for that event. To parents He sends the warning cry, Gather your children into your own houses; gather them away from those who are disregarding the commandments of God, who are teaching and practicing evil. Get out of the large cities as fast as possible. Establish church schools. Give your children the Word of God as the foundation of all their education… I am instructed by the Lord to warn our people not to flock to the cities to find homes for their families. To fathers and to mothers I am instructed to say, Fail not to keep your children within your own premises…
>
> Let children no longer be exposed to the temptations of the cities that are ripe for destruction. The Lord has sent us warning and counsel to get out of the cities. Then let us make no more investments in the cities. Fathers and mothers, how do you regard the souls of your children? Are you preparing the members of your families for translation into the heavenly courts? Are you preparing them to become members of the royal family? children of the heavenly King? 'What shall it profit a man, if he shall gain the whole world, and lose his own soul?' How will ease, comfort, convenience, compare with the value of the souls of your children?"

Also, on p. 8 of *Country Living* by E.G. White, she writes these words of counsel: "There are reasons why we should not build in the cities. On these cities, God's judgments are soon to fall… The time is near when large cities will be swept away, and all should be warned of these coming judgments… O that God's people had a sense of the impending destruction of thousands of cities, now almost given to idolatry."

Also, in my dream, I was quoting p. 21 from E.G. White's book, *Country Living*: "The Protestant world have set up an idol Sabbath in the place where God's Sabbath should be, and they are treading in the footsteps of the Papacy. For this reason I see the necessity of the people of God moving out of the cities into retired country places, where they may cultivate the land and raise their own produce. Thus they may bring their children up with simple, healthful habits. I see the necessity of making haste to get all things ready for the crisis."

In my dream, I was putting these things I had written into a bowl to give to God's people to eat and digest what I was trying to communicate to them the warnings and counsel of God's prophet, Sister White. **Read** Revelation 10. On p. 20, Sister White writes in her *Country Living* book, "We are not to locate ourselves where we will be forced into close relations with those who do not honor God... A crisis is soon to come in regard to the observance of Sunday... The Sunday party is strengthening itself in its false claims, and this will mean oppression to those who determine to keep the Sabbath of the Lord. We are to place ourselves where we can carry out the Sabbath commandment in its fullness… And we are to be careful not to place ourselves where it will be hard for ourselves and our children to keep the Sabbath. If in the providence of God we can secure places away from the cities, the Lord would have us do this. There are troublous times before us."

Read in *The Great Controversy* by E.G. White, pp. 603–612, "The Final Warning," chapter 38, especially pp. 604–605. Also, **read** *Last Day Events*, by E.G. White, chapter one, especially p. 14 and p. 42, "The Shortness of Time." (**Read** the whole chapter 3, "When Shall These Things Be?" pp. 32–42.)

> *I saw God's people, with their faces lighted up and shining with holy consecration, hastening from place to place to proclaim the message from heaven. They had their Bibles in their hands, opening the Scripture and sharing the truth with others*

Just recently, I had this dream: I saw God's people, with their faces lighted up and shining with holy consecration, hastening from place to place to proclaim the message from heaven. They had their Bibles in their hands, opening the Scripture and sharing the truth with others!

Read: *The Great Controversy* by E.G. White, pp. 611–612; the whole chapter 38, "The Final Warning," pp. 603–612; *Vol. 6 Testimonies for the Church*, pp. 60–62, "The Last Warning" by E.G. White; *The Great Controversy* chapter 25, pp. 433–450, "God's Law Immutable," especially p. 449–450.

Also, in *Book One, Selected Messages* by E.G. White, on p. 191, I dreamt on December 16, 2016, "It is our duty to watch and work and wait, to labor every moment for the souls of men that are ready to perish. We are to keep walking continually in the footsteps of Jesus, working in His lines, dispensing His gifts as good stewards of the manifold grace of God." (**Read** also, p. 192).

"A Storm is Coming!"
Written February 8, 2017

On January 26, 2017, the Lord gave me a dream, and the voice said to me in my dream, "A STORM IS COMING!" Then, on February 8, 2017, I dreamt I was quoting *Country Living* by Sister White to the people. (On February 7, 2017, I had sent out to God's people quotes from Sister White from *Country Living*.) Then, the Lord impressed me to write an article entitled, "A STORM IS COMING!"

In *Country Living* by Sister White on pp 20–21, 29, she gives this advice, "I see the necessity of making haste to get all things ready for the crisis… If in the providence of God we can secure places away from the cities, the Lord would have us do this. There are troublous times before us… God means that we shall not locate in the cities; for there are very stormy times before us."

In *Vol. 5 Testimonies for the Church* by E.G. White in the chapter, "The Coming Crisis," on p. 452, she tells us, "God has revealed what is to take place in the last days, that His people may be prepared to stand against the tempest of opposition and wrath. Those who have been warned of the events before them are not to sit in calm expectation of the coming storm, comforting themselves that the Lord will shelter His faithful ones in the day of trouble. We are to be as men waiting for their Lord, not in idle expectancy, but in earnest work, with unwavering faith. It is no time now to allow our minds to be engrossed with things of minor importance… The Sunday movement is now making its way in darkness… It is our duty to do all in our power to avert the threatened danger… Now is the time to lay hold of the arm of our strength."

Also, in *Vol. 5 Testimonies for the Church*, pp. 129–130, Sister White gives us this counsel, "A storm is arising that will wrench and test the spiritual foundation of every one to the utmost. Therefore avoid the sand bed; hunt for the rock. Dig deep; lay your foundation sure. Build, oh, build for eternity! Build with tears, with heartfelt prayers… 'He 'that is not with Me,'" said Christ, 'is against Me.' It is wholehearted, thoroughly decided men and women who will stand now. Christ sifted His followers again and again, until at one time there remained only eleven and a few faithful women to lay the foundation of the Christian church… To be great in God's kingdom is to be a little child in humility, in simplicity of faith, and in the purity of love. All pride must perish, all jealousy be overcome, all ambition for supremacy be given up, and the meekness and trust of the child be encouraged. All such will find Christ their rock of defense, their strong tower. In Him they may trust implicitly, and He will never fail them. Oh, that all who believe present truth would be warned to seek the Lord."

In *The Great Controversy* by E.G. White, we read in the chapter 37, "The Scriptures a Safeguard," on pp. 593–595, "The last great delusion is soon to open before us. Antichrist is to perform his marvelous works in our sight. So closely will the counterfeit resemble the true that it will be impossible to distinguish between them except by the Holy Scriptures. By their testimony every statement and every miracle must be tested. Those who endeavor to obey all the commandments of God will be opposed and derided. They can stand only in God. In order to endure the trial before them, they must understand the will of God as revealed in His word; they can honor Him only as they have a right conception of His character, government, and purposes, and act in accordance with them. None but those who have fortified the mind with the truths of the Bible will stand through the last great conflict. To every soul will come the searching test: Shall I obey God rather than men? The decisive hour is even now at hand. Are our feet planted on the rock of God's immutable word? Are we prepared to stand firm in defense of the commandments of God and the faith of Jesus?... The fearful judgments denounced against the worship of the beast and his image (Revelation 14:9–11), should lead all to a diligent study of the prophecies to learn what the mark of the beast is, and how they are to avoid receiving it… The apostle Paul declared, looking down to the last days: 'The time will come when they will not endure sound doctrine.' 2 Timothy 4:3. That time has fully come. The multitudes do not want Bible truth, because it interferes with the desires of the sinful, world–loving heart; and Satan supplies the deceptions which they love. But God will have a people upon the earth to maintain the Bible, and the Bible only, as the standard of all doctrines and the basis of all reforms... Before accepting any doctrine or precept, we should demand a plain 'Thus saith the Lord' in its support. Satan is constantly endeavoring to attract attention to man in the place of God. He leads the people to look to bishops, to pastors, to professors of theology, as their guides, instead of searching the Scriptures to learn their duty for themselves. Then, by controlling the minds of these leaders, he can influence the multitudes according to his will."

Read in *Last Day Events* by E.G. White, chapter 1, "Earth's Last Crisis" and chapter 2, "Signs of Christ's Soon Coming."

Read W.D. Frazee's book, *Coming Events and Crisis at the Close*. On p. 8 in the section, "Crisis at the Close," he says, "And in Revelation 13:6, 7, we read of church and state are going to unite to enforce the mark of the beast, and men won't be able to buy or sell unless they receive that mark… In other words, persecution is ahead of the remnant who follow the Lamb today… 'Satan hath desired to have you, that he may sift you as wheat'. Luke 22:31. And he foretold definitely that they were going to forsake their Lord because they had not prepared… 'And then shall many be offended, and shall betray one another, and shall hate one another'… We're going through the experience either of Jesus or of Judas, my friends. We can choose."

Read, also, p. 83 in *Desire of Ages* by E.G. White, "Many attend religious services, and are refreshed and comforted by the word of God; but through neglect of meditation, watchfulness, and prayer, they lose the blessing, and find themselves more destitute than before they received it."

In *Desire of Ages* on p. 121–122, we read what Sister White writes, "In the last great conflict of the controversy with Satan those who are loyal to God will see every earthly support cut off. Because they refuse to break His law in obedience to earthly powers, they will be forbidden to buy or sell. It will finally be decreed that they shall be put to death. See Revelation 13:11–17. But to the obedient is given the promise, 'He shall dwell on high: his place of defense shall be the munitions of rocks: bread shall be given him; his waters shall be sure.' Isaiah 33:16... Of all the lessons to be learned from our Lord's first great temptation none is more important than that bearing upon the control of the appetites and passions... His (Christ's) example declares that our only hope of eternal life is through bringing the appetites and passions into subjection to the will of God. In our own strength it is impossible for us to deny the clamors of our fallen nature."

In *Counsels on Diet and Foods* by Sister White on pp. 127, she tells us, "God requires of His people continual advancement. We need to learn that indulged appetite is the greatest hindrance to mental improvement and soul sanctification. With all our profession of health reform many of us eat improperly. Indulgence of appetite is the greatest cause of physical and mental debility, and lies largely at the foundation of feebleness and premature death. Let the individual who is seeking to possess purity of spirit bear in mind that in Christ there is power to control the appetite."

Read in *Counsels on Diet and Foods*, chapter 7 "Overeating." ("Natural" flavors put in our food makes us want to overeat.) Also, read chapter 8, "Control of Appetite." On p. 163, Sister White gives this counsel, "There are men of excellent natural ability whose labor does not accomplish half what it might if they were temperate in all things. Indulgence of appetite and passion beclouds the mind, lessens physical strength, and weakens moral power. Their thoughts are not clear. Their words are not spoken in power, are not vitalized by the Spirit of God so as to reach the hearts of the hearers... The controlling power of appetite will prove the ruin of thousands... But those who are slaves to appetite will fail in perfecting Christian character."

Proverbs 23:2, "And put a knife to thy throat, if thou be a man given to appetite."

On p. 83 in *Vol. 7 Testimonies for the Church*, Sister White says, "Out of the cities" is my message... The time is near when the large cities will be visited by the judgments of God. In a little while these cities will be terribly shaken."

In *Vol. 9 Testimonies for the Church*, Sister White tells us on p. 19, "God expects us to impart to others the knowledge that He has given us. It is His purpose that divine and human instrumentalities shall unite in the proclamation of the warning message. Ezekiel 33:7–9."

In *Vol. 2 Selected Messages* by E.G. White, she writes on p. 246, "I know that stormy times are before us, and we must know how to trust, how to lay hold on the Source of our strength. The Lord is good to those who trust in Him, and they shall not be overcome... Psalm 43:5."

In *Vol. 5 Testimonies for the Church* by E.G. White, on p. 546, she says, "Movements are being set on foot to enslave the consciences of those who would be loyal to God. The lawmaking powers will be against God's people. Every soul will be tested... Every position of our faith will be searched into; and if we are not thorough Bible students, established, strengthened, and settled, the wisdom of the world's great men will lead us astray."

In *Vol. 9 Testimonies for the Church*, p. 167, Sister White tells us, "We are living in the last days. The end of all things is at hand. The signs foretold by Christ are fast fulfilling. There are stormy times before us, but let us not utter one word of unbelief or discouragement... Let us remember that we bear a message of healing to a world filled with sin–sick souls."

On p. 211 in *Vol. 1 Testimonies for the Church* by Sister White, she warns us, "It is Satan's time to work. A stormy future is before us; and the church should be awake to make an advance move that they may stand securely against his plans. It is time that something was done."

We read in *Vol. 4 Testimonies for the Church*, p. 53, by Sister White, "Storms, earthquakes, whirlwinds, fire, and the sword will spread desolation everywhere, until men's hearts shall fail them for fear and for looking after those things which shall come upon the earth. You know not how small a space is between you and eternity. You know not how soon your probation may close... You may devote your entire existence to laying up treasures upon earth, but what will they advantage you when your life here closes, or when Christ makes His appearance? Not a farthing can you take with you... Your means are of no more value than sand, only as used to provide for the daily necessities of life and to bless others and advance the cause of God."

Sister White writes in *Vol. 2 Selected Messages*, on p. 52, "And see the storms and tempests. Satan is working in the atmosphere; he is poisoning the atmosphere, and here we are dependent upon God for our lives—our present and eternal life. And being in the position that we are, we need to be wide awake, wholly devoted, wholly converted, wholly consecrated to God. But we seem to sit as though we were paralyzed. God of heaven, wake us up!"

When reading this article to David and Jonathan, David said, "This kinda scares me. You think you're the Lord's, but are we really? Are we really getting our hearts ready for disaster, storms and the Sunday Law storm, so we can stand through the crises ahead of us, when it really breaks upon us with fury?! Are we grounded in our faith and trusting in the Lord with all our heart to see us through the storms and disasters ahead of us?" I agreed with what he was saying. Are we really searching our heart and getting rid of all our sins with God's help and developing a Christ-like character, so we can stand through the storms of life that will soon break upon us?! Yes, we know the storm clouds are coming and thickening around us. May Jesus please hold them back until we are ready and our loved ones are ready! Time is running out!!

Are we grounded in our faith and trusting in the Lord with all our heart to see us through the storms and disasters ahead of us?

It makes me think of when we recently listened to the weather on the weather radio. We had prayed God would please protect us and the "Ark" from any storm that they were forecasting. The weather radio said a serious storm was passing through our county bringing sleet, snow, ice, cold and strong winds. But praise the Lord, He let it pass by us, and we didn't have any dangerous storm, only strong winds blowing cold from the north! Praise God! Thank you Jesus! God is certainly looking out for us and the "Ark." Now is the time to get ready and prepare for the storms ahead of us! We all need the shelter of Jesus and His holy angels. On p. 136 in *Vol. 5 Testimonies for the Church* by E. G. White, we read, "Soon God's people will be tested by fiery trials, and the great proportion of those who now appear to be genuine and true will prove to be base metal... Already the judgments of God are abroad in the land, as seen in storms, in floods, in tempests, in earthquakes, in peril by land and by sea... Now is the time for God's people to show themselves true to principle."

Also, **read** in *The Great Controversy* by E.G. White, chapter 38, "The Final Warning," pp. 603–612. Especially read pp. 608–609. Sister White also has this counsel found in 5T 463, 129, 711, 716, 717, 452; 4T 251; *Christ's Object Lessons* p. 133.

Read the following quotes of E.G. White: *Gospel Workers* p. 323; *Prophets and Kings* p. 278, 537, 626; *9T* pp. 11, 43; *Evangelism* pp. 361–362; *Christian Service* p. 136; *8T* 315, 28, 307; *Adventist Home* p. 186; *The Great Controversy*, pp 594, 598, 593, 622, 625; *6T* pp. 17, 129; *Early Writings* p. 118; *Fundamentals of Christian Education* pp. 335–336, 526–527; *9T* pp. 167–172; *5T* pp. 129–130.

Read in the Bible: Mark 8:31–32; Mark 9:31; Mark 10:32–34; Matthew 26:56; Luke 24:6–8.

"Our Encounter with the Devil!"

(Ephesians 6:10–18)

Written February 12, 2017

I had made myself sick from trying to hurry and write out my dreams and materials and get them sent out to God's people to warn them of these things that are coming and quickly happening and prepare for these issues that are right upon us! In a dream I was saying, "Now I can relax." (God raised me back up to keep writing my book of dreams and the materials He was giving me quickly to share with others for time is running out!)

While sick in bed and feeling dizzy, because my blood sugar was out of control, because I'd be going night and day writing and also, working on the "Ark," moving big heavy furniture from place to place without a truck to haul it in, I had made myself sick from overwork and trying to keep up with everything else I had to do to cook, clean, washing and help Jonathan and work on the "Ark," etc.

It was at 8:15 p.m. that night that I was lying sick in bed and trying to recuperate from all I'd been doing! Jonathan was sitting in the front room in his easy chair watching sermons on DVDs. Dad was in his room studying Sister White's *Desire of Ages* book on "Gethsemane," chapter 74. There was a knock on the front door. I said, "What is it?" No answer. The dog came barking, hearing the knock, too, but stopped barking because no one or nothing was there! I asked Jonathan if he heard the knocking? He said he heard footsteps. There was no car sounds or headlights. The dog saw no one or nothing to bark at. I asked Daddy to please rub my back and feet, so I could relax and try and get some sleep. While he rubbed my back and feet, the fan, at the head of my bed turned on all by itself, and I had to turn it off! I know the devil is wroth with what I've been doing in sharing these dreams and articles I've been writing for others to try to arouse them and get them to realize the seriousness of the days we're living in now in earth's history, just before Jesus is to come. Satan is trying to harass us because of the work we're trying to do for Jesus to warn God's people to wake up to what's happening and taking place and prepare for what's coming! And like the Sunday Laws and Satan impersonating Christ, and the marvelous working of Satan to deceive God's people, and causing all this apostasy in the church, etc.

Satan is angry with my book I wrote, *Don't Be Trapped in the Cities!! Get Out NOW!* Like on pp. 72–82 of my book, the articles I wrote: "Step Fast!"; "God's People Wake Up!"; "Why Didn't Someone Warn Us?!"; "URGENT!"; "Satan is Wroth!"

Satan caused my right wrist I write with to hurt badly and my back to be terribly sore and caused my eye to hurt and felt like something was in it, irritating me! Satan caused David's nose to start bleeding, and Jonathan's eyes were hurting badly and he was feeling depressed. Satan was angry and harassing us and trying to make us miserable! We all are going to have to be determined to resist the devil, so he'll flee from us and draw nigh to God, so He will draw nigh to us. **Read** all James 4:7, 8.

One time while we were having our family worship, reading in *Desire of Ages* on the life of Christ, written by Ellen White, we were reading chapters 12, "The Temptation," and chapter 13, "The Victory," and I made the remark, "When Satan comes knocking at our heart's door to come in, let Jesus answer the door to send Satan away!"

Read in *Early Writings* by E.G. White, pp. 56–60, "Duty in View of the Time of Trouble" and "Mysterious Rapping." On p. 60, we read, "Could our eyes be opened, we should see forms of evil angels around us, trying to invent some new way to annoy and destroy us. And we should also see angels of God guarding us from their power; for God's watchful eye is ever over Israel for good, and He will protect and save His people, if they put their trust in Him. 'When the enemy shall come in like a flood, the Spirit of the Lord will lift up a standard against him.' (Isaiah 59:19) … Said the angel, 'Remember, thou art on the enchanted ground.' I saw that we must watch and have on the whole armor and take the shield of faith, and then we shall be able to stand, and the fiery darts of the wicked cannot harm us."

I think of poor Sister White and how Satan was constantly attacking her with problems and sicknesses and trying to take her life because of all her writing and exposing Satan and his wiles. Read her book, *The Great Controversy*, especially chapter 31, "Agency of Evil Spirits," and chapter 32, "Snares of Satan." On p. 518, we read, "The great controversy between Christ and Satan, that has been carried forward for nearly six thousand years, is soon to close; and the wicked one redoubles his efforts to defeat the work of Christ in man's behalf and to fasten souls in his snares." On p. 519, she continues to write, "He (Satan) tempts men to the indulgence of appetite or to some other form of self–gratification, and thus benumbs their sensibilities so that they fail to hear the very things which they most need to learn. Satan well knows that all whom he can lead to neglect prayer and the searching of the Scriptures, will be overcome by his attacks. Therefore he invents every possible device to engross the mind."

On pp. 528–530, she continues to write, "The followers of Christ know little of the plots which Satan and his hosts are forming against them. But He who sitteth in the heavens will overrule all these devices for the accomplishment of His deep designs. The Lord permits His people to be subjected to the fiery ordeal of temptation, not because He takes pleasure in their distress and affliction, but because this process is essential to their final victory. He could not, consistently with His own glory, shield them from temptation; for the very object of the trial is to prepare them to resist all the allurements of evil." On p. 529, we read, "Every temptation, every opposing influence, whether open or secret, may be successfully resisted, 'not by might, nor by power, but by My Spirit, saith the Lord of hosts.' Zechariah 4:6. 'The eyes of the Lord are over the righteous, and His ears are open unto their prayers... And who is he that will harm you, if ye be followers of that which is good?' 1 Peter 3:12, 13."

On p. 530, Sister White continues to tell us, "Only in humble reliance upon God, and obedience to all His commandments, can we be secure. No man is safe for a day or an hour without prayer. Especially should we entreat the Lord for wisdom to understand His word. Here are revealed the wiles of the tempter and the means by which he may be successfully resisted."

2 Timothy 3:12 says, "Yea, and all that will live godly in Christ Jesus shall suffer persecution." In *Review & Herald*, March 9, 1905, Sister White says, "… strive with all the power that God has given us to be among the hundred and forty-four thousand."

Read: *Last Day Events* by E.G. White, pp. 268–269 on the 144,000; *Acts of the Apostles*, p. 361 by E.G. White; *Vol. 1 Testimonies for the Church* p. 302, "Evil angels are upon our track every moment."

While I was recuperating in bed with my blood sugar out of control, I fell asleep and I dreamt I heard a rumbling sound! I don't know what it was! Maybe it could have been a rumbling sound of some kind of a storm coming?! We need to be preparing for the crises coming with the Sunday Law and also preparing for the disasters and calamities coming upon the earth! We are headed for stormy times! **Read** chapter one, "Earth's Last Crisis" in *Last Day Events* by E.G. White. On p. 11, she warns us, "The present is a time of overwhelming interest to all living. Rulers and statesmen, men who occupy positions of trust and authority, thinking men and women of all classes, have their attention fixed upon the events taking place about us. They are watching the relations that exist among the nations. They observe the intensity that is taking possession of every earthly element and they recognize that something great and decisive is about to take place—that the world is on the verge of a stupendous crisis… The calamities by land and sea, the unsettled state of society, the alarms of war, are portentous. They forecast approaching events of the greatest magnitude. The agencies of evil are combining their forces and consolidating. They are strengthening for the last great crisis. Great changes are soon to take place in our world, and the final movements will be rapid ones."

I had this dream some time back: "Even though we can't see them, we have angels all around us, watching over us, protecting us from the evil angels trying to destroy us (John 10:10). We will take the place of these evil angels when we get to heaven! **Read**: *The Great Controversy* by E.G. White, p. 610.

John 10:10 "The thief cometh not, but for to steal, and to kill, and to destroy: I am come that they might have life, and that they might have it more abundantly."

"Preparing for the Sunday Laws!!"

Written February 26, 2017

To be prepared for the soon–coming National Sunday Law, **read** E.G. White's book, *The Great Controversy*.

"Preparing for the Sunday Laws!!" I saw this written out in my dream. I also dreamt, "The Papal Power."

Our warning message to the world is found in Revelation 14:6–12, not to receive this mark of the beast. Our work as Seventh–day Adventists is to share the Three Angels Messages with the world, found in Revelation 14:6–12. **Read** in *Last Day Events* by E.G. White, chapter 14, "The Loud Cry" pp. 197–214. Read what Sister White writes on pp. 198–200 about God's last warning message. Sister White tells us, "This message is the last that will ever be given to the world." **Read** *The Great Controversy* by E.G. White where she says in chapter 38, "The Final Warning," on pp. 603–612, this is the "Loud Cry" message like the "Midnight Cry" given on October 22, 1844. **Read** Revelation 18:1–4. On p. 604 of *The Great Controversy*, Sister White writes, "These announcements, uniting with the third angel's message, constitute the final warning to be given to the inhabitants of the earth… Fearful is the issue to which the world is to be brought. The powers of earth, uniting to war against the commandments of God, will decree that 'all, both small and great, rich and poor, free and bond' (Revelation 13:16), shall conform to the customs of the church by the observance of the false sabbath. All who refuse compliance will be visited with civil penalties, and it will finally be declared that they are deserving of death. On the other hand, the law of God enjoining the Creator's rest day demands obedience and threatens wrath against all who transgress its precepts. With the issue thus clearly brought before him, whoever shall trample upon God's law to obey a human enactment receives the mark of the beast; he accepts the sign of allegiance to the power which he chooses to obey instead of God. The warning from heaven is: … Revelation 14:9, 10." On p. 605, we read, "The Sabbath will be the great test of loyalty, for it is the point of truth especially controverted. When the final test shall be brought to bear upon men, then the line of distinction will be drawn between those who serve God and those who serve Him not… While one class, by accepting the sign of submission to earthly powers, receive the mark of the beast, the other choosing the token of allegiance to divine authority, receive the seal of God." On p. 606–607 of *The Great Controversy*, we continue to hear Sister White's warning message given:

"But as the question of enforcing Sunday observance is widely agitated, the event so long doubted and disbelieved is seen to be approaching, and the third message will produce an effect which it could not have had before.

In every generation God has sent His servants to rebuke sin, both in the world and in the church. But the people desire smooth things spoken to them, and the pure, unvarnished truth is not acceptable... The words which the Lord gave them they uttered, fearless of consequences, and the people were compelled to hear the warning. Thus the message of the third angel will be proclaimed. As the time comes for it to be given with greatest power, the Lord will work through humble instruments, leading the minds of those who consecrate themselves to His service. The laborers will be qualified rather by the unction of His Spirit than by the training of literary institutions. Men of faith and prayer will be constrained to go forth with holy zeal, declaring the words which God gives them. The sins of Babylon will be laid open. The fearful results of enforcing the observances of the church by civil authority, the inroads of spiritualism, the stealthy but rapid progress of the papal power—all will be unmasked.

By these solemn warnings the people will be stirred. Thousands upon thousands will listen who have never heard words like these. In amazement they hear the testimony that Babylon is the church, fallen because of her errors and sins, because of her rejection of the truth sent to her from heaven. As the people go to their former teachers with the eager inquiry, Are these things so? the ministers present fables, prophesy smooth things, to soothe their fears and quiet the awakened conscience. But since many refuse to be satisfied with the mere authority of men and demand a plain 'Thus saith the Lord,' the popular ministry, like the Pharisees of old, filled with anger as their authority is questioned, will denounce the message as of Satan and stir up the sin–loving multitudes to revile and persecute those who proclaim it.

As the controversy extends into new fields and the minds of the people are called to God's downtrodden law, Satan is astir." *(Just like Satan attacked us. Read my article, "Our Encounter with the Devil!")* "The power attending the message will only madden those who oppose it. The clergy will put forth almost superhuman efforts to shut away the light lest it should shine upon their flocks. By every means at their command they will endeavor to suppress the discussion of these vital questions. The church appeals to the strong arm of civil power, and, in this work, papists and Protestants unite. As the movement for Sunday enforcement becomes more bold and decided, the law will be invoked against commandment keepers. They will be threatened with fines and imprisonment, and some will be offered positions of influence, and other rewards and advantages, as inducements to renounce their faith. But their steadfast answer is: 'Show us from the word of God our error'—the same plea that was made by Luther under similar circumstances. Those who are arraigned before the courts make a strong vindication of the truth, and some who hear them are led to take their stand to keep all the commandments of God. Thus light will be brought before thousands who otherwise would know nothing of these truths."

Continue to read in *The Great Controversy* Sister White's words of warning on pp. 603–606 and 608–612:

"Conscientious obedience to the word of God will be treated as rebellion… As the defenders of truth refuse to honor the Sunday–sabbath, some of them will be thrust into prison, some will be exiled, some will be treated as slaves… The heart can be very cruel when God's fear and love are removed. As the storm approaches, a large class who have professed faith in the third angel's message, but have not been sanctified through obedience to the truth, abandon their position and join the ranks of the opposition. By uniting with the world and partaking of its spirit, they have come to view matters in nearly the same light; and when the test is brought, they are prepared to choose the easy, popular side. Men of talent and pleasing address, who once rejoiced in the truth, employ their powers to deceive and mislead souls. They become the most bitter enemies of their former brethren. When Sabbathkeepers are brought before the courts to answer for their faith, these apostates are the most efficient agents of Satan to misrepresent and accuse them, and by false reports and insinuations to stir up the rulers against them. In this time of persecution the faith of the Lord's servants will be tried. They have faithfully given the warning, looking to God and to His word alone. God's Spirit, moving upon their hearts, has constrained them to speak… They remember that the words which they have spoken were not theirs, but His who bade them give the warning. God put the truth into their hearts, and they could not forbear to proclaim it… Wycliffe, Huss, Luther, Tyndale, Baxter, Wesley, urged that all doctrines be brought to the test of the Bible and declared that they would renounce everything which it condemned. Against these men persecution raged with relentless fury; yet they ceased not to declare the truth… Every new truth has made its way against hatred and opposition; those who were blessed with its light were tempted and tried. The Lord gives a special truth for the people in an emergency. Who dare refuse to publish it?"

> *Every new truth has made its way against hatred and opposition; those who were blessed with its light were tempted and tried*

It's like in my book, *Don't Be Trapped in the Cities!! Get Out Now!* I had this quote in a dream and I quoted Sister White's quote in *Vol. 3 Testimonies for the Church* p. 281, 'If God abhors one sin above another, of which His people are guilty, it is doing nothing in case of an emergency. Indifference and neutrality in a religious crisis is regarded of God as a grievous crime and equal to the very worst type of hostility against God. She goes on to say in *The Great Controversy*:

"He commands His servants to present the last invitation of mercy to the world. They cannot remain silent, except at the peril of their souls. Christ's ambassadors have nothing to do with consequences. They must perform their duty and leave results with God… No man can serve God without enlisting against himself the opposition of the hosts of darkness… The opposition of the enemies of truth will be restrained that the third angel's message may do its work. When the final warning shall be given, it will arrest the attention of these leading men through whom the Lord is now working, and some of them will accept it, and will stand with the people of God through the time of trouble. The angel who unites in the proclamation of the third angel's message is to lighten the whole earth with his glory… The work will be similar to that of the Day of Pentecost. As the "former rain" was given, in the outpouring of the Holy Spirit at the opening of the gospel, to cause the upspringing of the precious seed, so the "latter rain" will be given at its close for the ripening of the harvest. 'Then shall we know, if we follow on to know the Lord: His going forth is prepared as the morning; and He shall come unto us as the rain, as the latter and former rain unto the earth.' Hosea 6:3. 'Be glad then, ye children of Zion, and rejoice in the Lord your God: for He hath given you the former rain moderately, and He will cause to come down for you the rain, the former rain, and the latter rain.' Joel 2:23. 'In the last days, saith God, I will pour out of My Spirit upon all flesh.' 'And it shall come to pass, that whosoever shall call on the name of the Lord shall be saved.' Acts 2:17, 21… Here are "the times of refreshing" to which the apostle Peter looked forward when he said: 'Repent ye therefore, and be converted, that your sins may be blotted out, when the times of refreshing shall come from the presence of the Lord; and He shall send Jesus.' Acts 3:19, 20. Servants of God, with their faces lighted up and shining with holy consecration, will hasten from place to place to proclaim the message from heaven. By thousands of voices, all over the earth, the warning will be given. Miracles will be wrought, the sick will be healed, and signs and wonders will follow the believers. Satan also works, with lying wonders, even bringing down fire from heaven in the sight of men. Revelation 13:13. Thus the inhabitants of the earth will be brought to take their stand. The message will be carried not so much by argument as by the deep conviction of the Spirit of God. The arguments have been presented. The seed has been sown, and now it will spring up and bear fruit. The publications distributed by missionary workers have exerted their influence, yet many whose minds were impressed have been prevented from fully comprehending the truth or from yielding obedience. Now the rays of light penetrate everywhere, the truth is seen in its clearness, and the honest children of God sever the bands which have held them. Family connections, church relations, are powerless to stay them now. Truth is more precious than all besides. Notwithstanding the agencies combined against the truth, a large number take their stand upon the Lord's side."

In W. D. Frazee's book, *Another Ark to Build*, he says on pp. 31–38, the chapter, "Preparation." "Revelation 13:16–17. Here's a clear prediction that a mark will be enforced, and we know that mark is the mark of apostasy, the false rest day, the change of the Sabbath from Saturday, the seventh day to Sunday, the first day. That will be the issue. 'The Sabbath will be the great test of loyalty; for it is the point of truth especially controverted…'" *The Great Controversy*, p. 605. The way to prepare for this overwhelming surprise is to get in the habit of looking heavenward to Jesus rather than depending on men.

(In a dream, I saw these two quotes of Sister White, found in *8T* p. 28 and *2SM* p. 142.) Also, in my book, *Don't Be Trapped in the Cities!! Get Out <u>NOW</u>!* I warn God's people to leave the cities and move to the country for their spirituality and their safety and their preservation. Also, W.D. Frazee says in his book, *Another Ark to Build*, on pp. 21–29, he writes about "The Trap." On p. 21 he writes, "'The day of the Lord so cometh as a thief in the night', suddenly, unexpectedly. And what will "they" be talking about? 'Peace and safety; then sudden destruction cometh upon them… they shall not escape.'" 1 Thessalonians 5:2–3. But all this is told us so that <u>we</u> can escape. In Luke 21:34–36, we're warned to "take heed to yourselves, lest at any time your hearts be overcharged with surfeiting, and drunkenness, and cares of this life, and so that day come upon you unawares. For as a snare shall it come on all them that dwell on the face of the whole earth. Watch ye therefore, and pray always, that ye may be accounted worthy to escape all these things that shall come to pass, and to stand before the Son of man."

Another trap people get themselves in is debt. In *7T* p. 236, Sister White says, "Let all now seek most earnestly to avoid the mistakes of the past. Let them guard themselves as with a fence of barbed wire against the inclination to go into debt."

W.D. Frazee in his book, *Another Ark to Build* says on p. 28, "How can we prepare? By avoiding the trap, the trap of confederacies with the world, the trap of this ecumenical idea, the trap of debt, the trap of wanting to be rich, the trap of these labor unions, the trap of living for selfish ease, selfish pleasure, selfish indulgence. Avoid all that. Jesus says, Watch and pray and don't let your heart get overcharged with eating and drinking and the cares of this world. It's coming as a snare."

We are preparing for the Sunday Law now, and like Noah prepared for the Flood by obeying the Lord and getting ready for the crisis, so we are to prepare, like Sister White says in *Vol. 2 Selected Messages*, p. 359, "The Protestant world have set up an idol sabbath in the place where God's Sabbath should be, and they are treading in the footsteps of the Papacy. For this reason I see the necessity of the people of God moving out of the cities into retired country places, where they may cultivate the land and raise their own produce."

> *We are preparing for the Sunday Law now, and like Noah prepared for the Flood by obeying the Lord and getting ready for the crisis, so we are to prepare*

In *Vol. 2 Selected Messages* by Sister White, we read on p. 142, "The trades unions will be one of the agencies that will bring upon this earth a time of trouble such as has not been since the world began." **Read** Revelation 13. Also, read what Sister White says in *Vol. 2 Selected Messages*, pp. 355–356, "Who will be warned? We say again, 'Out of the cities.' Do not consider it a great deprivation, that you must go into the hills and mountains, but seek for that retirement where you can be alone with God, to learn His will and way. I urge our people to make it their lifework to seek for spirituality. Christ is at the door. This is why I say to our people, 'Do not consider it a privation when you are called to leave the cities and move out into the country places.'"

In Sister White's book *The Great Controversy*, we read on p. 38, in chapter 1, "The Destruction of Jerusalem," "The world is no more ready to credit the message for this time than were the Jews to receive the Saviour's warning concerning Jerusalem. Come when it may, the day of God will come unawares to the ungodly. When life is going on in its unvarying round; when men are absorbed in pleasure, in business, in traffic, in money–making; when religious leaders are magnifying the world's progress and enlightenment, and the people are lulled in a false security—then, as the midnight thief steals within the unguarded dwelling, so shall sudden destruction come upon the careless and ungodly, 'and they shall not escape.'" **Read** 1 Thessalonians 5.

Read the chapters in *The Great Controversy*, (35) "Liberty of Conscience Threatened"; (36) "The Impending Conflict." Sister White writes on pp. 588–592:

"Through the two great errors, the immortality of the soul and Sunday sacredness, Satan will bring the people under his deceptions... It is his (*Satan's*) object to incite the nations to war against one another, for he can thus divert the minds of the people from the work of preparation to stand in the day of God. Satan works through the elements also to garner his harvest of unprepared souls... and he uses all his power to control the elements as far as God allows... In accidents and calamities by sea and by land, in great conflagrations, in fierce tornadoes and terrific hailstorms, in tempests, floods, cyclones, tidal waves, and earthquakes, in every place and in a thousand forms, Satan is exercising his power... Destruction will be upon both man and beast... And then the great deceiver will persuade men that those who serve God are causing these evils... It will be declared that men are offending God by the violation of the Sunday sabbath; that this sin has brought calamities which will not cease until Sunday observance shall be strictly enforced; and that those who present the claims of the fourth commandment, thus destroying reverence for Sunday, are troublers of the people, preventing their restoration to divine favor and temporal prosperity... Those who honor the Bible Sabbath will be denounced as enemies of law and order, as breaking down the moral restraints of society, causing anarchy and corruption, and calling down the judgments of God upon the earth. Their conscientious scruples will be pronounced obstinacy, stubbornness, and contempt of authority. They will be accused of disaffection toward the government... The dignitaries of church and state will unite to bribe, persuade, or compel all classes to honor the Sunday. The lack of divine authority will be supplied by oppressive enactments. Political corruption is destroying love of justice and regard for truth; and even in free America, rulers and legislators, in order to secure public favor, will yield to the popular demand for a law enforcing Sunday observance. Liberty of conscience, which has cost so great a sacrifice, will no longer be respected. In the soon–coming conflict we shall see exemplified the prophet's words: 'The dragon was wroth with the woman, and went to make war with the remnant of her seed, which keep the commandments of God, and have the testimony of Jesus Christ.' Revelation 12:17."

On pp. 593–594, of *The Great Controversy* by E.G. White, in chapter 32, "The Scriptures a Safeguard," we read, "None but those who have fortified the mind with the truths of the Bible will stand through the last great conflict. To every soul will come the searching test: Shall I obey God rather than men? The decisive hour is even now at hand. Are our feet planted on the rock of God's immutable word? Are we prepared to stand firm in defense of the commandments of God and the faith of Jesus?... So in the prophecies the future is opened before us as plainly as it was opened to the disciples by the words of Christ. The events connected with the close of probation and the work of preparation for the time of trouble, are clearly presented... When God sends to men warnings so important that they are represented as proclaimed by holy angels flying in the midst of heaven, ... The fearful judgments denounced against the worship of the beast and his image (Revelation 14:9–11), should lead all to a diligent study of the prophecies to learn what the mark of the beast is, and how they are to avoid receiving it... 'The time will come when they will not endure sound doctrine.' 2 Timothy 4:3. That time has fully come."

Read: *Early Writings* pp. 254–288 by E.G. White; *Vol. 5 Testimonies for the Church* by E.G. White, "The Coming Crisis," pp. 449–454 and "The Church the Light of the World," pp. 454–467. On p. 452, she writes, "God has revealed what is to take place in the last days, that His people may be prepared to stand against the tempest of opposition and wrath… The Sunday movement is now making its way in darkness... It is our duty to do all in our power to avert the threatened danger… Now is the time to lay hold of the arm of our strength… Prayer moves the arm of Omnipotence."

Continue to read pp. 463–467 and pp. 468–476. (Joshua and the Angel). Sister White writes in *Vol. 8 Testimonies for the Church*, p. 28, "Transgression has almost reached its limit. Confusion fills the world, and a great terror is soon to come upon human beings. The end is very near. We who know the truth should be preparing for what is soon to break upon the world as an overwhelming surprise… Are we as a people asleep?... The Lord Jesus is calling for self–denying workers to follow in His footsteps, to walk and work for Him, to lift the cross, and to follow where He leads the way."

In *Desire of Ages* Sister White warns us in chapter 69, "On the Mount of Olives," pp. 627–636, and on p. 636, she writes, "Everything in the world is in agitation. The signs of the times are ominous. Coming events cast their shadows before. The Spirit of God is withdrawing from the earth, and calamity follows calamity by sea and by land. There are tempests, earthquakes, fires, floods, murders of every grade. Who can read the future? Where is security? There is assurance in nothing that is human or earthly. Rapidly are men ranging themselves under the banner they have chosen. Restlessly are they waiting and watching the movements of their leaders. There are those who are waiting and watching and working for our Lord's appearing… Few believe with heart and soul that we have a hell to shun and a heaven to win. The crisis is stealing gradually upon us… Satan sees that his time is short. He has set all his agencies at work that men may be deceived, deluded, occupied and entranced, until the day of probation shall be ended, and the door of mercy be forever shut."

Read: *Last Day Events* by E.G. White, "Sunday Laws," pp. 123–142, chapter 9; *National Sunday Law* by Jan Marcussen and W.D. Frazee's book *Coming Events and Crisis at the Close*; *Last Day Events* by E.G. White; *Vol. 1 Selected Messages* by E.G. White, chapter 24 and 25 "The Alpha and the Omega" and "The Foundation of our Faith" pp. 192–208 (The "Alpha" came through the medical and the "Omega" will come through the ministerial. These are very serious and solemn times we're living in); *Christ's Object Lessons* chapters "The Lord's Vineyard" and "Without a Wedding Garment"; Read 2 Timothy 2:15.

Satan is trying to keep us in a stupor and too busy to get ready for Christ's <u>soon</u> coming. Jesus is wanting to place His Seal on His people, and we're like in a stupor, and not getting ready! God of Heaven, wake us up! On pp. 711–720 read *Vol. 5 Testimonies for the Church* I dreamt this: "Watchmen, What of the Night?!" **Read** on pp. 120–137 in *Vol. 1 Testimonies for the Church*, and also pp. 129–137 in *Fundamentals of Christian Education*. **Read** *Early Writings* by E.G. White, pp. 2–45.

On February 24, 2017, I dreamt this song: "Breathe On Me, Breath of God."

On February 24, 2017, I was saying this in my dream to the people: "These things have been given me of the LORD."

Read: *Prophets and Kings* by E.G. White, chapter 22, especially pp. 275–278 and chapter 17.

Read: *Desire of Ages* chapter 69, especially pp. 632–636.

Read: 2 Corinthians 6:2.

Breathe on Me, Breath of God

1 Breathe on me, Breath of God, fill me with life a-new,
that I may love the way you love, and do what you would do.
2 Breathe on me, Breath of God, un-til my heart is pure,
un-til my will is one with yours, to do and to en-dure.
3 Breathe on me, Breath of God, so shall I nev-er die,
but live with you the per-fect life for all e-ter-ni-ty.

Text: Edwin Hatch, 1878, alt.
Tune: Robert Jackson, 1878

SM
TRENTHAM

This hymn is in the public domain. You may freely use this score for personal and congregational worship. If you reproduce the score, please credit Hymnary.org as the source.

"Linda's Dream on The Alpha and The Omega"

Written February 25, 2017

In my dream on February 25, 2017, I was in a building trying to destroy a big dangerous and deadly snake, who was loose and could attack anyone in the building. There were people in there who knew not that a big dangerous and deadly snake was loose! There were influential people who were counselors and educators in there, too. David was ready to come into the building, and I told him not to come in because of this big dangerous deadly snake loose in there and could attack anyone at any time, and that I was trying to destroy it before it attacked me or anyone else and destroy us. David began to try and help me to destroy it.

This is like Satan, the snake in the Alpha and the Omega and spiritual formation and the emergent church, etc., and all this falsehood and apostasy going on in the church and so many are not aware of its deadly heresy! In the *SDA Bible Commentary, Vol. 6*, p. 499, it says, "The poison of falsehood is as deadly as a serpent's venom." And how the Jesuits are getting more and more control of things in our own beloved SDA church and the people. We need to meet it! Like Rick Howard says in his book, *Meet It!* (Iceberg of Deception—A Look Beneath the Surface. Also, Rick Howard's other book, *The Omega of Rebellion –What Every Adventist Needs to Know…NOW*).

Read these two books and also, read Sister White's warnings found in references like *Evangelism*, pp. 119, 121; *Early Writings* pp. 124, 125; *Fundamentals of Christian Education*, p. 93; *Life Sketches* pp. 36, 51–64. **Read** Revelation chapters 12–15 and 17–19; Genesis 3 about Satan, the old serpent, deceiving Eve in the Garden of Eden. **Read** *Early Writings* pp. 118–121. On p. 10 in Rick Howard's book, *The Omega Rebellion*, I quote, "Reality check: We are all interested in last day events even as our leaders were in 1903. However, whether it is Sunday laws, papal resurgence, natural disasters, or spiritualism—one word trumps them all. That word is 'deception'."

Matthew 24:4: "And Jesus answered and said unto them, Take heed that no man deceive you."

1 Timothy 4:1: "Now the Spirit speaketh expressly, that in the latter times some shall depart from the faith, giving heed to seducing spirits, and doctrines of devils."

Read also: 2 Timothy 3:1–5 and 2 Timothy 4:2–4; *The Great Controversy* by E.G. White, on p. 593, "The Scriptures a Safeguard" and pp. 464, 523, 597; Sister White's book *Vol. 1 Selected Messages*, chapter 24, "The Alpha and the Omega," especially pp. 197, 200 and chapter 25, "the Foundation of Our Faith," pp. 201–208; *The Great Controversy* p. xi; *Vol. 3 Testimonies for the Church*, p. 361; *Vol. 2 Mind, Character and Personality*, pp. 275–276. The designers of this spiritual formation heresy is the Roman Catholic church!; *Vol. 6 Testimonies for the Church*, p. 91. "Christ said to His disciples: 'Ye are the light of the world. A city that is set on an hill cannot be hid.'"

Read: Matthew 4:4; Isaiah 8:19, 20. Get ready! Get ready! Get ready! The trumpet is to give a certain sound!; Isaiah 55:6–11; Isaiah 58; Isaiah 59:1–2; Isaiah 60:1–4; Isaiah 61:1–3; Joel 1:14–15; Joel 2:1, 12–32; Joel 3:10–16.

Remember: The "Alpha" came through the medical. The "Omega" will come through the ministerial.

Read Sister White's first vision and when she came out of vision found on pp. 13–24 in *Early Writings*. On p. 20, God said these words to Sister White, who was only a 17–year–old young lady, "Make known to others what I have revealed to you."

Several years ago, in a dream, the Lord said the very words to me, "Make known to others what I have revealed to you." I put this in my book, *Don't Be Trapped in the Cities!! Get Out NOW!* **Read** my book and see what all God has revealed to me that goes right along with the Bible and the writings of Sister White.

Read *Desire of Ages* by E.G. White, chapter 73, "Let Not Your Heart Be Troubled." My favorite page in all the book is page 668. Read it. She says, "They may expect large things if they have faith in His promises... We cannot depend for counsel upon humanity. The Lord will teach us our duty just as willingly as He will teach somebody else. If we come to Him in faith, He will speak His mysteries to us personally. Our hearts will often burn within us as One draws nigh to commune with us as He did with Enoch. Those who decide to do nothing in any line that will displease God, will know, after presenting their case before Him, just what course to pursue. And they will receive not only wisdom, but strength. Power for obedience, for service, will be imparted to them, as Christ has promised... And 'whatsoever we ask, we receive of Him, because we keep His commandments, and do those things that are pleasing in His sight.' 1 John 3:22."

Revelation 22:13: "I am Alpha and Omega, the beginning and the end, the first and the last."

"Robe of Christ's Righteousness"
Written March 11, 2017

Jonathan was taking a nap in his easy chair, and in his sleep he said, "Mom, help me find my robe! Hurry up!" I said to him, "You mean your Robe of Christ's Righteousness?" I then prayed, "Lord, please help Jonathan find his Robe of Christ's Righteousness, and put it on before it's too late! Thank you Jesus! Amen."

Read the parable, "Without a Wedding Garment," in *Christ's Object Lessons* by Sister White on pages 307–319. This parable is based on Matthew 22:1–14. On p. 310–311, we read, "By the wedding garment in the parable is represented the pure, spotless character which Christ's true followers will possess. Revelation 19:8; Ephesians 5:27… It is the righteousness of Christ, His own unblemished character, that through faith is imparted to all who receive Him as their personal Saviour. The white robe of innocence was worn by our first parents when they were placed by God in holy Eden… A beautiful soft light, the light of God, enshrouded the holy pair. This robe of light was a symbol of their spiritual garments of heavenly innocence… But when sin entered, they severed their connection with God, and the light that had encircled them departed… This covering, the robe of His own righteousness, Christ will put upon every repenting, believing soul." **Read** Revelation 3:18.

"Christ in His humanity wrought out a perfect character, and this character He offers to impart to us" (Isaiah 64:6).

On pp. 312–316, we read, "When we submit ourselves to Christ, the heart is united with His heart, the will is merged in His will, the mind becomes one with His mind, the thoughts are brought into captivity to Him; we live His life. This is what it means to be clothed with the garment of His righteousness. Then as the Lord looks upon us He sees, not the fig–leaf garment, not the nakedness and deformity of sin, but His own robe of righteousness, which is perfect obedience to the law of Jehovah… Righteousness is right doing, and it is by their deeds that all will be judged. Our characters are revealed by what we do. The works show whether the faith is genuine… 'Hereby we do know that we know Him if we keep His commandments.' 1 John 3:24; 1 John 2:3. This is the genuine evidence of conversion. Whatever our profession, it amounts to nothing unless Christ is revealed in works of righteousness."

Reading on p. 314, "He who becomes a partaker of the divine nature will be in harmony with God's great standard of righteousness, His holy law. This is the rule by which God measures the actions of men. This will be the test of character in the judgment… Could the law have been changed or set aside, then Christ need not have died. By His life on earth He honored the law of God. By His death He established it… But Christ came in the form of humanity, and by His perfect obedience He proved that humanity and divinity combined can obey every one of God's precepts. 'As many as received Him, to them gave He power to become the sons of God, even to them that believe on His name.' John 1:12. This power is not in the human agent. It is the power of God. When a soul receives Christ, he receives power to live the life of Christ."

On p. 315 we read, "God requires perfection of His children… The heavenly principles that distinguish those who are one with Christ from those who are one with the world have become almost indistinguishable." On p. 316, we read, "The professed followers of Christ are no longer a separate and peculiar people. The line of demarcation is indistinct. The people are subordinating themselves to the world, to its practices, its customs, its selfishness… Daily the church is being converted to the world. All these expect to be saved by Christ's death, while they refuse to live His self–sacrificing life… The righteousness of Christ will not cover one cherished sin… God is love… He will not connive at our sins or overlook our defects of character. He expects us to overcome in His name."

On pp. 318–319, we read, "Solemn will be the day of final decision. In prophetic vision the apostle John describes it: Revelation 20:11, 12… Sad will be the retrospect in that day when men stand face to face with eternity. The whole life will present itself just as it has been. The world's pleasures, riches, and honors will not then seem so important. Men will then see that the righteousness they despised is alone of value. They will see that they have fashioned their characters under the deceptive allurements of Satan. The garments they have chosen are the badge of their allegiance to the first great apostate. Then they will see the results of their choice. They will have a knowledge of what it means to transgress the commandments of God. There will be no future probation in which to prepare for eternity. It is in this life that we are to put on the robe of Christ's righteousness. This is our only opportunity to form characters for the home which Christ has made ready for those who obey His commandments. The days of our probation are fast closing. The end is near. To us the warning is given, 'Take heed to yourselves, lest at any time your hearts be overcharged with surfeiting, and drunkenness, and cares of this life, and so that day come upon you unawares.' Luke 21:34. Beware lest it find you unready. Take heed lest you be found at the King's feast without a wedding garment. 'In such an hour as ye think not the Son of man cometh.' 'Blessed is he that watcheth, and keepeth his garments, lest he walk naked, and they see his shame.' Matthew 24:44; Revelation 16:15."

In *Vol. 5 Testimonies for the Church*, p. 471, Sister White writes, "All that have put on the robe of Christ's righteousness will stand before Him as chosen and faithful and true. Satan has no power to pluck them out of the hand of Christ."

> *The professed followers of Christ are no longer a separate and peculiar people. The line of demarcation is indistinct. The people are subordinating themselves to the world, to its practices, its customs, its selfishness*

Read also by E.G. White: *5T* pp. 472, 510–512; *9T* 182–183; 7T p. 71; *Desire of Ages*, pp. 350–351, 680; *Testimonies to Ministers and Gospel Workers* pp. 363–373; *My Life Today* p. 277; Ministry of Healing, p. 506; Matthew 6:33.

In *Maranatha* by E.G. White, we read on p. 225, "Christ was obedient to every requirement of the law... By His perfect obedience He has made it possible for every human being to obey God's commandments. When we submit ourselves to Christ, the heart is united with His heart, the will is merged in His will, the mind becomes one with His mind, the thoughts are brought into captivity to Him; we live His life. This is what it means to be clothed with the garment of His righteousness. Then as the Lord looks upon us He sees, not the fig–leaf garment, not the nakedness and deformity of sin, but His own robe of righteousness, which is perfect obedience to the law of Jehovah... If you will stand under the bloodstained banner of Prince Emmanuel, faithfully doing His service, you need never yield to temptation; for One stands by your side who is able to keep you from falling." Jude 24.

"Watchmen, What of the Night?!"

(Read Ezekiel 3 and 33; and Joel 2 and 3)

Written March 14, 2017

I heard these words spoken to me in my dream: "Watchman, what of the night?!" Two times I've had this dream! Sister White says in *Vol. 9 Testimonies to the Church*, pp. 19–29, 61–63, "Called to Be Witnesses." On p. 19, she writes, "In a special sense Seventh–day Adventists have been set in the world as watchmen and light bearers. To them has been entrusted the last warning for a perishing world. On them is shining wonderful light from the word of God. They have been given a work of the most solemn import—the proclamation of the first, second, and third angels' messages. There is no other work of so great importance. They are to allow nothing else to absorb their attention. The most solemn truths ever entrusted to mortals have been given us to proclaim to the world. The proclamation of these truths is to be our work. The world is to be warned, and God's people are to be true to the trust committed to them… Christ says of His people: 'Ye are the light of the world.' Matthew 5:14… It is a wonderful privilege to be able to understand the will of God as revealed in the sure word of prophecy. This places on us a heavy responsibility. God expects us to impart to others the knowledge that He has given us. It is His purpose that divine and human instrumentalities shall unite in the proclamation of the warning message."

And what is our warning message to the world God has given us Seventh–day Adventists to share with the world? It's found in Revelation 14:6–12, the Three Angel's messages! **Read Ezekiel 33:7–9.**

On p. 20 of *Vol. 9 Testimonies for the Church*, Sister White continues her counsel saying, "We are to be consecrated channels, through which the heavenly life is to flow to others... Upon us is laid a sacred charge." That charge is found in Matthew 28:19, 20. Continue reading on p. 21, "Sin is a hateful thing… Those who receive Him are born again." On p. 22, we read, "The life that Christ lived in this world, men and women can live through His power and under His instruction. In their conflict with Satan they may have all the help that He had."

On p. 23, "They are to bear a plain, decided testimony against all evil practices, pointing sinners to the Lamb of God, who taketh away the sin of the world. He gives to all who receive Him, power to become the sons of God… Those who love Jesus will bring all in their lives into harmony with His will. They have chosen to be on the Lord's side, and their lives are to stand out in vivid contrast with the lives of worldlings." Page 24 reads, "Those who walk in the light as Christ is in the light will co–operate with the Saviour by revealing to others what He has revealed to them." Sister White continues to write these words, on p. 25, "Let us now take up the work appointed us and proclaim the message that is to arouse men and women to a sense of their danger."

On p. 26, we read, "The people of God are to come close to Christ in self–denial and sacrifice, their one aim being to give the message of mercy to all the world. Some will work in one way and some in another, as the Lord shall call and lead them. But they are all to strive together, seeking to make the work a perfect whole. With pen and voice they are to labor for Him." Also, on p. 27, God's prophet says to us, "What are we thinking of, that we cling to our selfish love of ease, while all around us souls are perishing? ... Is it in vain that God has given you a knowledge of His will? Is it in vain that He has sent you warning after warning of the nearness of the end? Do you believe the declarations of His word concerning what is coming upon the world? Do you believe that God's judgments are hanging over the inhabitants of the earth? How, then, can you sit at ease, careless and indifferent? Every day that passes brings us nearer the end. Does it bring us also near to God? Are we watching unto prayer? Those with whom we associate day by day need our help, our guidance. They may be in such a condition of mind that a word in season will be sent home by the Holy Spirit as a nail in a sure place. Tomorrow some of these souls may be where we can never reach them again. What is our influence over these fellow travelers? What effort do we make to win them to Christ? Time is short, and our forces must be organized to do a larger work."

Continue to read pp. 28–29, "An Impressive Scene," Sister White had about an immense ball of fire fall causing instant destruction. She said she heard someone say, "'We knew that the judgments of God were coming upon the earth, but we did not know that they would come so soon.' Others, with agonized voices, said: 'You knew! Why then did you not tell us? We did not know.' On every side I heard similar words of reproach spoken… If every soldier of Christ had done his duty, if every watchman on the walls of Zion had given the trumpet a certain sound, the world might ere this have heard the message of warning. But the work is years behind. While men have slept, Satan has stolen a march upon us."

Read Ezekiel 3:16–27; *6T* p. 166. Also, read in *9T* pp. 11–18, "The Last Crisis." I had this chapter in one of my dreams some time back. Read, also, chapters 10–13 in *Patriarchs and Prophets* by E.G. White. I had these chapters in one of my dreams to read, too!

Read, also, chapter 7 in *Patriarchs and Prophets* by E.G. White, especially p. 104 in the chapter, "The Flood." "'As it was in the days of Noah,' 'even thus shall it be in the days when the Son of man is revealed.' Luke 17:26, 30." **Read** 2 Peter 3:9–11. "When the reasoning of philosophy has banished the fear of God's judgments; when religious teachers are pointing forward to long ages of peace and prosperity, and the world are absorbed in their rounds of business and pleasure, planting and building, feasting and merrymaking, rejecting God's warnings and mocking His messengers—then it is that sudden destruction cometh upon them, and they shall not escape.' 1 Thessalonians 5:3."

Remember, for us to be faithful to the end, we need to decide to do what God says to do and not what man says to do. **Read** Isaiah 55:6–11; Isaiah 30:20–21; 1 Corinthians 14:8; 1 Peter

2:9; *The Great Controversy* by E.G. White, chapter 36, "The Impending Conflict"; chapter 37, "The Scriptures a Safeguard." On p. 602, we read, "When the testing time shall come, those who have made God's word their rule of life will be revealed... So the falsehearted professor may not now be distinguished from the real Christian, but the time is just upon us when the difference will be apparent. Let opposition arise, let bigotry and intolerance again bear sway, let persecution be kindled, and the halfhearted and hypocritical will waver and yield the faith; but the true Christian will stand firm as a rock, his faith stronger, his hope brighter, than in days of prosperity." **Read**, also, chapter 38 in *The Great Controversy*, "The Final Warning." In our S.D.A. Church, some say, "We cannot stop sinning." Watchmen, what of the night? We should not fear to call sin by its right name! Like the wild music in our church, spiritual formation, removing the old landmarks, the love of the world, Jesuits in our Church rejecting health reform and the Spirit of prophecy, the Sanctuary message and dress reform. Read Rick Howard's books, *Meet It!* and *The Omega Rebellion*.

I had a dream of Sister White's article, "The Impending Conflict" in *5T* pp. 711–718, especially p. 712. The Pope's "door of mercy" closed November 20, 2016, and he said that it would be severity to those who don't go along with him! There'll be fines, imprisonment, inducements, then no–buy–no–sell, then the death decree! Read chapter 38, "The Final Warning" in *The Great Controversy* by E.G. White, pp. 603–612. Study your Bible and *The Great Controversy* like never before! Jesus is at the door! Matthew 24; Mark 13; Luke 21. These are signs of Christ's soon coming! "Watchman, what of the night?!" Another dream God gave me was read "The Seal of God," in *5T*, pp. 207–216.

Read "An Appeal," pp. 217–235 in *5T* by E.G. White. Another dream God gave me was *5T*, pp. 568–580. **Read** also pp. 62–84 and pp. 98–105; pp. 132–148 and 628. Another dream God gave me was to read chapter 22, "Nineveh, That Great City," pp. 165–277 by E.G. White. **Read** especially pp. 274–278 in *Prophets and Kings; Patriarchs and Prophets* by E.G. White, chapter 14, "Destruction of Sodom"; *2T*, pp. 195–196; *Conflict and Courage*, p. 108; *The Upward Look*, "Watchmen, What of the Night?"; *Vol. 1 Selected Messages* by E.G. White, chapter 25, "The Foundation of our Faith"; Ezekiel 3 and 33, and Joel 2 and 3. "Watchmen, what of the night?!"; *Education* by E.G. White, pp. 262–271, "The Lifework," especially p. 269, 271 telling how God will use the common people and the youth rightly trained.

"Ye Are My Witnesses"

Written April 23, 2017

<u>Acts 1:8:</u> "But ye shall receive power, after that the Holy Ghost is come upon you: and ye shall be witnesses unto me both in Jerusalem, and in all Judaea, and in Samaria, and unto the uttermost part of the earth."

<u>Acts 22:15:</u> "For thou shalt be his witness unto all men of what thou hast seen and heard."

<u>Acts 2:16–21:</u> "But this is that which was spoken by the prophet Joel; And it shall come to pass in the last days, saith God, I will pour out of my Spirit upon all flesh: and your sons and your daughters shall prophesy, and your young men shall see visions, and your old men shall dream dreams: And on my servants and on my handmaidens I will pour out in those days of my Spirit; and they shall prophesy: And I will show wonders in heaven above, and signs in the earth beneath; blood, and fire, and vapour of smoke: The sun shall be turned into darkness, and the moon into blood, before that great and notable day of the Lord come: And it shall come to pass, that whosoever shall call on the name of the Lord shall be saved." (Also read Joel 2:28–32.)

Two times the Lord has given me this dream, "The Last Crisis" found in *9T*, pp. 11–18. **Read** also in *9T* "Called To Be Witnesses," pp. 19–29, and read in *9T*, pp. 125–136, "An Appeal to Laymen," especially pp. 134–136. These are words spoken by God's prophet, Sister White.

I also dreamt in *5T*, "The Impending Conflict," pp. 711–718. Read also in *5T*, pp. 132–137, "Laborers For God." Read also *5T*, pp. 217–235, "An Appeal."

In my dream I heard these words spoken, "Watchman, What of the Night?!" Also read *5T*, pp. 199–202. "Looking Unto Jesus" and *5T*, pp. 207–235, "The Seal of God."

After reading all this, we have been doing a lot of witnessing for Jesus. We know our time here in this old world is short, and we must be about our Father's business.

We know our time here in this old world is short, and we must be about our Father's business

I gave *Great Controversy* books to two of the ladies that work at Mental Health, who have seen Jonathan when he was depressed. I also gave them 3ABN sharing cards. When Jonathan was admitted to the hospital for his depression, I gave him a few 3ABN cards to share to help others with their problems. David and I pass them out like the leaves of autumn, and people are open to receive them and thank us for them. No matter where we go, we hand out 3ABN sharing cards. It brings us such joy to have a part in sharing the good news with those God lets us cross paths with. Like when we were buying Jonathan a pair of shoes at Walmart for his birthday, the lady who assisted us was so happy to get the card. When in the Emergency room where they were admitting Jonathan for his depression, David was handing them out to the patients in the E.R. waiting room, and to the nurses and people were so happy to receive them. On the 3ABN sharing card, it shows all the ways you can tune in and see 3ABN and also, it mentions on the card some of the many things you'll see on 3ABN like: Addiction Recovery; Children's Programs; Cooking Programs; Biblical Teaching; Health Education; Inspirational Music; Marriage Enrichment; Weight Loss & Exercise, etc.

I send the sharing cards in the envelopes when I pay our bills. When in the grocery stores, we give them to the cashier or people we get to talking to. People are very receptive and appreciative to receive the information and thank us for sharing it with them!

One time when going through line at the grocery store, I said to the lady checking out our food we were buying, and I said, "I guess you can tell with all these beans and fruits and vegetables and no meat or any animal products that we're vegetarians?" She smiled and said, "Yes! But I'm hooked on my meat!" I said, "You can get diseases 10 times greater by eating meat. And you'll feel so much better without meat and animal products." David spoke up and said, "Yes! My wife is 74 and she runs and lifts weights and rides her bicycle for miles." I handed her a card and showed the programs she could watch on 3ABN. She said, "I'll show this to my daughter too." I said, "Just think of all the benefits of being a vegetarian! We eat fruits and nuts, grains and vegetables and it's been over 20 years since I've had to see a doctor, just by following the eight natural health laws you'll learn about by watching 3ABN." She put the card in her pocket and thanked me for it. **Read** *Ministry of Healing* by E.G. White on p. 127 the natural remedies, "Pure air, sunlight, abstemiousness, rest, exercise, proper diet, the use of water, trust in divine power—these are the true remedies."

One time we went to Walmart and parked in the parking lot and when we came out of the store, our car wouldn't start! We prayed God would please help us with our car problem. Daddy got out and lifted the hood and banged around on the battery and as he was looking at things under the hood, a man drove into the empty parking space beside us and offered to help us with our problem. David said, "Thank you! If you'll tap the battery, I'll see if I can start it." David got in the car to turn the key on to try and start it as the man tapped on the battery. Nothing happened! I said, "Daddy, you don't have the car in 'Park.' It won't start unless you put it in 'Park.'" When he put it in 'Park,' it started right up! Praise the Lord! I said, "Daddy give that man a 3ABN card. God brought him in touch with us so we could get the truth into his hands!" The man thanked Daddy, and we thanked him for stopping to help us with our car problem!

We know the devil is wroth with us spreading these 3ABN sharing cards all over the place. Satan knows his time to work is short, and we know our time to work for Jesus and to save souls in God's kingdom is short. The great battle is going on!

Sister White, God's prophet, has let us Seventh–day Adventists realize our time here on this earth is short, and time is running out to witness and warn people of the dangers ahead and how to prepare for Christ's soon coming! In *Last Day Events* book by E.G. White, she says on pp. 41–42, "Transgression has almost reached its limit. Confusion fills the world, and a great terror is soon to come upon human beings. The end is very near. We who know the truth should be preparing for what is soon to break upon the world as an overwhelming surprise...

May the Lord give no rest, day nor night, to those who are now careless and indolent in the cause and work of God. The end is near. This is that which Jesus would have us keep ever before us—the shortness of time."

Read: chapter 4, "God's Last Day Church," and chapter 5, "Devotional Life of the Remnant," and chapter 6, "Lifestyle and Activities of the Remnant," found in *Last Day Events* by E.G. White; also *Christian Service* by E.G. White, p. 153, "None can estimate the influence that even a torn page containing the truths of the third angel's message may have upon the heart of some seeker after truth."

We always pray God will impress and direct us to the honest and sincere people out there who'll respond to the Holy Spirit when we give them a 3ABN sharing card.

God impressed me to give one to the man at the printing company, who makes copies of my articles, for him to give it to his dad, who is elderly and who had recently been in the hospital. We had already given one to the man who prints copies of my articles. He said he'd be sure and give the card to his dad and thanked us for it. We have been hurrying to get these 3ABN sharing cards out as fast as we can because 3ABN Campmeeting is coming up soon, and they're going to be "Exposing the Counterfeit."

While we were in town, we stopped to get gas. A young lady was standing there with a puppy in her arms, and I remarked how cute her little puppy was and what kind it was, and she said, "He's a Pit Bull." I asked what her puppy's name was and she mentioned some Egyptian god. I said, "Oh! It's too bad he has to have a name like that for such a cute puppy!" She said, "It wasn't my choice. I wanted to name him, "King." I said, "Yes! That would be a good name." We gave her a 3ABN sharing card and she was so happy to get it! Praise the Lord! God lets us cross paths with the right people. Thank you Jesus!

We pray in our worship each morning that the Lord will direct us to the right people to witness to, and He does! God gets all the praise! Like one morning when I woke up, I was talking to the Lord, and He impressed me to hurry and get up and take our bicycles to the bike trail in Pomona and pass out 3ABN sharing cards with the people we meet there.

So we hurried and packed our breakfast and put it in a backpack, and we had worship and asked the Lord to please help us to get these sharing cards into the right hands. When we got to the bike trail, we saw two cars parked there, but no one was around, so we took off on a 9–mile bike ride and didn't see one person to give the cards to. Then, as we were ready to pull into the parking lot, four people came in behind us on their bikes. It was husbands and wives, probably in their 50s or so. I gave them each a card and told them to be sure and watch the programs, that we really have enjoyed the programs. They thanked me for them.

After we ate our breakfast and we had prayed that God would please bless those cards we had just passed out, the Lord impressed me to go to the Pomona State Park and pass them out there, while it was the weekend and a lot of campers would be out there and to leave them in the many bathrooms out there and the laundromats. I said to Daddy, "Well, it sounds like the Lord wants us to do "bathroom evangelism" today!" So, we drove on over to the State Park that was packed with campers and began going into the bathrooms and leaving cards all over the campground. I'd leave it in the ladies' bathroom and then stick one in the door of the men's restroom, so it would fall out when they opened the door up. As we drove out of the campground, we prayed that God would please bless our efforts to sow this seed in the right places for the right persons to find the truth.

It makes us feel so good that we're having a part in being God's witnesses, to let Him use our hands and feet and voice to share the truth with those in darkness. I said to Daddy, "Maybe someday in heaven someone will come up to us and say, 'I'm here because you shared a 3ABN sharing card with me.'" Some day we will have stars in our crown because we put God's work first and witnessed for Him to save souls for His kingdom!

Read: *8T* pp. 196–197; *6T* pp. 310–312; *Last Day Events* by E.G. White chapter 11, pp. 197–214, especially p. 204 "The Loud Cry"; *9T* p. 19. We also pass out Jan Marcussen's *National Sunday Law* book and Danny Shelton's new book out called *Spiritual Vigilantes*.

Proverbs 11:30: "The fruit of the righteous is a tree of life; and he that winneth souls is wise."

March 21, 2017

David, Linda, & Jonathan Clore
2645 Arkansas Terrace
Quenemo, KS 66528

Dear Clore Family,

It's always a blessing to hear from you! Thank you for keeping me updated with the work you're doing on "The Ark," as well as your outreach and ministry for the Lord Jesus. I'm glad that you are able to pass out the 3ABN Share Cards, as this is a wonderful way to acquaint others with the life-saving truths found on 3ABN. Thank you for your faithful witness for Him!

I also appreciated you sharing your dreams and the things God has shown you regarding the danger of living in the cities, as well as the coming storm, the time of trouble that will soon come upon this world. At 3ABN, we feel that urgency as well, to do all we can to proclaim the undiluted three angels' messages to a lost and dying world while there's still time. You're right, we must study and know the Word of God for ourselves so we will not be ensnared by any of Satan's deceptions.

Know that your 3ABN family is praying for you, that God would continue to lead and guide you and bless you with His presence, His peace, and His power.

His Love and Ours,

Danny Shelton
President & CEO

DS:jm

3ABN.tv

Danny Shelton | President | CEO
danny.shelton@3abn.org

P.O. Box 220 | West Frankfort, IL 62896 | phone 618-627-4651 | fax 618-627-2726

Caleb Gibbs   03/17/2017
113 Fairwood Ct.
Smyrna, TN 37167
(214) 952-1521

David and Linda Clore
2645 Arkansas Ter.
Quenemo, KS 66528

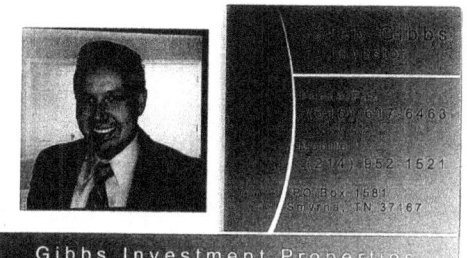

Dear David and Linda,

    Thank you so much for getting the executed contract back to me. I told my parents about the property, and they are ecstatic! My children will be very excited to know that their Grandma and Grandpa will be living so close! I'm so thankful for this blessing! Since writing you last, my wife unfortunately had a miscarriage, and it has been tough for her and I. I ask that you would you pray for her and for the child we lost.

    I bought your book Linda! <u>Don't Be Trapped in the Cities!!</u> I was really blessed by your words and I was touched by your story and prophecy. Your faith in the Lord is unwavering. It's truly inspirational, and I feel it's God's will that our families stay in contact after the sale. That is some useful information as I've been considering going in that direction. I would like to share something special with you. It's my account of an experience that has God has shared with me. It opened my eyes to the actuality of the spiritual gifts and that they are REAL! I was very skeptical of them in the past. Starting September 24th, 2016, God has been revealing himself to me and speaking directly to me though prayer, meditation, scripture and by introducing me to new people who are on FIRE for God. It has been an amazing journey so far. One morning in early October, I was meditating and praying in solitude. I asked that the Holy Spirit fill me with his presence, which is an awesome experience. While filled with the Holy Spirit, I asked the Lord to help me understand the Holy Trinity. After a few moments, I had my first vision, and I felt a presence I had never felt before. My body felt heavy, and I couldn't move. I felt somewhat suspended above my body. The vision was blurry, but I could make out a silhouette of a face. It had a long nose and distinct cheek bones. I felt anxiety, anticipation and fear but not terror or doom. I knew at that moment that I was in the presence of God the Father and the Holy Spirit reaffirmed me after I asked. My words just don't describe it right. I haven't experience God the Father again, but I'm so glad that he chose to share that with me. I know our meeting was not by chance or accident. I will continue to pray for you both and about your "ARK" that God would continue sending his blessings your way.

I have some business I want to discuss with you too. I want to clear up the wording of the contract that you signed regarding the use of the term "cash." I probably should have mentioned this in the previous letter but the term "cash" is commonly used in real-estate purchasing contracts in lieu of a financing contingency clause, and the term shouldn't be taken literally. I also do all real estate transactions through a title company for everyone's safety. That being said, I have given the contract to John Gleaves at Rudy Title & Escrow in Nashville who will be doing the title search and facilitating the closing. Here's how it works. After the title research is completed and shows a clear and unencumbered title, I will write a check for the $5000 plus closing costs to the Rudy Title. They take my payment for your property and deposit it in their protected Escrow bank account. Then Rudy Title will send you closing documents for you both to sign in front of a notary. After you send the signed documents back to Rudy Title, they will verify that everything is filled out correctly and send you a check from the protected Escrow account for the $5000. They will record everything with the Cheatham County Registrar's Office and the transaction will be finished. Listed below is John's contact information.

John Gleaves
Rudy Title and Escrow
2012 21st Ave S.
Nashville, TN 37212
(615) 383-2903 phone
(615) 515-3521 fax

If you have any questions, please feel free to write me.

Sincerely,

Caleb Gibbs

Acts 2:14-21
1 Peter 1:16-19
Ephesians 3:7-13
Philippians 4:19

Christian Television | Radio | Music

Counteracting the counterfeit by proclaiming the three angels' messages of Revelation 14 to the world.

May 23, 2017

David, Linda, and Jonathan Clore
2645 Arkansas Terrace
Quanemo, KS 66528

Dear Clore family,

It's always a blessing to hear from you! Thank you for keeping me updated on how the Lord is continuing to use you all in ministry for Him. You're right, God calls each one of us to be His witnesses, and I praise Him that you are able to use the 3ABN sharing cards as part of your witness for Him. Thank you for sharing the incredible stories, about God's leading and guiding in your lives, and His hand of protection over your family.

Know that your 3ABN family will be praying for you, as you continue your work on the Ark, and begin writing another book. Continue to have faith in God for He will supply all your needs, according to His riches in glory by Christ Jesus.

Let us pray for each other, that we would be faithful to the work God has called us to do, and would continue to proclaim this gospel message with power!

His Love and Ours,

Danny

Danny Shelton
President & CEO

DS:jm

3ABN.tv

Danny Shelton President CEO
danny.shelton@3abn.org

P.O. Box 220 West Frankfort, IL 62896 phone 618-627-4651 fax 618-627-2726

Christian Television | Radio | Music

Counteracting the counterfeit by proclaiming the three angels' messages of Revelation 14 to the world.

August 10, 2017

David & Linda Clore
2645 Arkansas Terrace
Quenemo, KS 66528

Dear Clore Family,

I always appreciate hearing from you, and learning what the Lord is doing in your lives! Thank you for keeping me updated on the doors God is opening for you all. Praise God that He can forgive and cleanse us, and empower us to live a life of victory. You're right, He wants to transform us into His image, so we will be like Him when He comes again soon. That's why 3ABN exists, as well, to proclaim this undiluted gospel message to a lost and dying world! Thank you for joining hands with us in helping to spread this message.

Know that your 3ABN Family will be praying for you, as you seek to raise funds for publishing your next book through Teach Services. I also so appreciate your prayers for 3ABN and my brother, Kenny, as he recovers after his heart surgery. Our God is faithful to hear and answer!

May God continue to bless your ministry for Him there in Kansas. Remain faithful to Him, and soon we'll hear those words, "Well done, My good and faithful servant."

His Love and Ours,

Danny

Danny Shelton
President & CEO

DS:jm

3ABN.tv

Danny Shelton | President | CEO
danny.shelton@3abn.org

P.O. Box 220 | West Frankfort, IL 62896 | **phone** 618-627-4651 | **fax** 618-627-2726

August 14, 2017

Galatians 6:9; Matthew 5:16

My dear Bro Danny,

It was <u>sooo</u> good to hear from you again! Thanks for writing! Your letters mean <u>sooo</u> much! I know you're a <u>very</u> busy man! We love you and 3ABN and pray for each of you! Thanks <u>sooo</u> much for your prayers for us!! We really do appreciate it!! I know God will hear your prayers! I wish you would have 3ABN prayer line pray for us too! Thanks! We have no phone to call them.

Our prayer requests are for our son, Jonathan. He's on a lot of doctor medicines, ruining his health and life and hard on us, as we try and care for him in the home. Pray he'll see what they are doing to him and listen to the Holy Spirit to change and be converted and be happy in the Lord, like he was as we raised him, as a child, for Jesus! Also, he's paralyzed in his ankles and can't walk! He's bound to a wheelchair. This was caused by his life in sin on drugs that took him away from Jesus and following Him! <u>Please</u> pray God will convict him and convert him <u>soon</u>, and be able to walk again, and want to win souls for Jesus! He loves Jesus, but not willing to change His ways and <u>please</u> the Lord! Your prayers will mean <u>soooo</u> <u>very</u> much to us!! Thanks! God bless each of you at 3ABN! God is using you <u>all</u> in a mighty way! We're <u>so</u> proud of <u>all</u> you're doing for the Lord and His cause! <u>Never</u> <u>give</u> <u>up</u>!

We just sent for 950 more 3ABN sharing cards! We pass them out like leaves of autumn, and we're <u>sooo</u> blessed having a part in sharing 3ABN to others, so they, too, can be blessed and helped to find the truth and be saved! It's such a joy to witness for Jesus by passing out 3ABN sharing cards! People seem <u>so</u> happy to receive them and say, "I'll check it out!" Thanks for making these cards available!

My other prayer request is another <u>BIG</u> prayer request that <u>only</u> God can do! We've been building the "Ark" (our 14 acres in the country) preparing for the time of trouble <u>soon</u> to come upon us! We began in 2001. We've had no trouble with the Building and Planning Committee all these years, and two years ago, an inspector and the sanitation inspector checked over what we were doing and there was no complaints in what we were doing as they checked over everything! Then, a few weeks ago, we received a letter to come to their office to talk about what we were doing out here! My husband stayed in the car and prayed for me, while I went before the "firing squad" to answer their questions! I was there two hours and praise God, He gave me the help and wisdom and knowledge to answer their questions. They said, "You're going to have to sell the cabins or use them as storage!" They said they're coming out to check it out! They haven't come out yet! I told them of the inspectors who came out two years ago, and there were no complaints! I said, "I wouldn't have invested in these cabins, if I had known I was doing anything wrong!"

So, this is where we're at right now! <u>Only</u> God can stop them from destroying the "Ark"!! We've put <u>all</u> our time and money and hard work to prepare the "Ark" for God's people to come to in the time of trouble, when you can't buy or sell and live off the land until we have to flee and leave our little "Arks of safety" for desolate and solitary places! God saved Noah and his Ark and family through the Flood! I know God can save our little "Ark of safety" prepared for God's people to have a refuse to come to when they need to leave these big wicked cities, and they'll have nowhere to flee to, except places God has impressed people in advance to prepare for such a time as this soon to break upon us! So, won't you please pray for our "Ark" to be saved and not destroyed by these people! Thanks! We know Satan is trying to put a stop to what we're doing for Jesus and His people who'll need a place when they can no longer remain safe in the big wicked cities and all these calamities! Thanks again for praying for God to show His power and intervene to save this little "Ark" made for the protection of His people when the storm really breaks upon us! We have faith in God! We claim His promises in *Ministry of Healing*, pp. 469–482, the chapter entitled, "Help in Daily Living" by E.G. White. Also, we claim the Bible promises found in Psalm 56:3; Psalm 55:22; 1 Peter 5:7; Luke 1:37; Mark 10:27; Matthew 21:22. God can do anything!! God can do anything!! We have faith in God!!! I know, Danny, in building 3ABN, you've seen lots of miracles and answers to prayers! Praise God! Thanks for praying for us in the situation we're in! 1 Thessalonians 5:18–28; Philippians 4; Psalm 121. God is all powerful! He's in control of each of His children that love and obey Him!

Now, one more very important prayer request!! I've been writing another book, which will cost us thousands of dollars to have typed and published! So, to have the money to do this, we had ten acres in the "Ark" we sold to a man in Texas. We signed his paper to sell it to him, but we never received the money he said he'd pay us for the land! That was three and a half months ago! Only God can work on his mind to be honest and give us the money he said he'd pay us for our ten acres. We know Satan doesn't want my new book to be published, because it would be a help and a blessing to those who read it, and Satan doesn't want people to be encouraged to get ready for what's soon to break upon us as an "overwhelming surprise," as *8T* p. 28 says, and also, what Sister White says in *Vol 2 Selected Messages* p. 142, "The work of the people of God is to prepare for the events of the future, which will soon come upon them with blinding force."

Please give my love to Kenny and Chris! They and their ministry are in our prayers, too! We need to band together in prayer for one another! There's power in prayer! God bless you all!

Love you, David, Linda & Jonathan xo

P.S. Danny, I really do like your new book out! We've read it two times! David's sister, Hilma Drako, bought us a box and we've spread them out! Several people have told us they're reading it that we've given it to! Praise God, Danny, for you and all you're doing for Jesus! You're amazing how God has been using you to witness for Him! Keep up the good work! God bless you!!!

"It Is More Blessed to Give than to Receive"

Written May 5, 2017

In Acts 20:35, we find this text, "I have showed you all things, how that so labouring ye ought to support the weak, and to remember the words of the Lord Jesus, how he said, It is more blessed to give than to receive."

We've been praying every day for the Lord to <u>please</u> send us money in the mail to help with all our needs! Our Honda car was still in the repair shop—it needed another computer before it could start. Our truck engine had blown, and we were without a truck to haul our building materials we need to build our 24' x 44' building, which we needed money to buy the building materials needed. We, also, needed a 12' x 20' building bought to store our fruit off the trees, and our garden things and our herbs to dry out and also, our walnuts and soybeans and field corn for winter use and when we can't buy or sell, when the Sunday laws will be passed and we won't go along with man's man–made Sunday sabbath but will remain true to God's 7th day Bible Sabbath.

We had been putting all our money on building the "Ark" on our 14 acres we purchased out in the country, where Sister White warns God's people to be, so they can grow their own produce. On p. 9, in E.G. White's book *Country Living* we read, "The time is fast coming when the controlling power of the labor unions will be very oppressive. Again and again the Lord has instructed that our people are to take their families away from the cities, into the country, where they can raise their own provisions; for in the future the problem of buying and selling will be a very serious one. We should now begin to heed the instruction given us over and over again: Get out of the cities into rural districts, where the houses are not crowded closely together, and where you will be free from the interference of enemies." (**Read** Sister White's whole book, *Country Living*. Also, read Elder W.E. Frazee's book, *Another Ark to Build*.) **Read** Genesis 6 and Hebrews 11, the faith chapter.

We've been trying to walk by faith as we've been building our "Ark" to be able to go through the crisis ahead when the Sunday Law will be passed and as Sister White writes in *Desire of Ages* on pp. 121–122, "In the last great conflict of the controversy with Satan those who are loyal to God will see every earthly support cut off. Because they refuse to break His law in obedience to earthly powers, they will be forbidden to buy or sell. It will finally be decreed that they shall be put to death. See Revelation 13:11–17. But to the obedient is given the promise, 'He shall dwell on high: his place of defense shall be the munitions of rocks: bread shall be given him; his waters shall be sure.' Isaiah 33:16. By this promise the children of God will live."

We've been praying about publishing possibly another book, which would cost us thousands of dollars. We prayed and sold some land in Tennessee to help pay for the cost. Then we put the most of it on a 12' x 20' cabin we needed to store our winter supplies in. We only had a little left to put on all our other urgent needs.

I had made out a grocery list and things we really had to have and gave the list to Dad to go to town and get the things we had to have. Jonathan was with him to go and pick up his medicine he had to have refilled and pay for them. When David went to pay for the things he had gotten, he couldn't find his billfold!! He came on home to see if he had left it at home. It wasn't here! We prayed and looked all over the car and his room and the house and outside, but no billfold could be found! We prayed again and looked all over everywhere again! But still no billfold was found! We had some other money that was to be used for other things we needed, so David took that and went on into town again to get the things we needed, but without his billfold and drivers license. We were thankful we had no credit cards to lose! We're free of debt and praise the Lord for that and don't use credit cards! (**Read** *Evangelism*, p. 63; *Counsels on Stewardship*, 257, 272 by E.G. White.)

While David and Jonathan were in town, I was planning on writing on my next book I was thinking of maybe publishing when we could come up with the money for that expense. Again, I prayed for money in the mail, as I went out to check the mail. We were in such desperate need for money to meet all our needs and bills, etc. In the mail, I received a letter from my dear friends, Bill and Mary and Don and Sharon. Mary had sent us two DVDs Don had made, and I sat down and read the letter and watched one of the DVDs, "At the Time Specified, Turkey." After watching it, I decided to give $10 of $65 we lost in David's billfold, if the Lord would please help us find it! I had told David not to report his driver's license lost yet, because maybe God would impress some honest person to find it and send it in the mail to us.

Well, this was on a Friday David lost his billfold, and when he and Jonathan returned from town, it still hadn't been found. He had checked in the parking lot where he had parked and gotten out, and thinking maybe it fell out of his pocket when he had gotten out of the car, but no billfold. When they returned home, we prayed again that the good Lord would please find our billfold for us. I told David that I had promised the Lord $10 to send to Bill and Mary and Don and Sharon to put on their many mission projects they had stepped out on faith to do for the Lord, trusting Him to please supply them with the thousands and thousands of dollars they needed to do this work for the Lord! I said, "If the Lord helps us get our billfold found, we'll donate $10 from the $65 that was in the billfold lost. We, then, on Sabbath Saturday sat down to watch the other DVD we had received in the mail Friday. The title was, "Blessed are the eyes which saw 1843–1844" by Don. After watching that DVD Sabbath morning, I said, "I think we should promise to send the whole $65 in the billfold, if we find it, and not just $10. They have stepped out in faith to do great things for the Lord, and they're praying and trying to raise money to do these wonderful things for the Lord and His cause and we can sacrifice to help them and do what we can to assist them in their projects for Jesus and showing faith that God will come through with the money to help meet our needs." We, then, prayed and promised the Lord to send them the $65 we had lost in our lost billfold, if He would just please help us find our lost billfold. I said to David, after we had prayed, "You go search the car again for the fifth time, and I'll go through the house and your room again and check the chairs and all around." David got his flashlight and went to search the car again, and I began turning the chairs upside down where he had been sitting.

Then, David came running into the house waving the lost billfold he had just found stuck between the two bucket seats in the car! We praised and thanked the good Lord for hearing our prayers to help us find our lost billfold and money! I took the $65 out of the torn–up billfold and said, "This is God's money to be used to help Bill and Mary and Don and Sharon to spread God's truth far and near!" Then, I said, "It's like the widow in Mark 12:42–44 who cast in all she had into the treasury." I said, "God will do exceedingly abundantly above all that we can ask or think, as Ephesians 3:19–21 promises. God will supply all our needs according to His riches in glory by Christ Jesus, as Philippians 4:19 promises! Jesus can do anything, I said, like Luke 1:37 promises, 'For with God nothing shall be impossible.' Also, in Luke 6:38, Jesus says, 'Give, and it shall be given unto you; good measure, pressed down, and shaken together, and running over, shall men give into your bosom. For with the same measure that ye mete withal it shall be measured to you again.' I like the promise in Matthew 6:33 that says, 'But seek ye first the kingdom of God, and his righteousness; and all these things shall be added unto you.'" I, then, said, "God didn't want us to send $10 of the $65, but the whole $65. Then, He found the billfold with the $65 in it, when we had promised to send the whole $65! We know God will somehow and some way, take care of our needs, as He always has! I think of what Jesus said in Acts, 20:35 '… it is more blessed to give than to receive.'" We were so happy to be a part in helping Bill and Mary and Don and Sharon in their faith outreach to do great things for God! We felt so blessed!"

> *Thank you Jesus! We have faith God will come through and continue to supply us with all our needs*

Oh, yes! David, while he was in town looking for his lost billfold and the money in it, went ahead and bought him a $5 billfold at Walmart since he had no billfold now, and the one he had lost was so torn up. So, God has already begun to supply our needs! Praise God! Thank you Jesus! We have faith God will come through and continue to supply us with all our needs. I love the chapter in *Ministry of Healing* by E.G. White, "Help in Daily Living," especially pp. 479–482:

> "Christ in His life on earth made no plans for Himself. He accepted God's plans for Him, and day by day the Father unfolded His plans. So should we depend upon God, that our lives may be the simple outworking of His will. As we commit our ways to Him, He will direct our steps… God never leads His children otherwise than they would choose to be led, if they could see the end from the beginning and discern the glory of the purpose which they are fulfilling as co–workers with Him… Today the Saviour calls us, as He called Matthew and John and Peter, to His work. If our hearts are touched by His love, the question of compensation will not be uppermost in our minds… Many who profess to be Christ's followers have an anxious, troubled heart because they are afraid to trust themselves with God. They do not make a complete surrender to Him, for they shrink from

the consequences that such a surrender may involve. Unless they do make this surrender they cannot find peace… Worry is blind and cannot discern the future; but Jesus sees the end from the beginning. In every difficulty He has His way prepared to bring relief… Our heavenly Father has a thousand ways to provide for us of which we know nothing. Those who accept the one principle of making the service of God supreme, will find perplexities vanish and a plain path before their feet. The faithful discharge of today's duties is the best preparation for tomorrow's trials… Let us be hopeful and courageous. Despondency in God's service is sinful and unreasonable. He knows our every necessity… He has means for the removal of every difficulty, that those who serve Him and respect the means He employs may be sustained. His love is as far above all other love as the heavens are above the earth. He watches over His children with a love that is measureless and everlasting. In the darkest days, when appearances seem most forbidding, have faith in God. He is working out His will, doing all things well in behalf of His people. The strength of those who love and serve Him will be renewed day by day. He is able and willing to bestow upon His servants all the help they need… 2 Corinthians 12:9, 10."

Read: *Vol 2 Selected Messages* pp. 142, 354; *Vol 8 Testimonies for the Church* p. 28 by E.G. White.

Hopefully this experience we had will encourage others to sacrifice to help finish the work and spread the Three Angels Messages while we still have time and money. <u>Soon</u> the doors will close! *Review & Herald* (3/21/1878), p. 91 we read, "Hoarded wealth will soon be worthless. When the decree shall go forth that none shall buy or sell, except they have the mark of the beast, very much means will be of no avail." **Read** in *Early Writings* pp. 42–58 what Sister White writes about making a commitment to sacrifice.

2 Corinthians 12:9–10: "And he said unto me, My grace is sufficient for thee: for my strength is made perfect in weakness. Most gladly therefore will I rather glory in my infirmities, that the power of Christ may rest upon me. Therefore I take pleasure in infirmities, in reproaches, in necessities, in persecutions, in distresses for Christ's sake: for when I am weak, then am I strong."

"Hunger and Thirst After Righteousness"

"Blessed are they which do hunger and thirst after righteousness: for they shall be filled." Matthew 5:6

Written May 14, 2017

Each year the Hummingbirds leave before winter comes on. Then, in Spring, they fly back to their very own spot they had left in the Fall. In April, a friend of ours told us her Hummingbirds hadn't returned yet to their feeder. She had put the nectar out several times for them, and still no sign of them. We had read how they're contaminating the air and the ocean and earth by poisoning the atmosphere with aluminum being sprayed out of the jets flying overhead and ruining the soil and crops and gardens and the water and killing off birds and ocean animals and trees and harmful to man and beasts.

We prayed our little feathered friends would return back home to us safe, after having to fly all those many miles in that contaminated atmosphere and contaminated food source. The birds that leave here for the winter and come back in the Spring are: Baltimore Oriole, Hummingbirds, Bluebirds, Golden Finch, Robins, etc. As we prayed for our birds to return again, we watched and noticed the different birds returning. One time while riding my bike around our circle driveway, I looked up and saw two birds on our electric wire line, and as I looked up to see what kind of birds they were, I lost control of my bike and fell off my bike onto my side onto the hard gravel driveway and hit my head hard on the gravel, and my bike fell on top of me! Praise God the Lord didn't let me get hurt! Thank you Jesus! My bike wasn't hurt either. Praise God!

We were so thankful to God for hearing our prayers to see our birds returning back home again, after being gone all winter. It was so good to hear and enjoy their pretty songs being sung again to their Creator God

I, then, put out the Hummingbird feeder in hopes of seeing our Hummingbirds again. I had already been putting out popcorn kernels to feed the other birds. I watched and saw a beautiful Baltimore Oriole come back home and was drinking from the nectar in the Hummingbird's feeder. We were so thankful to God for hearing our prayers to see our birds returning back home again, after being gone all winter. It was so good to hear and enjoy their pretty songs being sung again to their Creator God.

We had just finished having our morning worship and then, a Baltimore Oriole had drunk the Hummingbird feeder dry of its nectar, and it came to our patio window and sat there looking in the window begging for more nectar. I hurried to make up more nectar for the pretty bird begging at my patio window. Then, while making up the nectar at the kitchen sink, the Baltimore Oriole had flown to my kitchen window and sat there looking in at me making his nectar and chirping for me to hurry up! I said to Dad and Jonathan, "This bird must not feel any fear here in the house, but must feel his Creator God here, because we had just asked Jesus to bless us with His presence in our home and on the "Ark." We thanked God for the birds coming safely back home for us to enjoy. I prayed when I hung the Hummingbird feeder up again, for the Baltimore Oriole to drink from again, after begging at my window for more nectar, that God would please let me see my Hummingbirds coming back home. As I hung the feeder back up in the tree, I heard the sound of Hummingbirds wings fluttering, and then I saw some little Hummingbirds swarming around waiting to come and drink nectar from the feeder. I praised and thanked the good Lord for hearing my prayers to bring my Hummingbirds and other feathered friends back home to our little Garden of Eden place and our little heavenly place we call the "Ark."

It made me think of Psalm 19:7–11 and Psalm 119:131, how we creatures of God's creation, as we feed on His word each day, we should be yearning and pleading and begging for God to please give us more and more wisdom and knowledge of God's word and His truth and to know more and more of His will for our lives and how to please Him and be ready for His soon coming, as we feed on God's word and hunger and thirst after righteousness as Matthew 5:6 promises, and to prepare our lives and characters to be like Jesus and have more and more of His Holy Spirit power, and to be able to share more successfully His words of truth with those people God brings us in touch with to help them get ready and prepared for what's coming with the Sunday Laws soon to be passed and to be ready and prepared for Christ's soon coming. Like we share 3ABN's sharing cards like the leaves of Autumn to help people find the truth by watching 3ABN and to be ready and prepared to stand for Jesus and the true 7th day Sabbath, when the Sunday Law crisis will soon burst upon us! The following quotes of E.G. White will help you see where we are in history.

Read: *8T*, p. 28; *Vol. 2 Selected Messages*, p. 142; *Country Living*, pp. 20–21; *5T*, "The Coming Crisis," pp. 479–454; *5T*, "The Church the Light of the World," pp. 454–467, especially p. 463; Also, *5T*, "Joshua and the Angel," pp. 467–476.

Read, also, *Christ's Object Lessons*, pp. 269–271, and also, *Education*, pp. 262–271, "The Life Work." On p. 267, we read, "We need to follow more closely God's plan of life. To do our best in the work that lies nearest, to commit our ways to God, and to watch for the indications of His providence—these are rules that ensure safe guidance in the choice of an occupation."

Matthew 4:4 says, "But he answered and said, It is written, Man shall not live by bread alone, but by every word that proceedeth out of the mouth of God."

Psalm 40:8: "I delight to do thy will, O my God: yea, thy law is within my heart."

Psalm 50:15: "And call upon me in the day of trouble: I will deliver thee, and thou shalt glorify me."

Read also Isaiah 58, especially verses 5–12; Psalm 34, especially versus 6–9 and 14–20.

Psalm 120:1: "In my distress I cried unto the LORD, and he heard me."

"You Can Gain the Victory Over Sin!"

"I can do all things through Christ which strengtheneth me." Philippians 4:13

Written May 14, 2017

The following are some dreams the Lord gave me:

"Enoch pleased God—Make this your goal! Hebrews 11:5,6."

"No amount of sin—This is the condition we must be in to receive the Seal of God and give the Loud Cry message! Love the LORD! Love the LORD! Stay on the narrow path—The Watcher is measuring your course of action!"

"I saw the red book by E.G. White, *Counsels on Diet and Foods*. Study. Learn to eat smaller portions of food and get used to not eating so much!"

"Place yourself under the control of the Holy Spirit." Hebrews 12:1–7; 1 Corinthians 9:24–27; Isaiah 27:5; *Patriarchs and Prophets* pp. 153–154 by E.G. White on obedience. "Jesus wants to fill us with His Holy Spirit, so he can use us!"

"To have the Holy Spirit we must be obedient!" (1 Samuel 15:22, 23.)

Acts 5:29: "Then Peter and the other apostles answered and said, We ought to obey God rather than men." Also, **read** verses 30–32, "The God of our fathers raised up Jesus, whom ye slew and hanged on a tree. Him hath God exalted with his right hand to be a Prince and a Saviour, for to give repentance to Israel, and forgiveness of sins. And we are his witnesses of these things; and so is also the Holy Ghost, whom God hath given to them that obey him."

Remember, you can gain the victory over sin with God's help! Philippians 4:13 promises, "I can do all things through Christ which strengtheneth me."

Read: Jude 24, "Now unto him that is able to keep you from falling, and to present you faultless before the presence of his glory with exceeding joy."

Read the counsel given in Revelation 3:14–22 by Jesus, especially verse 21, "To him that overcometh will I grant to sit with me in my throne, even as I also overcame, and am set down with my Father in his throne."

Revelation 21:7, 8, 27: "He that overcometh shall inherit all things; and I will be his God, and he shall be my son. But the fearful, and unbelieving, and the abominable, and murderers, and whoremongers, and sorcerers, and idolaters, and all liars, shall have their part in the lake which burneth with fire and brimstone: which is the second death… And there shall in no wise enter into it any thing that defileth, neither whatsoever worketh abomination, or maketh a lie: but they which are written in the Lamb's book of life."

Revelation 22:14: "Blessed are they that do his commandments, that they may have right to the tree of life, and may enter in through the gates into the city."

Read in *Desire of Ages* by E.G. White, chapters 12, "The Temptation" and chapter 13, "The Victory," pp. 114–131. On p. 120, we read, "Jesus met Satan with the words of Scripture. 'It is written,' He said. In every temptation the weapon of His warfare was the word of God."

Matthew 4:4: "But he answered and said, It is written, Man shall not live by bread alone, but by every word that proceedeth out of the mouth of God."

Matthew 6:33: "But seek ye first the kingdom of God, and his righteousness; and all these things shall be added unto you."

On p. 121 of *Desire of Ages*, we continue to read, "When we learn the power of His word, we shall not follow the suggestions of Satan in order to obtain food or to save our lives. Our only questions will be, What is God's command? and what His promise? Knowing these, we shall obey the one, and trust the other." On pp. 122–123, Sister White gives this counsel:

"His (*Christ*) example declares that our only hope of eternal life is through bringing the appetites and passions into subjection to the will of God. In our own strength it is impossible for us to deny the clamors of our fallen nature. Through this channel Satan will bring temptation upon us… And by passing over the ground which man must travel, our Lord has prepared the way for us to overcome… 'Be of good cheer,' He says; 'I have overcome the world.' John 16:33. Let him who is struggling against the power of appetite look to the Saviour in the wilderness of temptation. See Him in His agony upon the cross, as He exclaimed, 'I thirst.' He has endured all that it is possible for us to bear. His victory is ours. Jesus rested upon the wisdom and strength of His heavenly Father. He declares, 'The Lord God will help Me; therefore shall I not be confounded: … and I know that I shall not be ashamed.… Behold, the Lord God will help Me.' Pointing to His own example, He says to us, 'Who is among you that feareth the Lord, … that walketh in darkness, and hath no light? let him trust in the name of the Lord, and stay upon his God.' Isaiah 50:7–10. 'The prince of this world cometh,' said Jesus, 'and hath nothing in Me.' John 14:30. There was in Him nothing that responded to Satan's sophistry. He did not consent to sin. Not even by a thought did He yield to temptation. So it may be with us. Christ's humanity was united with divinity; He was fitted for the conflict by the indwelling of the Holy Spirit. And He came to make us partakers of the divine nature. So long as we are united to Him by faith, sin has no more dominion over us. God reaches for the hand of faith in us to direct it to lay fast hold upon the divinity of Christ, that we may attain to perfection of character.

And how this is accomplished, Christ has shown us. By what means did He overcome in the conflict with Satan? By the word of God. Only by the word could He resist temptation. 'It is written,' He said. And unto us are given 'exceeding great and precious promises: that by these ye might be partakers of the divine nature, having escaped the corruption that is in the world through lust.' 2 Peter 1:4. Every promise in God's word is ours. 'By every word that proceedeth out of the mouth of God' are we to live. When assailed by temptation, look not to circumstances or to the weakness of self, but to the power of the word. All its strength is yours. 'Thy word,' says the psalmist, 'have I hid in mine heart, that I might not sin against Thee.' 'By the word of Thy lips I have kept me from the paths of the destroyer.' Psalm 119:11; 17:4."

References to study: Philippians 4:13; *Desire of Ages* by E.G. White, p. 324; 1 Timothy 2:5; *The Great Controversy*, pp. 45, 46–51, 55, 268–269, 80, 603–634; Revelation 12:17; 1 Timothy 6:11–17; Jude 14–25; *Last Day Events* p. 44; *Early Writings* p. 37; Revelation 22:11–12; *5T* pp. 172–173, 214; *The Great Controversy* pp. 371, 602, 605, 608; *7BC* p. 976; *Testimonies to Ministers and Gospel Workers* p. 233; *Christ's Object Lessons* p. 412; Revelation 3:18; *9T* p. 97; *Early Writings* pp. 269–272; *2SM* pp. 18, 380; *1T* p. 608; *15MR* p. 312, "… He will raise up from among the common people, men and women to do His work, even as of old He called fishermen to be His disciples."

> *We need to listen to the voice of the Lord speaking to us!*

David had a dream, and he heard the word, "Listen" spoken in his dream. We need to listen to the voice of the Lord speaking to us! (Isaiah 30:20–21; 1 Kings 19:11–13; Mark 14:38; Psalm 5:1–5; Psalm 95: 6–9.) **Read**: *6T* p. 393.

On p. 172–173 of *Desire of Ages* by E.G. White, we read:

"'Verily, verily, I say unto thee, Except a man be born of water and of the Spirit, he cannot enter into the kingdom of God.' Nicodemus knew that Christ here referred to water baptism and the renewing of the heart by the Spirit of God… No human invention can find a remedy for the sinning soul… The fountain of the heart must be purified before the streams can become pure… There is a death to self and sin, and a new life altogether. This change can be brought about only by the effectual working of the Holy Spirit… It can no more be explained than can the movements of the wind… Little by little, perhaps unconsciously to the receiver, impressions are made that tend to draw the soul to Christ. These may be received through meditating upon Him, through reading the Scriptures, or through hearing the word from the living preacher. Suddenly, as the Spirit comes with more direct appeal, the soul gladly surrenders itself to Jesus. By many this is called sudden conversion; but it is the result of long wooing by the Spirit of God,—a patient, protracted process.

While the wind is itself invisible, it produces effects that are seen and felt. So the work of the Spirit upon the soul will reveal itself in every act of him who has felt its saving power. When the Spirit of God takes possession of the heart, it transforms the life. Sinful thoughts are put away, evil deeds are renounced; love, humility, and peace take the place of anger, envy, and strife. Joy takes the place of sadness, and the countenance reflects the light of heaven. No one sees the hand that lifts the burden, or beholds the light descend from the courts above. The blessing comes when by faith the soul surrenders itself to God. Then that power which no human eye can see creates a new being in the image of God."

My aunt Ruby had memorized this quote and would repeat it often. This is what we pray the Lord will do for our son, Jonathan, soon and deliver him from the hold Satan has on him with these medicines he's on, with all their bad side effects.

Read: *Desire of Ages* the 69th chapter, "On the Mount of Olives," pp. 627–636, especially p. 636; Isaiah 45:22; John 3:3, 14–16; 2 Corinthians 3:18; Philippians 2:5, 12, 13; 1 John 1:7, 9; 2 Peter 3:9, 11; 2 Timothy 3:1–17; James 4:7, 8, 10; 1 Thessalonians 4:3, 4, 7; *Education* by E.G. White, chapter on "Faith and Prayer," pp. 253–261, especially pp. 257–258; Colossians 2:9, 10; Mark 11:22–26; Acts 3:19, 20; *Desire of Ages* by E.G. White, p. 466; *Christian Service* by E.G. White, pp. 68, 71, 154.

On p. 68 of *Christian Service* we read, "Those who stand as leaders in the church of God are to realize that the Saviour's commission is given to all who believe in His name. God will send forth into His vineyard many who have not been dedicated to the ministry by the laying on of hands." On p. 154, Sister White writes, "I saw that the work of present truth should engage the interest of all. The publication of truth is God's ordained plan, as a means of warning, comforting, reproving, exhorting, or convicting all to whose notice the silent, voiceless messengers may be brought. Angels of God have a part to act in preparing hearts to be sanctified by the truths published, that they may be prepared for the solemn scenes before them."

Read, also, the book, *The Crisis Ahead* by Robert Olson, the chapter 17, "Perfection in Christ," pp. 137–154. He quotes Hebrews 12:14, and then quotes Sister White in *Messages to Young People* p. 144, "He who enters heaven must have a character that is without spot or wrinkle or any such thing. Naught that defileth can ever enter there. In all the redeemed host not one defect will be seen." He quotes *Desire of Ages* by E.G. White on p. 311. He also quotes *Acts of the Apostles*, p. 531 by E.G. White and also *Vol 1 Selected Messages*, p. 82; *The Great Controversy*, p. 623; *Christ's Object Lessons*, p. 332; *Vol 5 Testimonies for the Church*, p. 53. **Read** what Sister White wrote in *Review & Herald* December 13, 1892, "And as we near the close of this earth's history, we either rapidly advance in Christian growth, or we rapidly retrograde toward the world."

Read in the book, *Thoughts From the Mount of Blessing* by E.G. White, pp. 116–119; Matthew 6:13; *Last Day Events* by E.G. White, the chapters, 4–6, 12–15. On p. 154, we read, "Afflictions, crosses, temptations, adversity, and our varied trials are God's workmen to refine us, sanctify us, and fit us for the heavenly garner." Also, we read in Sister White's book, *My Life Today*, the readings for November entitled, "A Victorious Life," pp. 309–338. The books by Sister White, *Steps to Christ* and *The Sanctified Life* are a must read. **Read** about the sanctified life in Sister's White's book, *My Life Today* for September's reading entitled, "Sanctification," pp. 248–277. On p. 248, we read, "Genuine sanctification ... is nothing less than a daily dying to self and daily conformity to the will of God." **Read** in *My Life Today* also February's readings, "A Spirit–filled Life," the gifts of the Holy Spirit, pp. 36–63. On p. 61, Sister White writes, "Those who had been the bitterest opponents of the truth became her champions."

Read in *Vol. 7 SDA Bible Commentary on E.G. White Comments*, pp. 908–909 on sanctification. Also, *Vol. 5 SDA Bible Commentary on E.G. White Comments* on p. 1,110. She writes about the two parties and two banners. "All rank either under the banner of the obedient or under the banner of the disobedient."

Read in *Christ's Object Lessons*, p. 319 what Sister White says, "There will be no future probation in which to prepare for eternity. It is in this life that we are to put on the robe of Christ's righteousness."

In *Vol 6 Testimonies for the Church* by E.G. White, we read on pp. 110–111, "In our work more attention should be given to the temperance reform. Every duty that calls for reform involves repentance, faith, and obedience. It means the uplifting of the soul to a new and nobler life… Christ is a risen Saviour, and there is healing in His wings… It is laying right hold of God through Jesus Christ that will gain the victory." Continue to read p. 140, "Obedience to every word of God is another condition of success. Victories are not gained by ceremonies or display, but by simple obedience to the highest General, the Lord God of heaven. He who trusts in this Leader will never know defeat… We must understand that a soldier's life is one of aggressive warfare, of perseverance and endurance. For Christ's sake we are to endure trials. We are not engaged in mimic battles. We have to meet most powerful adversaries; for 'we wrestle not against flesh and blood, but against principalities, against powers, against the rulers of the darkness of this world, against spiritual wickedness in high places.' Ephesians 6:12. We are to find our strength just where the early disciples found their strength: 'These all continued with one accord in prayer and supplication.' 'And they were all filled with the Holy Ghost, and they spake the word of God with boldness. And the multitude of them that believed were of one heart and of one soul.' Acts 1:14, 4:31, 32."

Read in *Vol 8 Testimonies for the Church* by E.G. White, on pp. 9–23. On p. 19, we read "It is His (*Christ's*) purpose that every Christian shall be surrounded with a spiritual atmosphere of light and peace. There is no limit to the usefulness of the one who, putting self aside, makes room for the working of the Holy Spirit upon his heart and lives a life wholly consecrated to God."

Read *Early Writings* by E.G. White "Preparation for the End," pp. 69–78. On p. 78, Sister White writes, "I recommend to you, dear reader, the Word of God as the rule of your faith and practice. By that Word we are to be judged. God has, in that Word, promised to give visions in the 'last days'; not for a new rule of faith, but for the comfort of His people, and to correct those who err from Bible truth. Thus God dealt with Peter when He was about to send him to preach to the Gentiles. (Acts 10.)"

Read in *Vol. 1 Testimonies for the Church* by E.G. White, pp. 185–195, "The Laodicean Church," especially read p. 187, "Those who come up to every point, and stand every test, and overcome, be the price what it may, have heeded the counsel of the True Witness, and they will receive the latter rain, and thus be fitted for translation."

Also, in *Vol. 1 Testimonies for the Church* pp. 123–137, **read** "Prepare to Meet The Lord." **Read**, 2 Thessalonians 2:9–12, 13; *Patriarchs and Prophets* by E.G. White, pp. 303–314, "The Law Given to Israel." (This chapter is based on Exodus chapters 19 to 24); *Prophets and Kings* by E.G. White, chapter 34, "Jeremiah," pp. 407–421 (especially pp. 415–417); *Prophets and Kings* chapter 22 "Nineveh, That Great City," pp. 265–278 (especially pp. 274–278).

On p. 278 we read, "God's message for the inhabitants of earth today is, 'Be ye also ready: for in such an hour as ye think not the Son of man cometh.' Matthew 24:44... The storm of God's wrath is gathering; and those only will stand who respond to the invitations of mercy, as did the inhabitants of Nineveh under the preaching of Jonah, and become sanctified through obedience to the laws of the divine Ruler."

In *Vol. 5 Testimonies for the Church*, **read** "The Testimonies Slighted," pp. 62–84. Also, **read** "The Seal of God," pp. 207–216; pp. 217–235, "An Appeal"; p. 425 how the Good Shepherd is searching out those who are wandering in crooked ways and wanting to bring them back to the path of safety and peace. On pp. 711–718 in *Vol 5 Testimonies for the Church*, we read "The Impending Conflict."

In a dream God gave me to read this chapter, "The Impending Conflict." In the dream God gave me, He said, "Watchman, what of the night?!" On p. 715, Sister White writes, "The people need to be aroused in regard to the dangers of the present time. The watchmen are asleep. We are years behind. Let the chief watchmen feel the urgent necessity of taking heed to themselves, lest they lose the opportunities given them to see the dangers."

Read E.G. White's book, *Maranatha—The Lord is Coming*. **Read** the whole book and read also, the whole book *The Great Controversy* by E.G. White; 2 Peter 3:9–14; *Vol 2 Selected Messages* p. 117; *Testimonies to Ministers and Gospel Workers* pp. 364–373 entitled, "Under Which Banner?"

Read in Sister White's book, *My Life Today*, p. 343, "The judgments of God are in the land. They speak in solemn warning, saying: 'Be ye also ready: for in such an hour as ye think not the Son of man cometh'... We are living in the closing scenes of this earth's history... We have no time—not a moment—to lose. Let us not be found sleeping on guard... Let us persuade men and women everywhere to repent and flee from the wrath to come. Let us arouse them to immediate preparation, for we little know what is before us." While writing this article, I had a dream. It was the song, "Is Your All on the Altar?"

I also dreamt the song, "I Surrender All."

I Surrender All

1. All to Jesus I surrender, All to Him I freely give;
2. All to Jesus I surrender, Make my, Savior, wholly Thine;
3. All to Jesus I surrender, Lord, I give myself to Thee;

I will ever love and trust Him, In His presence daily live.
Let me feel Thy Holy Spirit, Truly know that Thou art mine.
Fill me with Thy love and power, Let Thy blessing fall on me.

I surrender all, I surrender all;
I surrender all, I surrender all;

All to Thee, my blessed Savior I surrender all.

Text: Judson W. Van DeVenter, 1855-1939
Tune: Winfield S. Weeden, 1847-1908

87 87 Refrain
SURRENDER
www.hymnary.org/text/all_to_jesus_i_surrender

This hymn is in the public domain. You may freely use this score for personal and congregational worship. If you reproduce the score, please credit *Hymnary.org* as the source.

God's Ten Wonderful Provision for Victorious Living by Gordon Collier: 1. The Holy Spirit 2. Truth 3. Faith 4. Prayer 5. Suffering 6. The Health Message 7. Christian Service 8. Stewardship 9. The Angels 10. Obedience

Sister White writes in *Sons and Daughters of God* p. 45, "Exceeding great is our salvation for ample provision has been made through the righteousness of Christ, that we may be pure, entire, wanting nothing."

To help us be ready for Christ's soon return we need to:

Get rid of sin and watch and pray and prepare to meet the Lord and know the truth and share it with others and shine for Jesus. Hebrews 12:1–7. Remember, the Day of Judgment is coming, prepared for it or not. We all have to "Face Our Life's Record," (the Investigative Judgment) as *The Great Controversy* by Sister White writes on pp. 479–491. **Read** Philippians 4:13 and Jude 24. Also, read in *The Great Controversy*, chapter 27, "Modern Revivals," pp. 461–478, especially p. 464. God gave me three dreams. I heard these words spoken: "Press on soldiers! Press on!" Another dream was "Never give up! Jesus is coming!" And the other dream: I saw people experiencing the 7 Last Plagues and then Jesus coming, and people running and crying for the rocks and the mountains to fall on them and hide them from Jesus' coming! Revelation 6:14–17.

> *Get rid of sin and watch and pray and prepare to meet the Lord and know the truth and share it with others and shine for Jesus*

Read: *Ministry of Healing* by E.G. White, pp. 26, 66, 91, 114, 115, 509. Read: 1 John 4:10–12; 1 John 5:2, 3; 1 John 3:10–14; *Vol. 3 Selected Messages* by E.G. White, chapter 56, "As We Near the End," pp. 403–412; also, chapter 57 "The Last Great Struggle," pp. 413–431; *Last Day Events* by E.G. White, pp. 37–42, 64, 72, 74, 80, 90; *Maranatha* by E.G. White, p. 108 "A Time For Decision!"; Joshua 24:15; Matthew 12:30; Mark 12:29–31.

Study the book, *Counsels on Diet and Foods* by E.G. White, especially the first ten sections.

Read: 1 John 3; *Vol. 7 SDA Bible Commentary* pp. 908, 922; *Pacific Union Recorder* (1/5/1905); *Review & Herald* (1/7/1902); *Signs of the Times* (5/10/1910); *2 Manuscript Releases* pp. 185–186; *Spalding and Magan Collections* pp. 364, 365, 410; *Testimonies to Ministers and Gospel Workers* p. 79.

Read: 1 Corinthians 15:56, 57; Romans 1:16; 1 John 5:4, 5; Quotes of E.G. White: *The Great Controversy*, pp. 469, 619, 623; *Vol 2 Testimonies for the Church*, p. 140; *Testimonies to Ministers and Gospel Workers*, p. 50; *Vol 9 Testimonies for the Church*, pp. 154, 167–172; *Vol 5 Testimonies for the Church*, pp. 53, 207–216 "The Seal of God"; and also pp. 217–235, "An Appeal"; and also pp. 532–541, "Practical Godliness."

I once read this little caption somewhere that said, "A life not lived for others—is not worth living." Matthew 7:12.

Read: *Vol 4 Testimonies for the Church* by E.G. White, "The Testing Process," pp. 83–94, especially p. 87–90.

One day God impressed Dad to read in *Counsels on Diet and Foods* by E.G. White, the chapter on "Control of Appetite," pp. 145–170. He said to me, "Read this chapter and put it in your book you're writing to help people gain the victory over appetite." So, I added it to this article, "You Can Gain the Victory Over Sin!" (Read the whole book!)

Read the startling, but true books by Joe Crews, *Creeping Compromise* and *Reaping the Whirlwind*. Read this chapter, "Satan's War Against Perfection" in the *Reaping the Whirlwind* book. Consider these significant statements by E.G. White: *Vol 1 Testimonies for the Church*, pp. 187, 619; *Evangelism* p. 702; *Vol 5 Testimonies for the Church*, p. 214, 676; *Lift Him Up* p. 144.

Read: *Desire of Ages* by E.G. White, pp. 509, 671; *Vol 4 Testimonies for the Church*, pp. 28–43, "Indulgence of Appetite," by E.G. White, read especially p. 35.

In *Maranatha* by Sister White, we read on p. 224, "Everyone who by faith obeys God's commandments, will reach the condition of sinlessness in which Adam lived before his transgression." (Read, also, p. 225 in *Maranatha* and the August section on "Sanctification, the Sealing and the Sanctuary").

Read: *Testimonies to Ministers and Gospel Workers*, pp. 440–441 by E.G. White, "It is the privilege of every son of God to be a true Christian moment by moment; then he has all heaven enlisted on his side. He has Christ abiding in his heart by faith."

In *Counsels on Diet and Foods* by E.G. White, she writes on p. 163, "The controlling power of appetite will prove the ruin of thousands, when, if they had conquered on this point, they would have had moral power to gain the victory over every other temptation of Satan. But those who are slaves to appetite will fail in perfecting Christian character."

Read: Last Day Events by E.G. White, pp. 192–193, chapter 13, "The Latter Rain"; *Vol 7 SDA Bible Commentary of E.G. White Comments* on pp. 960–961

Is Your All on the Altar?

Elisha Albright Hoffman, 1905

Public Domain
Courtesy of the Cyber Hymnal™

154 | *The Just Shall Live by Faith*

Jesus, I My Cross Have Taken

1. Je - sus, I my cross have ta - ken, All to leave, and fol - low Thee;
Des - ti - tute, des - pised, for - sa - ken, Thou, from hence, my all shall be;
Pe - rish ev' - ry fond am - bi - tion, All I've sought or hoped or known;
Yet how rich is my con - di - tion: God and heav'n are still my own!

2. Let the world des - pise and leave me, They have left my Sa - vior, too;
Hu - man hearts and looks de - ceive me, Thou art not, like man, un - true;
And, while Thou shalt smile up - on me, God of wis - dom, love, and might,
Foes may hate, and friends may shun me: Show Thy face, and all is bright.

3. Haste thee on from grace to glo - ry, Armed by faith, and winged by prayer;
Heav'n's e - ter - nal days be - fore thee, God's own hand shall guide thee there;
Soon shall close thy earth - ly mis - sion, Swift shall pass thy pil - grim days;
Hope shall change to glad fru - i - tion, Faith to sight, and prayer to praise.

Text: Henry F. Lyte, 1793-1847
Tune: Attr. Wolfgang A. Mozart, 1756-1791,
  in Leavitt's *The Christian Lyre*, 1831;
  arr. Hubert P. Main, 1839-1925

87 87D
ELLESDIE
www.hymnary.org/text/jesus_i_my_cross_have_taken_all_to_le

This hymn is in the public domain. You may freely use this score for personal and congregational worship. If you reproduce the score, please credit *Hymnary.org* as the source.

"The Schools of the Prophets 1, 2, 3."

The Following Are 1, 2, 3 Parts

"PART ONE"

Written May 22, 2017

On March 12, 2017, I dreamt I saw this written in my dream: "The Schools of the Prophets 1, 2, 3." (Read chapter 58, "The Schools of the Prophets" in *Patriarchs and Prophets* by E.G. White on pp. 592–602.)

This is what our "Ark" is—a "school of the prophets"—to teach what was taught to the students back then in Samuel's day and Elijah's day in their schools and Elisha too, in his time working with the schools of the prophets. Read *Prophets and Kings* chapter 17, "The Call of Elisha," by E.G. White, pp. 217–228. On p. 217, it says, "In the quietude of country life, under the teaching of God and nature and the discipline of useful work, he received the training in habits of simplicity and of obedience to his parents and to God that helped to fit him for the high position he was afterward to occupy." On p. 218, we read, "By faithfulness in little things, Elisha was preparing for weightier trusts. Day by day, through practical experience, he gained a fitness for a broader, higher work. He learned to serve; and in learning this, he learned also how to instruct and lead. The lesson is for all. None can know what may be God's purpose in His discipline; but all may be certain that faithfulness in little things is the evidence of fitness for greater responsibilities. Every act of life is a revelation of character, and he only who in small duties proves himself 'a workman that needeth not to be ashamed' can be honored by God with higher service. 2 Timothy 2:15. He who feels that it is of no consequence how he performs the smaller tasks proves himself unfit for a more honored position."

Read on p. 219, "But because they can serve only in little things, they think themselves justified in doing nothing. In this they err. A man may be in the active service of God while engaged in the ordinary, everyday duties—while felling trees, clearing the ground, or following the plow. The mother who trains her children for Christ is as truly working for God as is the minister in the pulpit. Many long for special talent with which to do a wonderful work, while the duties lying close at hand, the performance of which would make the life fragrant, are lost sight of. Let such ones take up the duties lying directly in their pathway. Success depends not so much on talent as on energy and willingness. It is not the possession of splendid talents that enables us to render acceptable service, but the conscientious performance of daily duties, the contented spirit, the unaffected, sincere interest in the welfare of others. In the humblest lot true excellence may be found. The commonest tasks, wrought with loving faithfulness, are beautiful in God's sight."

On p. 220, we read, "Not for any worldly advantage would he forgo the opportunity of becoming God's messenger or sacrifice the privilege of association with His servant… Without hesitation he left a home where he was beloved, to attend the prophet in his uncertain life. Had Elisha asked Elijah what was expected of him,—what would be his work,—he would have been answered: God knows; He will make it known to you. If you wait upon the Lord, He will answer your every question. You may come with me if you have evidence that God has called you. Know for yourself that God stands back of me, and that it is His voice you hear. If you can count everything but dross that you may win the favor of God, come." On p. 221, continue reading, "Similar to the call that came to Elisha was the answer given by Christ to the young ruler who asked Him the question, 'What good thing shall I do, that I may have eternal life?' 'If thou wilt be perfect,' Christ replied, 'go and sell that thou hast, and give to the poor, and thou shalt have treasure in heaven: and come and follow Me.' Matthew 19:16, 21. Elisha accepted the call to service, casting no backward glance at the pleasures and comforts he was leaving. The young ruler, when he heard the Saviour's words, 'went away sorrowful: for he had great possessions.' Verse 22. He was not willing to make the sacrifice. His love for his possessions was greater than his love for God. By his refusal to renounce all for Christ, he proved himself unworthy of a place in the Master's service. The call to place all on the altar of service comes to each one. We are not all asked to serve as Elisha served, nor are we all bidden to sell everything we have; but God asks us to give His service the first place in our lives, to allow no day to pass without doing something to advance His work in the earth. He does not expect from all the same kind of service. One may be called to ministry in a foreign land; another may be asked to give of his means for the support of gospel work. God accepts the offering of each. It is the consecration of the life and all its interests, that is necessary. Those who make this consecration will hear and obey the call of Heaven."

On p. 222–227:

"Individually we are to stand in our lot, saying, 'Here am I; send me.'… Elisha's life after uniting with Elijah was not without temptations. Trials he had in abundance; but in every emergency he relied on God. He was tempted to think of the home that he had left, but to this temptation he gave no heed. Having put his hand to the plow, he was resolved not to turn back, and through test and trial he proved true to his trust. Ministry comprehends far more than preaching the word. It means training young men as Elijah trained Elisha, taking them from their ordinary duties, and giving them responsibilities to bear in God's work—small responsibilities at first, and larger ones as they gain strength and experience. There are in the ministry men of faith and prayer, men who can say, 'That which was from the beginning, which we have heard, which we have seen with our eyes, which we have looked upon, and our hands have handled, of the Word of life; … that which we have seen and heard declare we unto you.' 1 John 1:1–3. Young, inexperienced workers should be trained by actual labor in connection with these experienced servants of God. Thus they will learn how to bear burdens… God has honored them by choosing them for His service and by placing them where they can gain greater fitness for it, and they should be humble, faithful, obedient, and willing to sacrifice. If they submit to God's discipline, carrying out His directions and choosing His servants as their counselors, they will develop into righteous, high–principled, steadfast men, whom God can entrust with responsibilities… As the gospel is proclaimed in its purity, men will be called from the plow and from the common commercial business vocations that largely occupy the mind and will be educated in connection with men of experience. As they learn to labor effectively, they will proclaim the truth with power. Through most wonderful workings of divine providence, mountains of difficulty will be removed and cast into the sea."

"PART TWO"

Continue reading Sister White's book, *Prophets and Kings*, on pp. 224–228:

"As Elijah's successor, Elisha, by careful, patient instruction, must endeavor to guide Israel in safe paths. His association with Elijah, the greatest prophet since the days of Moses, prepared him for the work that he was soon to take up alone… The schools of the prophets, established by Samuel, had fallen into decay during the years of Israel's apostasy. Elijah re–established these schools, making provision for young men to gain an education that would lead them to magnify the law and make it honorable… Especially did he [Elijah] instruct them concerning their high privilege of loyally maintaining their allegiance to the God of heaven. He also impressed upon their minds the importance of letting simplicity mark every feature of their education. Only in this way could they receive the mold of heaven and go forth to work in the ways of the Lord.

> *I pray the Lord will please give us a triple portion of God's Spirit to be upon us and help us to stand through the trying times ahead of us*

The heart of Elijah was cheered as he saw what was being accomplished by means of these schools… Unknown to Elijah, the revelation that he was to be translated had been made known to his disciples in the schools of the prophets, and in particular to Elisha. And now the tried servant of the man of God kept close beside him… Elisha asked not for worldly honor, or for a high place among the great men of earth. That which he craved was a large measure of the Spirit that God had bestowed so freely upon the one about to be honored with translation. He knew that nothing but the Spirit which had rested upon Elijah could fit him to fill the place in Israel to which God had called him, and so he asked, 'I pray thee, let a double portion of thy Spirit be upon me.'"

I pray the Lord will please give us a triple portion of God's Spirit to be upon us and help us to stand through the trying times ahead of us! She continues:

"Elijah was a type of the saints who will be living on the earth at the time of the second advent of Christ and who will be 'changed, in a moment, in the twinkling of an eye, at the last trump,' without tasting of death. 1 Corinthians 15:51, 52. It was as a representative of those who shall be thus translated that Elijah, near the close of Christ's earthly ministry, was permitted to stand with Moses by the side of the Saviour on the mount of transfiguration. In these glorified ones, the disciples saw in miniature a representation of the kingdom of the redeemed. They beheld Jesus clothed with the light of heaven; they heard the 'voice out of the cloud' (Luke 9:35), acknowledging Him as the Son of God; they saw Moses, representing those who will be raised from the dead at the time of the second advent; and there also stood Elijah, representing those who at the close of earth's history will be changed from mortal to immortal and be translated to heaven without seeing death. In the desert, in loneliness and discouragement, Elijah had said that he had had enough of life and had prayed that he might die. But the Lord in His mercy had not taken him at his word. There was yet a great work for Elijah to do; and when his work was done, he was not to perish in discouragement and solitude. Not for him the descent into the tomb, but the ascent with God's angels to the presence of His glory. 'And Elisha saw it, and he cried, My father, my father, the chariot of Israel, and the horsemen thereof. And he saw him no more: and he took hold of his own clothes, and rent them in two pieces. He took up also the mantle of Elijah that fell from him, and went back, and stood by the bank of Jordan; and he took the mantle of Elijah that fell from him, and smote the waters, and said, Where is the Lord God of Elijah? and when he also had smitten the waters, they parted hither and thither: and Elisha went over. And when the sons of the prophets which were to view at Jericho saw him, they said, The Spirit of Elijah doth rest on Elisha. And they came to meet him, and bowed themselves to the ground before him.' 2 Kings 2:12–15. When the Lord in His providence sees fit to remove from His work those to whom He has given wisdom, He helps and strengthens their successors, if they will look to Him for aid and will walk in His ways. They may be even wiser than their predecessors; for they may profit by their experience and learn wisdom from their mistakes. Henceforth Elisha stood in Elijah's place. He who had been faithful in that which was least was to prove himself faithful also in much."

Read: *Vol 6 Testimonies for the Church* by E.G. White, section 3; *Education*, pp. 126–144. I once read this thought: "The main problem with common sense, is that it is so uncommon."

In *Vol 6 Testimonies for the Church*, p. 128, we read, "The third angel's message, the great testing truth for this time, is to be taught in all our institutions... Time is short. The perils of the last days are upon us, and we should watch and pray, and study and heed the lessons that are given us in the books of Daniel and the Revelation."

On p. 129, "By pen and voice, knowledge should be imparted which will be meat in due season, not only to the young, but to those of mature years also." On p. 130, "Throughout the world there should be a reform in Bible study, for it is needed now as never before... A knowledge of God and of Jesus Christ 'whom He has sent' is the highest education… Bible study is especially needed in the schools. Students should be rooted and grounded in divine truth. Their attention should be called, not to the assertions of men, but to the word of God. Above all other books, the word of God must be our study, the great textbook, the basis of all education."

On p. 132, "Christ must be brought into all the studies, that students may drink in the knowledge of God and may represent Him in character… The study of God's word should take the place of the study of those books that have led minds into mysticism and away from the truth. Its living principles, woven into our lives, will be our safeguard in trials and temptations; its divine instruction is the only way to success. As the test comes to every soul, there will be apostasies. Some will prove to be traitors, heady, high–minded, and self–sufficient, and will turn away from the truth, making shipwreck of faith. Why? Because they did not live 'by every word that proceedeth out of the mouth of God.' They did not dig deep and make their foundation sure."

On p. 133, "What, then, shall be the character of the education given in our schools? Shall it be according to the wisdom of this world or according to that wisdom that is from above? Will not teachers awake to their responsibility in this matter and see that the word of God has a larger place in the instruction given in our schools?" On p. 134, "It should never be forgotten that Christ Himself has charge of our institutions. The best ministerial talent should be employed in teaching the Bible in our schools." On p. 137, "It is possible to have too many educational facilities centered in one place. Smaller schools, conducted after the plan of the schools of the prophets, would be a far greater blessing."

On p. 139, "Schools should be established, not such elaborate schools as those at Battle Creek and College View, but more simple schools with more humble buildings, and with teachers who will adopt the same plans that were followed in the schools of the prophets… In the work of reform, teachers and students should co–operate, each working to the best advantage to make our schools such as God can approve. Unity of action is necessary to success… The soldiers of Christ also must act in harmony… When we are one with Christ, we shall be united among ourselves."

In *Ministry of Healing* by E.G. White, p. 186, "Various industries were taught in the schools of the prophets, and many of the students sustained themselves by manual labor."

"PART THREE"

Read in Sister White's book, *Education*, pp. 45–50 entitled, "The Schools of the Prophets." On p. 45:

"Through unfaithfulness in the home, and idolatrous influences without, many of the Hebrew youth received an education differing widely from that which God had planned for them. They learned the ways of the heathen.

To meet this growing evil, God provided other agencies as an aid to parents in the work of education. From the earliest times, prophets had been recognized as teachers divinely appointed. In the highest sense the prophet was one who spoke by direct inspiration, communicating to the people the messages he had received from God. But the name was given also to those who, though not so directly inspired, were divinely called to instruct the people in the works and ways of God. For the training of such a class of teachers, Samuel, by the Lord's direction, established the schools of the prophets. These schools were intended to serve as a barrier against the wide-spreading corruption, to provide for the mental and spiritual welfare of the youth, and to promote the prosperity of the nation by furnishing it with men qualified to act in the fear of God as leaders and counselors. To this end, Samuel gathered companies of young men who were pious, intelligent, and studious. These were called the sons of the prophets. As they studied the word and the works of God, His life-giving power quickened the energies of mind and soul, and the students received wisdom from above. The instructors were not only versed in divine truth, but had themselves enjoyed communion with God, and had received the special endowment of His Spirit… The pupils of these schools sustained themselves by their own labor in tilling the soil or in some mechanical employment. In Israel this was not thought strange or degrading; indeed, it was regarded as a sin to allow children to grow up in ignorance of useful labor. Every youth, whether his parents were rich or poor, was taught some trade. Even though he was to be educated for holy office, a knowledge of practical life was regarded as essential to the greatest usefulness. Many, also, of the teachers supported themselves by manual labor. In both the school and the home much of the teaching was oral; but the youth also learned to read the Hebrew writings, and the parchment rolls of the Old Testament Scriptures were open to their study. The chief subjects of study in these schools were the law of God, with the instruction given to Moses, sacred history, sacred music, and poetry. In the records of sacred history were traced the footsteps of Jehovah. The great truths set forth by the types in the service of the sanctuary were brought to view, and faith grasped the central object of all that system—the Lamb of God, that was to take away the sin of the world. A spirit of devotion was cherished. Not only were the students taught the duty of prayer, but they were taught how to pray, how to approach their Creator, how to exercise faith in Him, and how to understand and obey the teachings of His Spirit. Sanctified intellect brought forth from the treasure house of God things new and old, and the Spirit of God was manifested in prophecy and sacred song. These schools proved to be one of the means most effective in promoting that righteousness which 'exalteth a nation.' Proverbs 14:34… The principles taught in the schools of the prophets were the same that molded David's character and shaped his life. The word of God was his instructor… In the early life of Solomon also are seen the results of God's method of education… Above every earthly good he asked of God a wise and understanding heart… In the reigns of David and Solomon, Israel reached the height of her greatness…

But in the midst of prosperity lurked danger… As he cast off his allegiance to God, Solomon lost the mastery of himself… Solomon dishonored himself, dishonored Israel, and dishonored God…

Though he afterward repented, his repentance did not prevent the fruition of the evil he had sown. The discipline and training that God appointed for Israel would cause them, in all their ways of life, to differ from the people of other nations. This peculiarity, which should have been regarded as a special privilege and blessing, was to them unwelcome. The simplicity and self-restraint essential to the highest development they sought to exchange for the pomp and self-indulgence of heathen peoples. To be 'like all the nations' (1 Samuel 8:5) was their ambition. God's plan of education was set aside, His authority disowned.

In the rejection of the ways of God for the ways of men, the downfall of Israel began. Thus also it continued, until the Jewish people became a prey to the very nations whose practices they had chosen to follow…

The experiences of Israel were recorded for our instruction… 1 Corinthians 10:11. With us, as with Israel of old, success in education depends on fidelity in carrying out the Creator's plan. Adherence to the principles of God's word will bring as great blessings to us as it would have brought to the Hebrew people."

Also, read on p. 61, *Education* by E.G. White,

"The lesson is for all. None can know what may be God's purpose in His discipline; but all may be certain that faithfulness in little things is the evidence of fitness for greater responsibilities. Every act of life is a revelation of character, and he only who in small duties proves himself 'a workman that needeth not to be ashamed' (2 Timothy 2:15) will be honored by God with weightier trusts."

In *Vol. 5 Testimonies for the Church*, pp. 156–157, Sister White writes, "Brethren, awake from your life of selfishness, and act like consistent Christians… The wants of the cause will continually increase as we near the close of time. Means is needed to give young men a short course of study in our schools, to prepare them for efficient work in the ministry and in different branches of the cause. We are not coming up to our privilege in this matter. All schools among us will soon be closed up. How much more might have been done had men obeyed the requirements of Christ in Christian beneficence… The first Christian church had not the privileges and opportunities we have… They cast in their all and held themselves in readiness to go or come at the Lord's bidding… Let us individually go to work to stimulate others by our example of disinterested benevolence."

Read: *Counsels to Parents, Teachers and Students* by E.G. White, pp. 168, 465–484; *Last Day Events* by E.G. White, pp. 80–82; *Vol 6 Testimonies for the Church*, p. 162–167, "Words From a Heavenly Instructor"; chapter 35, "The Rebellion of Korah" in *Patriarchs and Prophets*, pp. 395–405, by E.G. White. This chapter 35 is based on Numbers 16 and 17; *Vol 5 Testimonies for the Church* pp. 66 and 290 by E.G. White and pp. 62–84, "The Testimonies Slighted." Sister White was more than a prophet, and so was Moses and John the Baptist, Matthew 11:7–11.

Read also *Vol. 2 SDA Bible Commentary*, p. 1,036, on 2 Kings 2:1–8.

"THE ARK"

There is a place of safety,
It's found <u>only</u> in the Lord!
He's our City of Refuge,
He's our Anchor in the storm!

He's "<u>THE ARK</u>" of our salvation,
It is in Him we can trust.
He's the Rock of our foundation,
He'll never leave nor fail us!

Cause He'll never leave nor fail us,
We can abide in His love.
We can go to Him in prayer,
Knowing He watches from above!

When He warns us of His coming,
When He tells us we're to prepare,
Then we'll do what the Lord tells us,
Having faith and trust without fear!

By daily studying God's Word,
We're to follow His directions,
Then we know what we are to do,
We're to build "THE ARK" for protection!

Angels are promised to watch,
While we prepare for the storm.
Before the Sunday laws are passed,
Like Noah, the people we will warn!

Like the Schools of the prophets,
Way back there in Bible times,
We'll teach the people God's Word,
And how to live through hard times!

In "<u>THE ARK</u>," we will teach them how to
Grow gardens and depend on God,
Also, to learn God's promises,
And to have faith and trust in God!

We'll teach Medical Missionaries
How to heal the sick and help the poor,
How to share God's Final message,
And then help them learn so much more!

Like having a Christ–like character,
And keeping <u>all</u> God's commandments,
Being filled with His Holy Spirit,
And reaching higher attainments!

Being in "THE ARK" of safety
Just like back in Noah's day,
We'll be able to ride the storms,
Until comes God's delivery day!

So even though the time will come
For the 'death sentence' on our life,
We'll be ready and trusting in God,
Waiting for our eternal life!

So, now while probation lingers,
And we're sheltered in His arms of love,
Let us not put off deeds of kindness,
Nor fail to enter our home above!

There awaits our Master's words
Of admonition and words, "WELL DONE,"
Because we've followed our Saviour,
And the victory we've finally won!

Isaiah 33:15 and 16,
God's promise is given,
To care for those who'll do His will,
And a Christ–like life they'll be livin'!

So get in "THE ARK" of safety,
While there is still a little time,
Since there's still a lot of storms ahead,
We'll need Jesus till the end of time!

So, heed His call and heed His warnings,
Take that final step and get aboard!
Be a part of God's closing work,
By giving your all to the Lord!

Written by Linda Clore with the help of the Lord! March 9, 2010

"Experiences"

Written May 31, 2017

That morning on May 29, 2017, when we got up, we noticed it was looking terribly stormy, so we turned on the radio weather station and it said, "In the forecast for today, there are tornadoes with hail the size of baseballs and 70 mph damaging winds with heavy rains."

We knew the devil delights in destruction and to steal and kill, as John 10:10 says. We were having our morning worship and praying for God's protection over us and the "Ark" in these dangerous storms forecasted. As we continued to have our worship, the clouds grew heavy, and it began to thunder and grow darker and darker! We could see the angry clouds forming, and we kept praying God would please let the storm pass by us and protect us and our house trailer and windows and car and garden and fruit on our fruit trees!

I remarked about them forecasting hail the size of baseballs and how in Revelation 16, it describes the 7 last plagues and in verse 21, it says, "And there fell upon men a great hail out of heaven, every stone about the weight of a talent: and men blasphemed God because of the plague of the hail; for the plague thereof was exceeding great." (Some scholars have estimated a talent to be 66 pounds in weight or more.)

We could see the angry clouds forming, and we kept praying God would please let the storm pass by us and protect us and our house trailer and windows and car and garden and fruit on our fruit trees

I prayed God would please put His protective right hand over us, like I had seen, one time, in a cloud formation over our place, an enormous gigantic cloud in the form of a right hand covering over the "Ark." I prayed, also, that God would please send His angels wings drawn over us and protect us, like I had seen one time in a cloud formation covering over our place, an angel with his wings spread out and covering over our whole "Ark"!

Read in *Early Writings* by E.G. White, "The Open and Shut Door" on pp. 42–45. On p. 43, she writes, "Satan is now using every device in this sealing time to keep the minds of God's people from the present truth and to cause them to waver. I saw a covering that God was drawing over His people to protect them in the time of trouble; and every soul that was decided on the truth and was pure in heart was to be covered with the covering of the Almighty." On p. 44, she continues to say, "Satan was trying his every art to hold them where they were, until the sealing was past, until the covering was drawn over God's people, and they left without a shelter from the burning wrath of God, in the seven last plagues. God has begun to draw this covering over His people, and it will soon be drawn over all who are to have a shelter in the day of slaughter. God will work in power for His people; and Satan will be permitted to work also."

As we continued to have our worship, we could see the dark angry clouds pass by and the storm passed, and the sun came out! Praise the Lord! Thank you Jesus! We prayed and thanked the good Lord for protecting us from the fierce storm that had just passed by, and we didn't lose our electricity either! God is so good!

Then, the next day on May 30, 2017, we were having our evening worship, and as we were praying and studying God's word, it grew really dark and threatening clouds, black and heavy, and the wind came up strong, and we heard the thunder rolling! Again, we prayed for God's protection over us and the "Ark." Then, it passed on by us with no dangerous or damaging storm hitting us on the "Ark." Praise the Lord! We, again, prayed and thanked the good Lord for sparing us again from what could have been a disaster!

Then, David spoke up and said, "Turn the radio weather station on and see what they were saying." They were saying, "A severe storm warning threat for East Osage County was cancelled, and the storm was no longer a threat! Also, the severe storm threat for N.W. Franklin County had moved out of the area and was no longer a threat of damaging tornadoes!"

This was the exact spot where we were at! We prayed again and thanked the good Lord for hearing our earnest prayers again for His loving protective care over us and the "Ark" and for taking care of us from these terrible damaging storms that He let pass by us with no damage done to us or our place! We just praised the Lord for His covering placed over us and the "Ark" we're preparing for God's people to come to for protection during the Sunday Law crisis, when we won't be able to buy or sell, and we'll need this "Ark," God has helped us to build and has protected over and over again from Satan trying to destroy us and our place of refuge to go through the time of trouble soon to be upon us! Now's the time to prepare spiritually and physically for the storms ahead of us, when every earthly support will be cut off to those who stay true and loyal to God's 7th day Sabbath and all His Ten Commandments, as *Desire of Ages* by E.G. White, pp. 121–122 says.

Again, on May 31, 2017, another storm was forecast on the radio weather station with possible tornadoes, hail, damaging winds and heavy rains! Again, we had our morning worship and again prayed for God's protection over us in the dangerous storms forecast! The terribly dangerous dark, black clouds formed over us, and it began to thunder and rain! We prayed God would please give us a much-needed rain, but no bad storms or tornadoes! Again, God heard our sincere prayers for protection over us and the "Ark" and for rain! Thank you Jesus! Praise the Lord! God is so good to look out for us and the "Ark." We didn't lose our electricity either. The radio weather station said we'll have these terrible storms all week. We pray God will spare us from any dangerous storm blowing around out there! We serve a great and wonderful and mighty God! We love you Lord!

Another experience we had was, we were air-popping our popcorn to eat for breakfast. I had been praying and asking God to please, TODAY, convert Jonathan! Then, as I was eating my popcorn, a kernel of popcorn stuck on my finger, and it looked like a "?" (question mark). I know God won't force us to serve and obey Him! God gives us the power of choice to make our decision to follow and obey Him or not. (I had Dad take a picture of the piece of popcorn looking like a question mark.)

It's up to Jonathan, and each one of us, when we'll decide to surrender all to Jesus! Jesus loves us and woos us to Him.

God, Dad and I want Jonathan "TODAY" to love and obey and follow Jesus and go all the way with Jesus NOW and see how much happier and healthier he'll be serving the Lord with all his heart and going all the way with the Lord! But we know God won't force His will on any of us. We know it has to be Jonathan's decision when that choice and decision will be made! We just keep praying for him!

Psalm 95:7, 8, we claim for Jonathan. He's wanting to go back into a nursing home and not stay here with us, because we're taking his nicotine and coffee pills away. Read in *Ministry of Healing* the chapter, "The Co–Working of the Divine and the Human" by E.G. White, pp. 111–124.

> *I know God won't force us to serve and obey Him! God gives us the power of choice to make our decision to follow and obey Him or not*

Jonathan became depressed and wanted to be taken to the Emergency room and be admitted to the hospital for his depression, and from there be taken to a nursing home facility to be cared for and not come back home. We had prayer with him and tried to encourage him to stay home with us and improve his health, getting off his nicotine and coffee pills. He had had a blood pressure of 210/110, and we were afraid he'd have a stroke or a heart attack! The doctor had had to put him on a second blood pressure medicine to try and bring it down. But he still wanted to leave and be put in a nursing home where he could take what he wanted and do what he wanted.

So, I got his things together. The weather station radio was saying severe storms and hail and strong winds and possible tornadoes. But Jonathan still wanted to be taken to the Emergency room and admitted for his depression in a hospital.

We prayed with Jonathan that he would change his mind and that he'd get well and want to come on home. As Dad and Jonathan drove off to Ottawa, it began to sprinkle. By the time Dad and Jonathan had reached Ottawa, there had been a terrible storm go through Ottawa before they got there! At the Emergency room entrance, Dad saw two ladies sitting outside on the bench, and he said, "What has happened in this city with all the debris all over the streets and everywhere?!"

They both started telling him of the terrible storm that just passed through with golf ball sized hail and strong winds and tons of rain smashing windows in houses and cars and denting in cars and causing terrible damage all over town! Dad gave each of them a 3ABN sharing card and said, "That is so terrible about the storm!" Both the ladies were so happy to get the 3ABN sharing card telling of all the different programs they offer and thanked David for sharing the cards with them.

Jonathan was seen in the Emergency room and admitted to a rehabilitating center to help his depression. Dad then began his journey home. It just poured and poured, and he had to drive 30 mph, because he couldn't see! Praise God! The Lord got him safely home through the storm! There was no damage here. We thanked the good Lord for His protective care over us and our place! God heard our prayers! We continue to pray for Jonathan's healing and protection and his conversion! Jonathan is in God's hands! We pray God will be in control of Jonathan and his life. It's <u>so</u> sad to have him leave home. We have no idea what will be in Jonathan's future at this time! All we can do is pray that God will help him through this crisis he's going through! God impressed Jonathan to come on home after his rehab in the hospital. Praise the Lord! He heard our prayers for Jonathan to return home! Thank you Jesus!

"Be Ready and Be Prepared!"

Written July 29, 2017

I hadn't slept well that night, and I felt sleepy and tired as I ate my breakfast. We had our worship, and I went out to exercise after eating. I rode my bike around the circle driveway a few times, and I fell off my bike and landed in the gravel. The Lord kept me from being hurt. I thought, "I might as well go back inside. I'm too tired to exercise." Then, I thought, "I'll just walk down the driveway to the entrance and back and then go back inside." So, I neared the entrance of our driveway, I saw a car slowly drive into my driveway and stop and a man and a young man with ties on got out of the car and another man remained in the car in the front seat. The two that got out of the car introduced themselves and gave their names, and I shook their hands. They began introducing their paper. I knew they were Jehovah's Witnesses. Some of them had been here before and left that paper with me. They asked me questions from the Bible, and I prayed God would please help me answer their questions and be able to quote Scripture to them to back up my answers. The man kept saying, "I'm so impressed with your knowledge of the Scripture!" I said, "I give God the glory and thank Him for helping me know His word." He said, "I've not had people be able to answer these questions I'm asking you!" I said, "Praise the Lord! I give God the glory for helping me know His word!" Finally, when it came time for them to leave, I said, "Let's have a word of prayer together." I bowed my head and began my prayer with "Our loving Heavenly Father," then I prayed for them and closed my prayer with the words, "In Jesus' name I pray! Amen."

We never know where or how and when God may use us to witness for Him! That's why it's so important to be ready and prepared to give an answer of what we believe

We shook hands goodbye and then they drove off.

I thought now I know why Satan made me fall off my bike to make me want to go on inside. Then, David, my husband, would have been the one to go out to the car when they drove up the drive to our house trailer, but God wanted to use me to witness to them, by answering their questions by quoting Scripture. We never know where or how and when God may use us to witness for Him! That's why it's so important to be ready and prepared to give an answer of what we believe. "Study to show thyself (*ourselves*) approved unto God, a workman that needeth not to be ashamed, rightly dividing the word of truth." 2 Timothy 2:15.

Read chapter 37 in *The Great Controversy* book by E.G. White, "The Scriptures a Safeguard." On p. 593, we read, "None but those who have fortified the mind with the truths of the Bible will stand through the last great conflict. To every soul will come the searching test: Shall I obey God rather than men? The decisive hour is even now at hand. Are our feet planted on the rock of God's immutable word? Are we prepared to stand firm in defense of the commandments of God and the faith of Jesus?"

Reading on p. 594, "The words which they needed to remember were banished from their minds; and when the time of trial came, it found them unprepared. The death of Jesus as fully destroyed their hopes as if He had not forewarned them. So in the prophecies the future is opened before us as plainly as it was opened to the disciples by the words of Christ. The events connected with the close of probation and the work of preparation for the time of trouble, are clearly presented. But multitudes have no more understanding of these important truths than if they had never been revealed. Satan watches to catch away every impression that would make them wise unto salvation, and the time of trouble will find them unready."

Continue reading on pp. 594–595, "When God sends to men warnings so important that they are represented as proclaimed by holy angels flying in the midst of heaven, He requires every person endowed with reasoning powers to heed the message. The fearful judgments denounced against the worship of the beast and his image (Revelation 14:9–11), should lead all to a diligent study of the prophecies to learn what the mark of the beast is, and how they are to avoid receiving it. But the masses of the people turn away their ears from hearing the truth and are turned unto fables. The apostle Paul declared, looking down to the last days: 'The time will come when they will not endure sound doctrine.' 2 Timothy 4:3. That time has fully come. The multitudes do not want Bible truth, because it interferes with the desires of the sinful, world-loving heart; and Satan supplies the deceptions which they love.

But God will have a people upon the earth to maintain the Bible, and the Bible only, as the standard of all doctrines and the basis of all reforms… Satan is constantly endeavoring to attract attention to man in the place of God. He leads the people to look to bishops, to pastors, to professors of theology, as their guides, instead of searching the Scriptures to learn their duty for themselves. Then, by controlling the minds of these leaders, he can influence the multitudes according to his will." On p. 596, it says, "Notwithstanding the Bible is full of warnings against false teachers, many are ready thus to commit the keeping of their souls to the clergy."

On p. 598, we read, "God has given us His word that we may become acquainted with its teachings and know for ourselves what He requires of us. When the lawyer came to Jesus with the inquiry, 'What shall I do to inherit eternal life?' the Saviour referred him to the Scriptures, saying: 'What is written in the law? how readest thou?'… It is not enough to have good intentions; it is not enough to do what a man thinks is right or what the minister tells him is right. His soul's salvation is at stake, and he should search the Scriptures for himself… He has a chart pointing out every waymark on the heavenward journey, and he ought not to guess at anything… We should day by day study the Bible diligently, weighing every thought and comparing scripture with scripture. With divine help we are to form our opinions for ourselves as we are to answer for ourselves before God."

We read these words on pp. 599–600, "We must come with a humble and teachable spirit to obtain knowledge from the great I AM. Otherwise, evil angels will so blind our minds and harden our hearts that we shall not be impressed by the truth… The Bible should never be studied without prayer. The Holy Spirit alone can cause us to feel the importance of those things easy to be understood, or prevent us from wresting truths difficult of comprehension. It is the office of heavenly angels to prepare the heart so to comprehend God's word that we shall be charmed with its beauty, admonished by its warnings, or animated and strengthened by its promises. … Psalm 119:18. Temptations often appear irresistible because, through neglect of prayer and the study of the Bible, the tempted one cannot readily remember God's promises and meet Satan with the Scripture weapons. But angels are round about those who are willing to be taught in divine things; and in the time of great necessity they will bring to their remembrance the very truths which are needed (Isaiah 59:19)."

That was like it was for me when I was talking to the Jehovah's Witnesses, and I was praying God would help me to be able to quote Scriptures to them, and that amazed them of my knowledge of the Scriptures, but I gave God the glory! He answered my prayer for help! Praise God!

Continue reading on p. 600, "But the teachings of Christ must previously have been stored in the mind in order for the Spirit of God to bring them to our remembrance in the time of peril (Psalm 119:11)."

"The very pillars of truth will be assailed." On p. 601–602, we read these very serious and solemn words, "We are living in the most solemn period of this world's history. The destiny of earth's teeming multitudes is about to be decided. Our own future well–being and also the salvation of other souls depend upon the course which we now pursue. We need to be guided by the Spirit of truth. Every follower of Christ should earnestly inquire: 'Lord, what wilt Thou have me to do?' We need to humble ourselves before the Lord, with fasting and prayer, and to meditate much upon His word, especially upon the scenes of the judgment. We should now seek a deep and living experience in the things of God. We have not a moment to lose. Events of vital importance are taking place around us; we are on Satan's enchanted ground. Sleep not, sentinels of God; the foe is lurking near, ready at any moment, should you become lax and drowsy, to spring upon you and make you his prey.

Many are deceived as to their true condition before God. They congratulate themselves upon the wrong acts which they do not commit, and forget to enumerate the good and noble deeds which God requires of them, but which they have neglected to perform. It is not enough that they are trees in the garden of God. They are to answer His expectation by bearing fruit. He holds them accountable for their failure to accomplish all the good which they could have done, through His grace strengthening them. In the books of heaven they are registered as cumberers of the ground. Yet the case of even this class is not utterly hopeless. With those who have slighted God's mercy and abused His grace, the heart of long–suffering love yet pleads. 'Wherefore He saith, Awake thou that sleepest, and arise from the dead, and Christ shall give thee light. See then that ye walk circumspectly, … redeeming the time, because the days are evil.' Ephesians 5:14–16.

When the testing time shall come, those who have made God's word their rule of life will be revealed… So the falsehearted professor may not now be distinguished from the real Christian, but the time is just upon us when the difference will be apparent. Let opposition arise, let bigotry and intolerance again bear sway, let persecution be kindled, and the halfhearted and hypocritical will waver and yield the faith; but the true Christian will stand firm as a rock, his faith stronger, his hope brighter, than in days of prosperity.

Says the psalmist: 'Thy testimonies are my meditation.' 'Through Thy precepts I get understanding: therefore I hate every false way.' Psalm 119:99, 104.

We need to be preparing now for what's ahead, so we'll be ready and be prepared

'Happy is the man that findeth wisdom.' 'He shall be as a tree planted by the waters, and that spreadeth out her roots by the river, and shall not see when heat cometh, but her leaf shall be green; and shall not be careful in the year of drought, neither shall cease from yielding fruit.' Proverbs 3:13."

Also, **read** chapter 38, "The Final Warning" and chapter 39, "The Time of Trouble" in E.G. White's book in *The Great Controversy*.

We need to be preparing now for what's ahead, so we'll be ready and be prepared! *Vol 8 Testimonies for the Church* p. 28; *Vol 2 Selected Messages* by E.G. White, I had these two references in a dream.

Read: *Southern Watchman* (January 19, 1909) "Prepare to Meet Thy God." Amos 4:11–12.

To be prepared to meet the Lord, read: Hebrews 12. We're being judged whether we're ready or not. These are serious and solemn times we're living in! Sister White writes in *Early Writings* p. 119, "Get ready! Get ready! Get ready!" **Read** also, in *Vol 5 Testimonies for the Church*, pp. 680–691, "Neglect of the Testimonies" by E.G. White, especially p. 680.

I had a dream that I was saying to God's people, "Let the people know to get ready!"

Read: "Pray for the Latter Rain," by E.G. White in *Testimonies to Ministers and Gospel Workers*, pp. 506–512; *Ministry of Healing* by E.G. White, "Development and Service," pp. 497–502; *Last Day Events* by E.G. White, pp. 183–214, "The Latter Rain and The Loud Cry."

Sometime back, I dreamt: "Who, what when, where, why, how? Psalm 119:11. This is the condition we must keep in mind. <u>NOW</u>! The judgment is going on right now, since October 22, 1844, and it will change to the cases of the living, and we will not know when our names will come up! So keep straight, <u>NOW</u>!

Read: *The Great Controversy* by E.G. White, chapter 28, "Facing Life's Record"—The Investigative Judgment; *Early Writings* by E.G. White, "The Open and Shut Door," pp. 42–45, especially p. 43, "Satan is now using every device in this sealing time to keep the minds of God's people from the present truth and to cause them to waver. I saw a covering that God was drawing over His people to protect them in the time of trouble; and every soul that was decided on the truth and was pure in heart was to be covered with the covering of the Almighty."

Please listen to Hal Mayer's CD entitled, "Deceptive Moves," to let you know where we are in history! Things are shaping up FAST! Let's be ready!

"What Do People See in You?"
Written October 9, 2017

Each morning, as I begin my day, I pray that the Lord will "let me live in the sunlight of God, and radiate Jesus Christ."

Jonathan had become depressed and feeling suicidal and having a panic attack. It was around 10 p.m. in the evening, and he asked to be taken to the Emergency room in Ottawa for help. I got his things together, and Dad and I prayed with him and asked the Lord to please be with him and help him and heal him and that he would be admitted to the right place to get the help he so much needed! We hate to see him on these mental health drugs that he feels he needs, but they have all these bad side effects to put up with. But he feels he needs them, so he stays on them. We pray for his conversion and that he'll want off these bad drugs.

Once he arrived at the Emergency room, they evaluated him and the only opening they could find to send him to for help was at our SDA Hospital, Shawnee Mission Medical Center in Shawnee Mission, Kansas. The ambulance came, and they admitted him to the Mental Health floor. That was on a Thursday. We have no phone to call him or for him to call us, or for the hospital to call us and let us know how he was doing. So, all we could do was to pray for him and leave him in God's tender loving care to get well. It was 150 miles round trip to go see him, so we were asking the good Lord to please take care of him and help him get the help he needed. We were thankful he was in our SDA hospital. It was the same hospital my husband, David, worked in back when Jonathan was young, and we lived in Wellsville, Kansas and raised Jonathan out in the country. Daddy worked in the Boiler and Maintenance department at the time. It has grown into around an 800–bed hospital now.

We kept praying for Jonathan that he would get well. Jonathan said that they would probably keep him four or five days and adjust his medicine and then dismiss him to come on home.

On Friday night, God gave me a dream. In my dream, I heard Jonathan calling, "MOM!" When I woke up, Sabbath morning, I prayed for Jonathan that he'd be doing okay. (God had given me this dream twice in the same night, with Jonathan calling "MOM"!) Dad and I prayed for him and we decided to drive on up to the hospital and see for ourselves how he was doing. Since we have no phone for Jonathan or the hospital to be able to call us, we figured God was giving me a dream to encourage us to go see Jonathan and pray with him and encourage him in the Lord, and to come on home when he was dismissed and not be admitted to a depression facility.

So, Dad and I prayed and made the trip up to the hospital. We had no idea when visiting hours were, so, we prayed in faith that they'd let us see him. We arrived safe at 2 p.m., thinking visiting hours might be from 2 to 4 p.m. At the entrance desk of the hospital, we found out where Jonathan was, and I left a 3ABN sharing card with the lady at the desk, and she was so happy to get it. While we were there, we left cards all over the hospital and in the bathrooms. Then, we made our way up to see Jonathan on the Mental Ward.

At the patient desk, we had to sign papers who we were and when they found out we were his parents, and we had driven 75 miles up there to see our son, Jonathan, they let us go back to his room to visit with him, even though it wasn't visiting hours. Praise the Lord! Before we had gone up to the hospital to see Jonathan, God had given me a poem, after I woke up that very morning on Sabbath. I wrote it out and took it up to read to Jonathan, along with another poem I had written on the day he was admitted to the hospital. The two poems were: "Have Faith in God" and "More Time."

When we arrived in his room, he was just sitting in his wheelchair all alone in his private room. When he saw us, he was so happy to see us! We had prayer together, and we gave him hugs and let him know how much we love him and miss him! I told him of the two dreams I had that night of him calling, "MOM"! And, so we decided to make the 150–mile round trip up to see him and pray with him and encourage him to come on home when dismissed. He just smiled and was so happy we were there! I read him my two poems that God had helped me to write, and he enjoyed them.

He wanted to go out in the big room where there was a table and chairs for visiting. He got him a cup of coffee, and I said to him, "Jonathan, that can cause you to be depressed." While we sat at the table visiting, I asked him to get his Bible, and we'd pray and read promises from God's word and pray and sing and have our little worship time together since it was Sabbath. Dad fell asleep in the big easy chair they had there in the room and Jonathan and I worshipped together.

As we were reading the Bible and praying and I sang some songs to him, a patient lady who looked depressed and had been walking up and down the halls came into the room, where we were having our little worship, and she walked over to the phone on the wall, and then she walked over to where we were sitting at the table, and she looked all around at us, and I said, "Hi," and then she just turned around and walked out. Then, within a minute, Jonathan's nurse came in and walked over to the phone on the wall, and she just stood there looking and staring at us having our little quiet worship time, and I said "Hi" to her, and then, after a while, without a word, she left. I thought to myself, "what are these people seeing when they come into this room and just stare at us and then without a word, they just leave?" I was wondering if maybe they're seeing bright light about us glowing or something, as we worshipped the Lord on His holy Sabbath day? The Lord has promised in Matthew 18:19, 20 that Jesus will be in the midst of two or three gathered in His name, and that if two of you shall agree as touching anything that they shall ask, it shall be done for them by the Father in heaven. Praise God!

Jonathan wanted to go to his room for a while, and as we passed the nurses station, I asked if they could please call and have an SDA chaplain come and have prayer with Jonathan. She was real nice and got right on the phone and said that a chaplain was on his way. I gave her a 3ABN sharing card and thanked her for her help and thanked her for taking care of my boy. She was happy to receive the card and thanked me, and I gave the other nurses standing around behind the desk, cards too, and they thanked me and seemed interested in the information on the card.

We, then, went into Jonathan's room, and I noticed his bag of clothes I sent with him wasn't there. I went out to the desk and explained that Jonathan's clothes weren't in his room. She told me that he hadn't had any clothes with him when he was admitted, and we concluded they had been either left in the Emergency room in Ottawa or in the ambulance. We noticed the nurse had gotten him a couple shorts and a shirt to wear when he took his bath, and we thanked her for doing that.

While we waited for the chaplain to come and see Jonathan and pray with him, we prayed and I sang a song. The door was shut and then the chaplain knocked and came in, and he wasn't a SDA chaplain but was filling in for the SDA chaplains who were in church that day. We let him know we were SDAs and appreciated him coming and praying for Jonathan. In his visiting, he mentioned he was working on a sermon for his church Sunday morning taken from Mark 9 and that the Lord said how important it was to pray for people who are possessed. I added, "It also says in verse 29 of Mark 9, '… this kind can come forth by nothing, but by prayer and fasting.'" I said to him, "We've been eating light and praying for help for Jonathan to get well."

Then, Jonathan spoke up and said how he had gotten into drugs growing up and took LSD, and he had a flashback that caused him to go into the hospital. The chaplain prayed for Jonathan and when he said, "Amen," then I prayed for the chaplain and his dear family he had told us about, and as I prayed for Jonathan, I had my hand on his right shoulder. When we finished praying, I gave the chaplain a 3ABN sharing card and thanked him for coming and praying with Jonathan. He seemed real interested in the card.

I then told him how when S.M.M.C. was just a little hospital before it grew to be an 800–bed hospital, how we'd bring Jonathan, as a little boy, to sing with us on the singing bands. And, also, when he was in his teens, he had volunteered at the hospital as a messenger to deliver information to the different departments.

When he went to leave, I asked him if he would please leave a note for the SDA chaplain to <u>please</u> come Sunday and have prayer with Jonathan. He said he would sure do that. We shook his hand goodbye and thanked him again for coming and praying for our boy. It meant so much. He said, "Let me write down your names." So, he wrote down David and Linda Clore and Jonathan.

After he left, we went back to the visitor's room and sat and prayed and read the Bible and sang. Jonathan drank more coffee. Then, a doctor stepped into the room to visit with Jonathan and see how he was doing and adjusted his medication. He asked Jonathan what the date was, and he spoke right up and said, "October 7, 2017." That pleased the doctor, and I was so proud of him, too, that he could still think clear, even though he was on mental health drugs. Then, the doctor said to me, "I'm a psychiatric doctor. You know what they call us?" I said, "Yes, a shrink." He said, "That's right." After he adjusted Jonathan's medicines, he got up to leave, and I shook his hand and thanked him for coming and caring for Jonathan. I handed him a 3ABN sharing card, and he thanked me for it.

There was another patient that kept coming around us and wanted to talk to us, and he was way out of in left field on all the medicines they had him on, making no sense. He seemed to like us, and I asked to pray for him, and he said, "Yes." After I prayed, he thanked me and shook my hand. I gave him a hug. He thanked me.

It came time to leave, and Jonathan wanted us to come back to get him on Tuesday on the 10th, so he could return home. That's when Jonathan thought they would dismiss him and for us to be there to get him. We had prayer together, and we gave him hugs goodbye. I left the two poems with him to read. I thanked the nurses for letting us enjoy visiting with Jonathan and for taking care of Jonathan and thanked them for getting a chaplain to pray with Jonathan and that we really appreciated it and that he was a nice chaplain. The nurse said, "He seemed to enjoy getting to visit with you, too."

We then left and headed to Ottawa Emergency room and prayed we'd be able to find Jonathan's bag of clothes still there. Praise the Lord, they were still in the Emergency room for us to pick them up! Thank you Jesus!

On the drive home, I was telling Daddy all that had taken place at the hospital, since he slept through most of it. I told him how the lady patient and then the nurse came into the room where we were having our worship and how they each just stood and stared at us and then, without a word, left the room. I said, "Do you think God let them see an angel beside us or a heavenly light shining around us for them to just stare at us and say nothing?!" Daddy replied, "It seems like they had to have seen something they were staring at." He said, "You are a rare breed you know. You're friendly and outgoing and pray and witness with people and give them literature, and you dress and act like a true Christian and are polite and courteous and appreciative of things you receive, and people can see Jesus in you, and you're loving and kind to people, and you give them hugs, and you pray with people. People can tell you're a Christian and have the love of Jesus in your heart." I said, "Thank you. Praise the Lord!

> *People can tell you're a Christian and have the love of Jesus in your heart*

God gave us a safe trip home, and we were so thankful God had been with us in our witnessing and so thankful we found Jonathan doing okay. **Read** 2 Corinthians 3, especially verse two, "Ye are our epistle written in our hearts, known and read of all men."

The date came for us to go up to S.M.M.C. and bring Jonathan home. We put more 3ABN sharing cards in our pockets and had prayer that Jonathan would be doing okay and get to come on home. We prayed the Lord would please get these 3ABN sharing cards into the right people's hands. We prayed for a safe trip up there and back again. It looked like it could storm. When we arrived, we began passing out 3ABN sharing cards. We found Jonathan sleeping in bed. We asked if he would be dismissed today, and the nurse said, "the doctor hasn't made his rounds yet." Then the doctor came and dismissed him, and the social worker came and wanted to make sure all was okay, and Jonathan said, "Yes." His nurse came in too, to go over his doctor's charge paperwork and medicines. We gave her a card.

The hospital dietitian came into see how everything was for him to go home. She was real nice, and I handed her a 3ABN sharing card and began explaining to her about the programs and how good they were, and she spoke up and said, "I'm a SDA too, and I love 3ABN and watch it all the time!" I thanked her for the beautiful and nutritious meals they served Jonathan and how very much he enjoyed their food. She was so happy to hear that. She asked me if she could keep the 3ABN sharing card, and I said, "Yes! You can order a bunch of them and share them." I said, "We've been giving them to people all over the hospital, and they've all been very happy to get them!" She said, "That's good!"

When she left, a lady with her Dalmatian dog was standing outside Jonathan's door. Jonathan said to her, "Please bring your dog in here." The lady came in with her dog, and we petted the dog and she said, "I bring my dog here once a month for the patients to see her do tricks." She began having her dog do all kinds of tricks. I asked if she was a teacher? She said, "Yes." She said, "People are taught and trained and dogs have to be taught and trained, too. Obedience is so important to learn." I thought to myself, "Yes, obedience to God and His word and His will is so important for people to learn, too, so we can rightly represent Jesus and His truth and prove what we believe and live it, so we can be a blessing and a help to others and make Jesus happy and proud of us. Just like that lady was so proud of her dog showing others what she had learned from her master and making her master happy, and the people watching the dog were made happy. Jesus wants us to be like Him in word and deed, so we can bring joy into other people's lives, too, and be good representatives and good witnesses for Jesus by the things they've learned and live." **Read** 2 Timothy 2:15.

We then were directed off the floor, for Jonathan to return home. We thanked everyone for Jonathan's good care he had received.

When we got into the car, we prayed for a safe trip home. On the way home, it just poured and poured and poured, and it was so very hard to see, and cars and trucks were just flying around us so fast in the rain, but praise the Lord, we arrived safely home! Thank you Jesus! And we were so thankful to have our son safely back home with us and doing okay. Praise the Lord!

As we all three were visiting at home and going over the rain storm God had just pulled us through and how it poured so hard, and we couldn't see, and we kept praying and praying for God's watch care over us and to protect us, even though our wipers would not go real fast to clear the rain off our windshield! They were on slow speed, and we could not get them to go fast, so we could see the road. We felt God had spared us from having an accident and saved our lives! Praise the Lord! Thank you Jesus! We know the devil would love to snuff us all out and get rid of us for witnessing all over the hospital and me writing another book to encourage people to remain true to God in the storms ahead of us and the Sunday law crisis, and we'll have to have faith and trust for the Lord to take care of us through those trying and dangerous days ahead of us who will remain true and faithful to Jesus and His 7th day Bible Sabbath and all His Ten Commandments. We felt God had overruled Satan, who was keeping our wipers on slow speed, so we couldn't see the road, and we were driving by faith, trusting the Lord to send angels all around us, so we didn't have a bad accident and be killed! David went out and checked the wipers, and they have a fast speed and a real fast speed, but the old devil was keeping them from working, so we couldn't see the road in the bad down pour. David saw that they are working just fine now!

We also talked about how Satan would love to have Jonathan put out of the way, so he wouldn't be converted and win souls for Jesus either. Satan tries to keep Jonathan on these terrible devil drugs with all their dangerous side effects, even making him depressed and suicidal. God keeps pulling Jonathan through these terrible experiences he's been going through on Satan's drugs, and God keeps overruling Satan and sparing his life, so he can work for Jesus and win souls from Satan to the Lord's side. We just keep praying for God's help and protection to see all three of us through Satan's attacks he brings on us to destroy us! Praise God, our God is stronger than Satan!

We were also remarking to one another about the things that were happening while we were waiting for Jonathan's doctor to dismiss him. I was going over how the head nurse kept opening Jonathan's door to tell us things, and then she'd shut the door and leave. One time, she left the door opened up all the way, so she could look from her desk right in at us. We had been praying, and I was singing songs and read out of Jonathan's Bible promises, and we were handing out 3ABN sharing cards with all who came into Jonathan's room. I remarked to David and Jonathan as we went over the experience we had with the nurse who kept opening Jonathan's door to say something to us, then she'd close it, then she finally left it open so she could look in and see us. I said to David and Jonathan, "I wonder what she was seeing in there when she kept opening the door and would say a little something and then close the door, then she finally left it all the way open and left. Do you think she was seeing a heavenly glow like maybe the other head nurse on Sabbath, when we were there seeing Jonathan and having a worship time with him, and she came in and stared at us, like she was seeing something, like a heavenly glow about us? We all remarked that we may never know, but things were happening that were surely strange, and we couldn't account for it.

It makes you wonder what people see in you when they look at you and observe your life?

Sister White says in *Patriarchs and Prophets* on p. 144, "From every Christian home a holy light should shine forth… They would indeed be the 'light of the world.'" Matthew 5:16 says, "Let your light so shine before men, that they may see your good works, and glorify your Father which is in heaven." (**Read** Galatians 6:9).

In *The Great Controversy* book by E.G. White, we read on p. 612, "Servants of God, with their faces lighted up and shining with holy consecration, will hasten from place to place to proclaim the message from heaven. By thousands of voices, all over the earth, the warning will be given."

Read: *Vol 8 Testimonies for the Church*, p. 19, "It is His purpose that every Christian shall be surrounded with a spiritual atmosphere of light and peace."

"The Seizure"
Written October 22, 2017

Jonathan has been having pain in his right shoulder and low back. Many months ago the doctor ordered an x–ray of his right shoulder and they came to the conclusion it must be arthritis causing all the pain, and why it was hard for him to move it. Off and on he'd take pain pills for it, but he'd become addicted to the pain pills and had to be taken off the pain pills.

This pain in his right shoulder and in his low back was making him very uncomfortable, so again he asked for some pain pills to give him relief for a while from his pains. The doctor ordered a one–week supply until he had it x–rayed again and possibly he'd have to have surgery on his right shoulder.

The day he was to go get his x–ray and have the doctor surgeon examine him, he had a seizure in his chair. He had taken more pain pills than he should and most of his medicines he's on cause seizures as a side effect.

Dad and I were sitting at the breakfast table and from where I sit at the table, I can look into the front room and see Jonathan sitting in his chair. I saw him shaking all over and his arms moving furiously. I ran into the front room to him and knew immediately he was having a seizure! Dad and I both were frantically praying God would please help him and spare his life. He was chewing on his tongue and blood was coming out of his mouth onto his beard. His eyes rolled back in his head, and he stopped shaking and fell over to one side. Dad was crying and saying, "He's dead! Check his pulse!" His pulse was slow and real faint. I kept calling his name, "Jonathan! Jonathan!" He wouldn't respond! His eyes began to stare and were glassy looking! His face was blood red! I put cold washcloths to his face and neck. Dad said, "That's how red my mom got just before she died!" and I said, "Yes, my dad's eyes glazed and stared and glassy looking just before he died, just like Jonathan's eyes are looking right now." He was sweating and I took off his shirt and turned the fan on him. We kept praying and trying to arouse him and help him and call his name and tell him, "You're okay Jonathan! You're going to be okay! Jesus is helping you!"

He slowly started to come around. I asked him who I was? He didn't know. I asked him the date. He didn't know. I asked him how he felt? He said, "My stomach hurts." I asked his name; he didn't know. I said, "Jonathan, let's take you to the Emergency room and let them check you over." He got out of his chair and started to crawl toward the door, then he got back into his chair. I said, "Jonathan, you need medical help! Please crawl for the door and get in your wheelchair, so we can get you into the car and take you to the Emergency room." He again got out of the chair and started rolling back and forth, from side to side on the floor. Then got back into his chair saying, "I don't want to go to the Emergency room."

We kept praying with him and explained to him that he had had a seizure. He began to know his name, who I was and where he was, but still didn't want to go to the Emergency room. It took a while for him to get awakened to what had just happened to him. He said he still couldn't remember things, but it was slowly coming back.

We prayed and thanked God he was still alive and doing okay. We had just witnessed a miracle

We prayed and thanked God he was still alive and doing okay. We had just witnessed a miracle!

Several days later he said, "I need to make another appointment to see the doctor and get an order for an x–ray on my right shoulder that hurts."

I said to him, "You said you didn't want to go through a surgery on your shoulder."

He said, "But I'd like to have an x–ray and see why I'm in such pain." I said, "the last x–ray showed you have arthritis."

I said, "No more pain pills."

He said his right eye was hurting real bad and he needed to have the doctor look into his eye and see why he's in such pain, ever since he had the seizure. He went to the Emergency room in Ottawa and the doctor had a cat scan done on his head, and Praise the Lord, everything checked out okay! Thank you Jesus! Jonathan said his memory was back to normal too! Praise the Lord!

I said, "God has certainly been looking out for you!" We all agreed and prayed and thanked the good Lord for healing Jonathan and seeing him through this terrible seizure he went through.

"Jesus, Come into My Heart, TODAY!"

God wants to rid you of your sins,
So, in your heart, He can come in,

And take away your hate and strife,
And make you new and your wrongs right.

Only in Christ can you find peace,
Only with Christ's help can you teach,

Through God's power, souls you will reach.
And their salvation you will seek.

Pray for the Holy Spirit power.
On you, God's blessings will shower.

To get victory over sin,
Let the Holy Spirit come in.

See how much happier you'll be,
From all your sins, being set free.

When Jesus comes into your heart,
Then Satan will have to depart.

Put Christ in control of your life,
Then He'll give you eternal life.

So, let Christ in your heart today,
And see your sorrows fade away.

He'll give you a new life and joy,
He's spared your life from a boy,

And has plans for you, even now,
To show you the Christian way now.

Don't delay! Let Him in today!
And walk the Christian road today.

Begin now to open your heart.
Jesus will give you a new start.

Ask Him to come into your heart,
And obey Him with all your heart,

And be a soul–winner for Him,
Helping others get rid of sin,

Finding the joy, you've found in Him,
Gaining victory over sin.

When the "Pearl of Great Price" you've found,
Then the "Loud Cry" you'll want to sound,

And warn others to get ready,
And their life and heart get ready.

Then like Isaiah 58,
You'll help others in their bad state,

To find truth before it's too late,
Prepared for the Sunday Law's date.

Helping them know what they're to do,
Obey God's Sabbath and be true,

To all God's Ten Commandments, too,
And stay faithful to God and true.

These souls will be stars in your crown.
You'll have God's smile and not His frown.

There're people just waiting for you,
To share what God has done for you.

So, help them find a better life,
Choosing to have eternal life.

Jesus is wanting to use you,
To win souls and to Him be true.

So, won't you make that choice today,
And ask Christ in your heart today?

These are serious times we're in.
Now's the time to get rid of sin,

And have a Christ–like character,
And not be a Satan Actor.

Surrender all to Christ today.
Don't put it off! Do it today!

Life is so uncertain for us.
It's only in Christ we can trust.

But Satan will lie and steal and kill.
Your only safety is God's will.

And it is God's will to save you,
But it's up to you what you'll do.

Will it be Heaven you will choose?
The choice is yours. What will you choose?

Christ and Satan, both want your life,
Choose Jesus and eternal life.

Get rid of Satan in your life,
Follow Jesus and do what's right.

See what peace and joy will come in.
Put Christ first and let Him come in.

You can do it! Trust God's power,
Flee to Christ as your strong tower.

His arms of love are opened wide,
When you choose in Him to abide.

Christ will free you from Satan's hold,
Just come to Christ and His hand hold.

Just day by day stay in His will,
His promises He will fulfill.

And when He comes, you'll be ready,
And the souls you've helped get ready.

When we look upon Jesus' face,
We'll be glad we chose Him in life's race.

Now's the time to ask Jesus in,
And get free of Satan and sin.

Do it right now! Don't put it off!
Make Jesus your Friend and your Boss,

Obey God's orders and be saved,
Get rid of Satan and be saved.

There's strength in God's Word to help you,
To overcome in all you do.

Whatever sacrifice it takes,
Do it now, before it's too late!

You don't know what Satan might do!
You need Christ to take care of you!

So ask Jesus into your heart,
And from His love never depart!

Jesus is stronger than Satan.
A new home, for you He's makin'.

So, choose Christ and a new life for you,
Old things passed away, all things new.

> Let Christ come in and restore you,
>
> And to Him be faithful and true.
>
> You will be so thankful you did.
>
> And in Christ your sins will be hid.

Written by Linda Clore (April 30, 2016)

Based on: Hebrews 3:7, 8, 12–15; Philippians 4:13, 19; Isaiah 53:1–12; Isaiah 52:7; John 14:1–31; John 15:1–27; Matthew 28:18–20; 2 Corinthians 5:17; 2 Corinthians 6:2; Psalm 51; James 4:7, 8; Psalm 61:1–5; 1 John 1:9; Hebrews 12:1–7; Revelation 22:14; Ephesians 3:17–21; 1 John 2:1–6; Proverbs 18:10; Hebrews 5:9; Matthew 1:21; Matthew 5:1–48; John 3:14–21; Matthew 11:28–30; Luke 9:23–26.

Read: *Desire of Ages*—chapter 27 Thou Canst Make Me Whole; chapter 37 "The First Evangelist"; chapter 73 "Let Not Your Heart Be Troubled"; chapter 74 "Gethsemane"; chapter 78 "Calvary"; chapter 84 "Peace Be Unto You"; chapter 86 "Go Teach All Nations"; chapter 87 "To My Father and Your Father."

This poem was written for our son, Jonathan Clore, to encourage him to surrender all to Jesus.

Song to Sing: "I Surrender All."

"The One Lost Sheep"

Written October 22, 2016

A little lost sheep had strayed from the fold,
Got lost out in the wilds and in the cold.

The good Shepherd left the comforts of Home,
To find His lost sheep that had from Him roamed.

He searched through the night and all through the wilds,
As a parent would search for their lost child!

Never giving up, He heard the faint cry,
Coming from His lost sheep, ready to die!

Though tired and bleeding, He rescued him!
Jesus finds us and saves us from our sins.

All we like the lost sheep have gone astray,
All we like the lost sheep have disobeyed.

Jesus reaches out with His loving arm,
And carries us home from dangers and harm.

Back to the fold and the ninety and nine,
There safe from Satan and cared for and fine.

But this ordeal cost the good Shepherd's life,
To suffer and bleed to save the sheep's life!

What more could Jesus have done to save us?
He left all Heaven and died to save us!

We should be willing to part with our sins,
And then trust our life and keeping to Him.

But too many times we want it our way,
Like the little lost sheep, we go astray.

It cost so much to bring us back again,
And some lost sheep never come back again!

Oh! What a terrible thought to be lost!
To lose out on Heaven and what it cost!

Let's surrender all to Jesus right now!
Let's be determined to be saved right now!

Give up this world and its pleasures of sin,
Be determined to never sin again!

Jesus loves you and wants you to be saved,
Give your heart to Jesus without delay!

Jesus wants to carry you to Heaven,
And enter those pearly gates in Heaven.

That decision is up to you and me,
Come to Him, as you are, and be set free!

And like the lost sheep, come back to the fold,
And the smiling face of Jesus behold!

Make the good Shepherd rejoice in Heaven,
'Cause you've come back and have chosen Heaven!

This poem was written from a dream I had on October 22, 2016 about "The One Lost Sheep."

It also makes me think of the songs, "The Ninety and Nine" and "Jesus is Calling," "Lord, I'm Coming Home," "Rescue the Perishing," "Softly and Tenderly."

For Further Reading: Proverbs 22:6; Luke 15; Isaiah 53; John 3:16; *Christ's Object Lessons* by E.G. White, pp. 186–192, "The Lost Sheep"; *Last Day Events* by E.G. White, p. 211.

God gave me this song in a dream: "Shepherd of Love!"

Linda Clore's Dream About "The One Lost Sheep."

October 22, 2016

In my dream I was seeing this: A little lost sheep had strayed from the fold and got lost in the mountains out in the wilds and the cold. The Good Shepherd left the comforts of His home and went searching and hunting for His one lost sheep out in the wilds and in the cold, lost and hurt and frightened. The Good Shepherd went all through the night and all through the mountains and all through the cold and all through the dangers, calling and trying to find and rescue His one little lost sheep. He finally heard the sheep's faint cry and when He had found him stuck in the thorns and thicket, hurt and bleeding, He picked him up in his own hurt and torn and bleeding hands and feet and carried the little lost sheep in His loving arms and on His shoulders safely back to the fold with the other ninety and nine sheep. There the Good Shepherd tenderly cared for His little lost sheep's needs by cleaning him up and feeding him and lovingly bound up his wounds. But this terrible ordeal, the good Shepherd had to go through to save His one lost sheep, He loved so much, cost the life of the good Shepherd.

This made me think of the songs, "The Ninety and Nine" and "Rescue the Perishing." It also made me think of our son, Jonathan, and the sinner who strays from Jesus and goes out into the cold cruel world, lost and sad and lonely and how Jesus comes searching for him and finds him all hurt and bruised and brings him safely back to the fold and cares for his needs. But it cost the life of Jesus, our good Shepherd, to be able to rescue this one lost sinner. But there was such great joy, the lost sheep was found!

This world is but an atom in the vast dominions over which God presides, yet this little fallen world— the one lost sheep—is more precious in His sight than are the ninety and nine that went not astray from the fold

Read: *Christ's Object Lessons*, by E.G. White, pp. 186–192, "The Lost Sheep." Isaiah 53; John 3:16. *In Last Day Events* by E.G. White, she says, "Many who have strayed from the fold will come back to follow the great Shepherd." On p. 187 in *Christ's Object Lessons*, Sister White makes this comment, "In the parable the shepherd goes out to search for one sheep—the very least that can be numbered.

So if there had been but one lost soul, Christ would have died for that one." On p. 190, she continues saying, "By the lost sheep Christ represents not only the individual sinner but the one world that has apostatized and has been ruined by sin. This world is but an atom in the vast dominions over which God presides, yet this little fallen world—the one lost sheep—is more precious in His sight than are the ninety and nine that went not astray from the fold."

God impressed me to write the following poem, "The One Lost Sheep," when I had this dream about "The One Lost Sheep," on October 22, 2016.

Read: *Desire of Ages* by E.G. White, chapter 52, "The Divine Shepherd."

"NOW – Don't Put It Off!"
Written June 6, 2017

Don't put it off, what you can do today,
So you can make your life a better way!

For no one knows what tomorrow may hold!
Obey Jesus and do as you are told!

Make your choice to put your life in God's hand!
And remain true to Him and take your stand!

This old world is soon to come to an end!
<u>Now</u> is the time for you to part with sin!

And surrender your <u>all</u> to Jesus Christ,
And be determined to end all your strife!

And choose to be at peace with God and man!
Choose to enter into that better land!

It's there where <u>all</u> our trials we will lay down!
And there receive our robe and harp and crown!

The decisions we're making day by day,
Determines how our journey ends some day!

So, don't put it off, give Jesus your heart!
And with Gods' help, <u>now</u> with your sins depart!

We're living in serious and solemn times!
Lives are hanging in the balance all the time!

How we're living now decides our destiny!
<u>Now's</u> the time for you to gain the victory!

Be ready to look in Christ's face without fear!
Because we know His coming is drawing near!

So, don't put it off! Get rid of your sins now!
And enjoy the smiles of God, and not His frown!

Jesus left all Heaven and died to save you!
Won't you prove your love to Jesus and be true?!

All you have is <u>now</u>! Tomorrow may be too late!
Don't put it off! Decide <u>**NOW**</u> what will be your fate!

Surrender all to Jesus without delay!
And be ready and prepared for "Judgment Day"!

Be ready to look in Christ's face without fear!
Because we know His coming is drawing near!

There's no one that can make this decision for you!
<u>**NOW**</u> is all you have! What are you going to do?!

Song to Sing: "Each Step I Take"

Read: *Thoughts from the Mount of Blessing*, by E.G. White, pp. 116–119 on Matthew 6:13.

"My New Song!"
Written June 28, 2017

I have finally come to you, Lord!
Thanks for not shutting mercy's door!

Thanks for being long–suffering!
I come to you, my heart to bring!

Please accept me as I am now,
Humbly at Thy feet I bow!

Forgive me for all my bad past!
I'm surrendering all at last!

Make something beautiful of my life!
For your glory I'll live my life!

Yes! Heaven will be worth it all!
I've decided to heed God's call!

And come to Christ with all my heart!
And in my life, make a new start!

Jesus will be first in my life!
Surrendering all with no strife!

Coming to Christ with all my sins!
Giving them up and Heaven win!

I wish I had done this before,
And avoided all life's horrors!

It's better late than not at all,
To heed God's counsel and His call!

I'll step by step and day by day,
Stay on the straight and narrow way!

Be faithful and true till the end,
Gain the victory over sin!

Then Jesus will place on your head,
The victor's crown for souls you've led,

To follow Christ and obey Him,
And give up their idols of sin!

Don't get off the path to Heaven!
Live for Christ and your goal, Heaven!

Satan will try in every way,
To sidetrack you to sin each day!

Don't listen to him and his sins!
Stay true to Christ and Heaven win!

You have all the power you need,
To become like Christ and succeed!

Don't let Satan discourage you!
Learn God's word and to Him be true!

We know Jesus is soon to come!
The war with Satan will be won!

Be faithful and true till the end!
Gain the victory over sin!

Don't lose hope or become distressed!
Look to Christ and don't be depressed!

You'll win over Satan at last!
Don't let yourself fall in his traps!

Keep your eyes on Christ and your goal!
And go to Heaven winning souls!

You will be so glad that you did!
In Christ all your sins will be hid!

Determine to be like Jesus!
And live forever with Jesus!

There's nothing else that can compare,
To be like Christ and be up there!

Having no more sickness or pain!
To be in Heaven to remain!

Enjoy the joys of Heaven, too!
Being with Christ and loved ones, too!

And souls you've won to Christ's Kingdom!
And no more sins to overcome!

Heaven will be a happy place!
No more Satan to have to face!

Lay all your trials at Jesus' feet!
Your Saviour you'll finally meet!

Thank Him for all He's done for you!
For the problems He's seen you through!

Just can't wait to look in His face,
And thank Him for winning the race!

And cast my crown at His dear feet!
There my guardian angel meet!

Heaven's going to be so sweet!
To see the souls I've won and meet!

Lord! help me in my walk with You,
To never stray away from You!

Please! always be there at my side,
So with you I'll always abide!

Thanks Lord for taking care of me,
While living a life of folly!

I want now to live to please You!
And do all You want me to do!

Forgive my sins and make me new!
So I can live and be like You!

And someday meet You face to face!
Thanks for getting me through life's race!

Hold me up and carry me on!
Help me now to sing my new song!

Based on: Isaiah 42:10; Psalm 40; Psalm 33:3; Psalm 144:9; Psalm 149:1; Revelation 14:1–5
Sing the Song: "Sing Unto the Lord a New Song."
Read: *Great Controversy* by E.G. White, pp. 648–649.

"LORD! Make Me New!"
Written July 31, 2017

Never give up! Never give in!
Stand true to Jesus 'til the end!

My friend, it will be worth it all!
Just listen to God's Final Call!

To be in Heaven with no sin!
To enjoy our loved ones again!

In Heaven, there'll be no more pain!
In Heaven, life won't be the same!

No more sorrows and no more fears!
No more dying and no more tears!

To be there and enjoy it all!
By answering God's Final Call!

Don't let Satan discourage you!
Stay close to Christ—He'll see you through!

When tempted to throw in the towel!
Turn your eyes on Jesus—<u>Right</u> <u>Now</u>!

Stay in the race and don't give up!
Even though things here can get rough!

Through thick or thin, He'll see you through!
He'll always be there to help you!

Jesus is stronger than Satan!
Fighting with spiritual weapons!

Put the whole armor of Christ on!
Sing and pray as you journey on!

Christ and angels are on your side!
Day and night, with you they'll abide!

God has a plan for each of us!
Even though things get kinda tough!

Christ is waiting! Give Him your heart!
And begin today a new heart!

Living for Christ will bring such joy!
You were <u>so</u> happy, when a boy!

You loved Jesus with <u>all</u> your heart!
You can begin now a new start!

Tell Jesus you love Him today!
And never from Him will you stray!

Now, put Satan out of your heart!
And from Jesus never depart!

Life will begin anew for you!
Now, Live for Jesus and be true!

Wait and see what Christ plans for you!
Christ is your power behind you!

Through <u>all</u> your trials He'll see you through!
Just see what Christ will do for you!

Keep your eyes on your goal – Heaven!
Taking souls with you to Heaven!

It will be worth it <u>all</u>, my friends!
Stay faithful to Christ, 'till the end!

Jesus is soon to come my friend!
To end this world of strife and sin!

Now, Jesus is counting on you!
It's up to you! What will you do?!

Today, the LORD is calling you!
Choose you this day, what you will do!

Tomorrow it may be too late!
Your soul's salvation is at stake!

Jesus gives <u>all</u> the help you need!
Obey His Word and His call heed!

Time is running out for us all!
Don't turn a deaf ear to God's call!

Christ waits for your answer to Him!
Won't you come and be freed from sin?!

Christ strengthens me, so I won't sin!
I choose to come and follow Him!

Giving up my sinful pleasures!
And in Christ's power I'll endure!

Lord! Take me just now as I am!
Cleanse me from all my worldly sins!

Lord! Help me to be just like you!
And with your help—I'll make it through!

Throw open those pearly gates wide!
Lord! I want to enter inside!

And be with You—through eternity!
To praise You through eternity!

Thank You LORD, for sparing my life!
So I can have eternal life!

I was out in the world of sin!
Not knowing when my life would end!

LORD! Then, I heard You call my name!
I answered You! I'm not the same!

I'm giving up my life of sin!
I choose to follow You again!

Please clean me up and make me new!
I want to follow only You!

And do Your will, and not my own!
I'm sorry for the seeds I've sown!

Please take me back into your fold!
I'll follow You, and do as told!

I'm tired of my sinful life!
And hurting You, with all my strife!

You've been patient and kind to me!
I want to have Your company!

Accept me <u>NOW</u>, on bended knee!
A new man in Christ You will see!

I'm coming Home to be with You!
Enjoy Heaven and live with You!

Forgive me, LORD, for hurting You!
I love and worship only You!

Take me now, LORD, and make me new!
LORD, I want to be just like You!

Based on: Ezekiel 36:25–28; Psalm 51:10.

Read: *Steps to Christ* by E.G. White; *The Great Controversy* by E.G. White, chapter 38, "The Final Call."

Songs to Sing: "I Would Be Like Jesus" and "Never Give Up."

(The Lord inspired me to write this poem about my son, Jonathan. Thank You Jesus! May it be a help and a blessing to those who read it!)

"Do It Today!"

Written Sept. 2, 2017

The life you and I are living day by day,
Will determine where we will end up someday.

The LORD has power to calm the raging sea,
He has the power to calm the sea in me.

To give me the victories I need in life,
So I can have and enjoy eternal life.

Satan is trying to keep his hold on me,
Make me sick and sin and full of misery.

Jesus died on the cross to save me from sin,
So that I can begin a new life in Him.

I want to go to Heaven and be with Christ,
Where there'll be no more sorrow, pain, death or strife.

I am getting sick of this old world of sin,
I want to start over and begin again.

Only Jesus can help me make my wrongs right,
I'm depending on Him, the devil to fight.

I'm so tired and worn to begin again,
I need help and strength from Christ to cleanse my sins.

LORD, I am choosing to follow You today,
LORD, won't You please touch me and heal me today?

LORD, I'm sorry I hurt You and went astray,
Please, LORD, forgive me and take my sins away.

I want the peace and joy only You can give,
I see now it's in a Christ–like life to live.

LORD, I want to turn my life over to You,
And, LORD, do those things only that will please You.

LORD, I see my mistakes and want to repent,
Father, I want to accept Jesus You sent.

Who takes away my sins and cleanses my past,
I am finally coming to You, LORD, at last.

I wish LORD, I had done this sooner, You know,
And saved myself all this pain, sickness and woe.

LORD, You have always known what was best for me,
But in my selfish pride, I just could not see.

I kept going back to the pleasures of sin,
Not wanting to begin life over again.

I wanted to do what I wanted to do,
Not thinking of what You wanted me to do.

LORD, then I heard you speak in Your still small voice,
"Jonathan, what is going to be your choice?"

"Do you want Me or Satan to control you?
Do you want Heaven or Hell? What will you do?"

"I'm just about ready to come and end sin,
I don't want you to have to burn for your sins."

"I came to Earth, died for you and paid the price,
So you could be saved and have eternal life."

"But you have ignored Me all these years in tears,
Going on in your life of sin, pain and fears."

"When will you ever come back to Me again?
I have tried to help you overcome your sins."

"But you keep listening to Satan to sin,
I keep pleading for you to begin again."

"Don't listen to Satan, he's out to kill you!
But I'm out to save you and make your life new."

"Jonathan, the choice you make is up to you,
Mom, Dad, or anyone can't do it for you."

All your choices and plans you're making right now,
To follow Jesus or to follow the crowd.

The majority are walking the broad road,
They won't come to Jesus and lay down their load.

But Jesus has given you chance after chance,
Won't you look into your heart and take your stance?

Today is all you may have to make your choice,
Won't you listen to your Saviour's still small voice?

No one is sure of tomorrow to make plans,
All we have is the right now to take our stand.

It is a serious thing to play in sin,

Tonight, could be the night you could die in sin.

Without the Saviour to save you from your sins,

Won't you decide right now to get rid of sin?

And begin a new life, free from all your sins,

Christ is right there with you to help you begin.

Jesus loves you and died so you could be saved,

The road to Heaven, with His blood, has been paved.

It is all up to you which way you will go,

But remember this, "you will reap what you sow."

Jesus is pleading, "What will your answer be?

The choice you make will decide your destiny."

Won't you please come to Him now, with all your heart?

And make plans with Jesus to make a new start.

This could be your last chance to make your new start,

Won't you decide now to give Him all your heart?

Jesus is soon to come for His chosen ones,

Do not reject the Spirit and from Him run.

Make your calling and election sure today,

Do it now, don't put it off. Do it TODAY!

You do not have tomorrow nor yesterday,

All you have is right now, so do it TODAY!

Based on: Joshua 24:14, 15; Hebrews 3:7–15; Psalm 90:12.
Song to Sing: "Choose Ye This Day Who Ye Will Serve."

"Getting Ready for Jesus to Come!"
Written September 6, 2017

I can't think about winning a beauty contest,
Time to give the Battle Cry, and win the conquest.

The Big Great Test for God's people is not here yet,
And the image of the Beast has not quite been set.

How much longer will the angels, the four winds hold?
The final work we do now for God must be bold!

No time now to fold our hands, Satan is at war!
He knows his time is short, and at God's saints he wars!

We need now the power of God to take our stand,
Pray for the Holy Spirit and the promised Land.

We must conquer ourselves, before we conquer foes,
We must surrender all to Christ, and His hand hold.

Soon the heat of the Battle will be going on,
The life we're living will decide whose side we're on.

It's no time now for God's people to play in sin,
We have to overcome sin, and victories win.

Now our enemy is fighting behind the scenes,
But very soon his motives and plans will be seen.

As an overwhelming surprise it comes on us,
We need now to have faith, and in God put our trust.

We need now to be thinking of perishing souls,
Not of ease and pleasures, but of sinners take hold.

Hurrying to let them know—Christ is <u>soon</u> to come!
Get ready for the crisis when Jesus will come!

All these calamities coming upon the world,
Is Christ's sign He's coming to end this sinful world!

For all this that is soon coming, we must step fast!
For no one knows how much longer his life will last.

We must prepare now for all that is soon to come,
When we can't buy or sell, and have to flee and run!

We need now the Seal of God to be placed on us,
And develop faith in God and in His word trust.

My friends, we can make it through to the promised Land,
If we'll remain true to Christ—keep hold of His hand.

Friends, this Battle that is raging will soon be done,
Make plans to win souls and the fight with Satan's won!

Then from Christ we'll hear words spoken, "My child, well done!
You deserve to be in Heaven, 'cause sin you've shunned."

So, get in the race now, and don't be left behind,
Have a Christ–like character, and joys you will find.

You'll be so glad you've chosen to be on God's side,
Where in Heaven, peace, joy and happiness abide.

My dear friends, just stay in the race, and don't lose out!

Be part of those who'll give the "Loud Cry" with a shout!

So, remain true to Christ until the end of sin,

And, my friends, your goal, Heaven, you will surely win!

Read: *8T* 28; *2 SM* 142; *Early Writings* p. 119; *Maranatha* pp. 158, 164 – All these were written by E.G. White. Also read 1 Thessalonians 5.

One should read all of the *Maranatha* book by E.G. White through. It's like another *Great Controversy* book, which must be read at this time too!

Song to Sing: "Are You Ready for Jesus to Come?!"

"More Time"

Written October 5, 2017

God is so merciful and kind,
He is giving us all more time.

And time to make all our wrongs right,
And laying aside all our strife.

Putting our faith and trust in God,
Preparing to walk on His sod.

To be overcomers at last,
And forgetting all our bad past.

We will trust and wait patiently,
For God to give us victory.

Through God's help we can gain power,
Receive the Latter Rain showers.

And with God's help we can press on,
And give the Loud Cry message song.

To encourage those in the LORD,
To use their Bibles as their sword.

To stand true to God and His word,
To speak with power Gods' true word.

And stand courageously for Him,
Rescuing sinners from their sins.

The, keep our eyes on our goal,
We will be workers to win souls.

And make it to Heaven at last,
And at His feet our crowns we'll cast.

We'll thank Him for seeing us through,
And helping us His will to do.

My friends, it will be worth it all,
To be able to hear His call.

Hearing Him say, "Child, welcome Home!"
For now you will never more roam!

You're now safe in My loving arms,
For you there will be no more harm.

You've made the supreme sacrifice,
Giving up sin, with all its vice.

To have a character like God's,
Worthy to walk on Heaven's sod.

Now you can enjoy heaven's joys,
With all God's children—girls and boys.

To never more have pain or weep,
And worship at the Saviour's feet.

Enjoying the bliss of Heaven,
Singing songs of joy in Heaven.

Never more to feel sin again,
And be able to reign with Him.

Won't it be wonderful my friends,
Never to have to sin again?!

God's made this possible for us,
Just put in Him your faith and trust.

Jesus loves you, died to save you,
Now, what are you going to do?!

Friends, only you can make the choice,
To listen to God's pleading voice.

To lay your burdens at His feet,
And walk on Heaven's golden streets.

To do just that, make up your mind,
And Jesus will give you more time!

Based on: Acts 3:19

"Have Faith in God!"

Written October 7, 2017

Have faith in God,
No matter come what may.
Have faith in God,
And Jesus' will obey.

Have faith in God,
Keep your eyes on Him.
Have faith in God,
And don't let yourself sin.

Have faith in God,
To bring you through it all.
Have faith in God,
On His holy Name call.

Have faith in God,
To help you overcome.
Have faith in God,
Be ready when He comes.

Have faith in God,
Let your faith grow in God.
Have faith in God,
Then walk on Heaven's sod.

Have faith in God,
Prepare to meet thy God.
Have faith in God,
Avoid meeting the rod.

Have faith in God,
Find peace and joy in God.
Have faith in God,
By winning souls for God.

Have faith in God,
Trust Him to see you through.
Have faith in God,
And see what He will do!

Have faith in God,
And make Heaven your goal.
Have faith in God,
And trust God with your soul.

Have faith in God,
And passing every test.
Have faith in God,
Then find real happiness!

Have faith in God,
Jesus is on your side.
Have faith in God,
And in His love abide!

Based on: Acts 14:8–10; Luke 7:50; Luke 17:5; Luke 18:1–8; Luke 22:31, 32; Acts 3:16, 19; Mark 11:22–24; Amos 4:12; Hebrews 11; Galatians 3:11; Matthew 9:22, 29; Matthew 17:20, 21.

David and Linda Clore, 2010

Our son, Jonathan Clore, sitting in our front room in our 14'x80' house trailer. Jonathan attended our SDA schools.

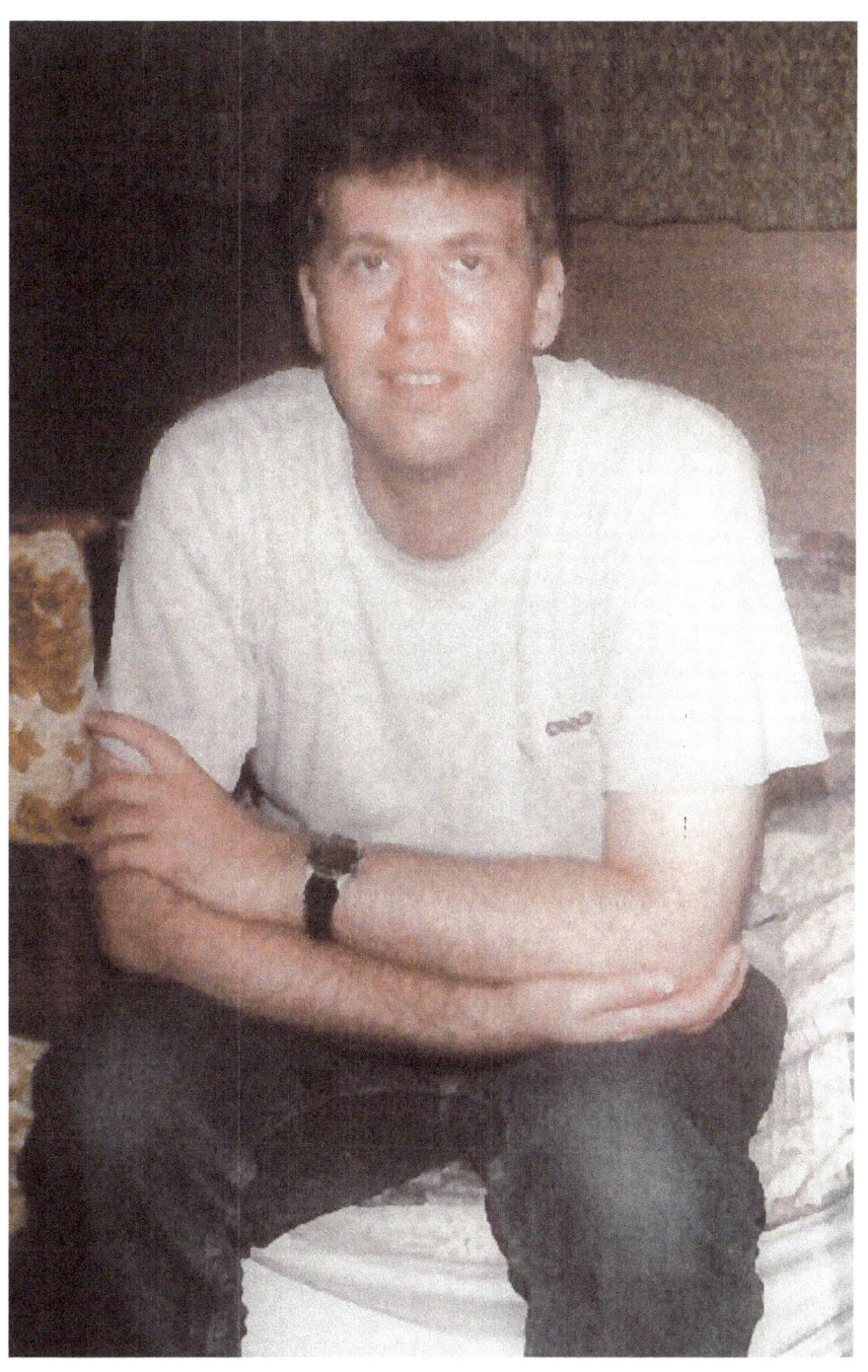

Our son, Jonathan Clore, taken when he was 27 years old …
2 ½ months before he became totally paralyzed in 1996.

On left is our sanitarium treatment room. In the center on the left is the library/chapel cabin, 12'x20'. In the center is the dining hall, 12'x24'. In the center in the distance is our metal pole barn storage. On the right is a little of our 12'x14' screened-in porch showing. On the right is our enclosed 10'x10' porch connected to our 14'x80' house trailer. In the center is the 3ABN dish.

The "Ark" is located in the Chippewa Hills Forest on 14 acres. On the left is our 12'x14' screened in porch. In the middle is our 10'x10' enclosed porch, attached to our 14'x80' mobile home. On the right in the center is our 12'x24' dining hall. In the back of the dining hall is our sanitarium treatment room. On the far right is our library/chapel cabin 12'x20'.

Our Lincoln Mark VIII given to us for free, parked in front of our new 12'x20' cabin for sleeping. Praise God! Read the story "For With God, Nothing Shall Be Impossible."

Our 12'x20' library/chapel new cabin with picnic tables and cherry tree and little green house in the distance on the left. The dining hall is on the right where the propane tank is and a picnic table. In Kansas on our 14 acres on the "Ark," in the Chippewa Hills Forest.

Our 12'x20' barracks cabin with 4 beds.

An airplane view over "The Ark"

ASPECT Books

We invite you to view the complete
selection of titles we publish at:
www.ASPECTBooks.com

We encourage you to write us
with your thoughts about this,
or any other book we publish at:
info@ASPECTBooks.com

ASPECT Books' titles may be purchased in
bulk quantities for educational, fund-raising,
business, or promotional use.
bulksales@ASPECTBooks.com

Finally, if you are interested in seeing
your own book in print, please contact us at:
publishing@ASPECTBooks.com

We are happy to review your manuscript at no charge.

www.ingramcontent.com/pod-product-compliance
Lightning Source LLC
Chambersburg PA
CBHW080538300426
44111CB00017B/2785